HUMAN ADAPTATION

A functional interpretation

HUMAN ADAPTATION

A functional interpretation

A. ROBERTO FRISANCHO, Ph.D.

Professor of Anthropology and Research
Scientist of the Center for Human Growth
and Development, The University of Michigan,
Ann Arbor, Michigan

with **170** illustrations

The C. V. Mosby Company

ST. LOUIS • TORONTO • LONDON   1979

The C. V. Mosby Company
11830 Westline Industrial Drive, St. Louis, Missouri 63141

Library of Congress Cataloging in Publication Data

Frisancho, A   Roberto, 1939-
   Human adaptation.

   Bibliography：p.
   Includes index.
    1. Adaptation (Physiology). 2. Man—Influence of environment. I. Title.
QP82.F74   573   78-31913
ISBN 0-8016-1693-X

GW/VH/VH 9 8 7 6 5 4 3 2 1   03/B/300

IN MEMORY OF

my father   **Augusto**

AND DEDICATED TO

my mother   **Rebeca**

my wife   **Hedy** and

my sons   **Roberto Javier** and **Juan Carlos**

Preface

In recent years increased interest in the interaction between environmental conditions and the adaptive capacity of humans has led physiologists, biologists, and physical anthropologists to study the effects of climatic factors such as heat, cold, and humidity, as well as high-altitude hypoxia, solar radiation, undernutrition, and overnutrition on an organism's cellular, biochemical, and morphological functioning during both developmental and adult states. Results of these investigations have been published in specialized research articles or symposia. The goal of this book is to integrate such scattered and specialized knowledge into a single work that evaluates human adaptation from a physiological and anthropological perspective.

This book evaluates the short- and long-term responses that enable humans to function normally under the stress of heat, cold, solar radiation, high-altitude hypoxia, and undernutrition. In addition, because of their importance and influence on the well-being of humans and to show the interaction between technological adaptation and biological function, the effects of Westernization of dietary habits on the pattern of disease are briefly discussed.

Because this book is addressed to students of several disciplines and to facilitate understanding of the mechanisms of human adaptation to environmental stress, major topics are always preceded by either a chapter or section outlining initial responses observed in laboratory studies with humans and experimental animals. Emphasis is also given to the short adaptive mechanisms that enable an organism to acclimate itself to a given environmental stress. Subsequently, the long-term adaptive mechanisms that enable humans to acclimatize themselves to natural, stressful environmental conditions are discussed.

Throughout the book emphasis is given to the effects of environmental stress and the adaptive responses that an organism makes during its growth and development. For example, current evidence suggests that population differences in adaptation to the stresses of heat, cold, and high-altitude hypoxia result in part from adaptations made during growth and development. In some cases the evidence is only suggestive, and I hope that the postulated hypotheses will stimulate researchers to prove or disprove them. If further research is so motivated, my efforts will have been worthwhile.

I would like to acknowledge my indebtedness to Professors Paul T. Baker and Thelma S. Baker of the Department of Anthropology of Pennsylvania State University, whose guidance, teaching, and friendship have been a major influence throughout my graduate training and professional life. Discussions with my colleagues of the University of Michigan have been of great benefit. My thanks to Professors Loring C. Brace, George J. Brewer, Stanley M. Garn, Frank P. Livingstone, Robert E. Moyers, Roy Rappaport, and Arthur Vander. Nello Pace, Professor Emeritus of Physiology at the University of California, Berkeley, Professor Elsworth R. Buskirk, Director of the Laboratory for Human Performance at Pennsylvania State University, and Joel M. Hanna, Associate Professor of Physiology at the University of Hawaii at Manoa all provided prepublication reviews of the manuscript, and their numerous recommendations have been most helpful.

I especially thank my Peruvian colleagues Drs. Roger Guerra-Garcia, Carlos Monge, Emilo Picon-Reategui, Cesar Reynafarje, and Tulio Velasquez of the Institute of High Altitude Studies and Institute of Andean Biology of the University of San Marcos and the University of Cayetano Heredia for their invaluable assistance and cooperation in my studies of high-altitude adaptation.

Many persons contributed to the preparation of this book. I wish to express a deep appreciation to all for their assistance. Special thanks are extended to my coresearcher and former graduate student of the Department of Anthropology of the University of Michigan, Jane E. Klayman, who from the onset of this work helped me industriously. Theryl Schessler, a former graduate student of Biological Anthropology, patiently traced all the line drawings and illustrations. I am grateful to the secretarial staff of the Center for Human Growth and Development of the University of Michigan, and I especially thank Rosanne Arnowitz, June Bixler, Barbara Nesbit, Margaret Owen, and Carol Thompson.

A. Roberto Frisancho

Contents

1 | Principles and definitions in the study of human adaptation

DEFINITIONS

Although the term *adaptation* has been widely used by biologists, social scientists, and laymen, there is no general agreement as to its meaning. Part of this difficulty is because humans adjust to their environment through a complex set of interrelationships between themselves and their physical, biological, and social environment. Consequently, both scientists and laymen use the term adaptation to indicate a multiplicity of physiological, psychological, social, and genetic characteristics. For example, among geneticists the term refers to genetic adaptation, implying that natural selection is involved[1-12]; in this context, it refers specifically to populations and not individuals. However, most nongeneticists apply the term adaptation to both individuals and populations.[13-33]

The concept of adaptation cannot be reduced to a single definition without gross oversimplification. Throughout this book the term adaptation is used in the broad generic sense of functional adaptation, and it is applied to all levels of biological organization from individuals to populations. A basic premise of this approach is that adaptation is a process whereby the organism has attained a beneficial adjustment to the environment.[1-34] This adjustment can be either temporary or permanent, acquired either through short-term or lifetime processes, and may involve physiological, structural, behavioral, or cultural changes aimed at improving the organism's functional performance in the face of environmental stresses. If environmental stresses are conducive to differential mortality and fertility, then adaptive changes may become established in the population through changes in genetic composition and thus attain a level of genetic adaptation. In this context functional adaptation, along with cultural and genetic adaptation, is viewed as part of a

continuum in an adaptive process that enables individuals and populations to maintain both internal and external environmental homeostasis. Therefore the concept of adaptation is applicable to all levels of biological organization from unicellular organisms to the largest mammals and from individuals to populations. This broad use of the concept of adaptation is justified not only in theory but also because it is currently applied to all areas of human endeavor so that no discipline can claim priority or exclusivity in the use of the term.[20] In this chapter the various forms of adaptation will be defined, and their relationship to each other, as well as their applicability to the study of human adaptation to environmental stress, will be discussed.

Functional adaptation

Functional adaptation involves changes in organ system function, histology, morphology, biochemical composition, anatomical relationships, and body composition, either independently or integrated in the organism as a whole. These changes can occur through acclimatization, acclimation, or habituation.

Acclimatization. Acclimatization refers to changes occurring within the lifetime of an organism that reduce the strain caused by stressful changes in the natural climate or by complex environmental stresses.[21,22,34] If the adaptive traits are acquired during the growth period of the organism, the process is referred to as either *developmental adaptation* or *developmental acclimatization*.[23,32]

Acclimation. Acclimation refers to the adaptive biological changes that occur in response to a single experimentally induced stress[21,22] rather than to multiple stresses as occurs in acclimatization. As with acclimatization, changes occurring during the process of growth may also be referred to as developmental acclimation.[32]

Habituation. Habituation implies a gradual

reduction of responses to, or perception of, repeated stimulation.[21,22] By extension, habituation refers to the diminution of normal neural responses, for example, the decrease of sensations such as pain. Such changes can be generalized for the whole organism (general habituation) or can be specific for a given part of the organism (specific habituation). Habituation necessarily depends on learning and conditioning, which enable the organism to transfer an existing response to a new stimulus. The extent to which these nonphysiological responses are important in maintaining homeostasis depends on the severity of environmental stress. For example, with severe cold stress or low oxygen availability, failure to respond physiologically may endanger the well-being and survival of the organism.

Acclimatization vs acclimation. Studies on acclimatization are done with reference to both major environmental stresses and several secondary, related stresses. For example, any difference in the physiological and structural characteristics of subjects prior to and after residence in a tropical environment are interpreted as a result of acclimatization to heat stress. In addition, because tropical climates are also associated with nutritional and disease stresses, individual or population differences in function and structure may also be related to these factors. On the other hand, in studies of acclimation any possible differences are easily attributed to the major stress to which the experimental subject has been exposed in the laboratory. For understanding the basic physiological processes of adaptation, studies on acclimation are certainly better than those of acclimatization. However, since all organisms are never exposed to a single stress but instead to multiple stresses, a more realistic approach is that of studying acclimatization responses. Thus, both studies on acclimation and acclimatization are essential for under-

standing the processes whereby the organism adapts to a given environmental condition. This rationale becomes even more important when the aim is to understand the mechanisms whereby humans adapt to a given climatic area, since humans in a given area are not only exposed to diverse stresses but have also modified the nature and intensity of these stresses as well as created new stresses for themselves and for generations to come.

Cultural and technological adaptation

Cultural adaptation refers to the nonbiological responses of the individual or population to modify or ameliorate an environmental stress. As such, cultural adaptation is an important mechanism that facilitates human biological adaptation. It may be said that cultural adaptation both during contemporary times and in evolutionary perspective represents humanity's most important tool. It is through cultural adaptation that humans have been able to survive and colonize far into the zones of extreme environmental conditions. Human beings have adapted to cold environments by inventing fire and clothing, building houses, and harnessing new sources of energy. The construction of houses, use of clothing in diverse climates, certain behavioral patterns, and work habits represent biological and cultural adaptations to climatic stress. The development of medicine from its primitive manifestations to its high levels in the present era and the increase of energy production associated with agricultural and industrial revolutions are representative of human cultural adaptation to the physical environment.

Culture and technology have facilitated biological adaptation, but they have also created and continue to create new stressful conditions that require new adaptive responses. A modification of one environmental condition may result in the change of another. Such a change may eventually result in the creation of a new stressful condition (Chapter 14). A classic example of such an interaction of culture and biology is the development of malaria. In West Africa malaria became hyperendemic when the *Anopheles gambiae* mosquito, the major vector of malaria, was propagated because of the development of agriculture in the tropical rain forest of West Africa.[7] It was in response to this new stress that the adaptive qualities of the abnormal hemoglobins, such as sickle cell and thalassemia, became important to the survival of man in tropical climates. In the same manner, advances in the medical sciences have successfully reduced infant and adult mortality to the extent that the world population is growing at an explosive rate, and unless world food resources are increased, the twenty-first century will witness a world famine. Western technology, although upgrading living standards, has also created a polluted environment that may become unfit for good health and life. If this process continues unchecked, environmental pollution will eventually become another selective force to which humans must adapt through biological or cultural processes or face extinction. Therefore, the ability to adapt to the unforseeable threats of the future remains an indispensable condition of survival and biological success.[29] Adaptation to the world of today may be incompatible with survival in the world of tomorrow unless humans learn to adjust their cultural and biological capacities.

Genetic adaptation

Genetic adaptation refers to specific heritable characteristics that favor tolerance and survival of an individual or a population in a particular total environment. A given biological trait is considered genetic when it is unique to the individual or population and

when it can be shown that it is acquired through biological inheritance. A genetic adaptation becomes established through the action of natural selection, the central theme of Darwinian evolution. Natural selection refers to the mechanisms whereby the genotypes of those individuals showing the greatest adaptation or "fitness" (leaving the most descendants through reduced mortality and increased fertility) will be perpetuated, and those less adapted to the environment will contribute fewer genes to the population gene pool. Natural selection favors the features of an organism that bring it into a more efficient relationship with its environment. Those gene combinations fostering the best-adapted phenotypes will be "selected for," and inferior genotypes will be eliminated. The selective forces for humans as for other mammals, include the sum total of factors in the natural environment. All the natural conditions, such as hot and cold climates and oxygen-poor environments, are potential selective forces. Food is a selective force by its own abundance, eliminating those susceptible to obesity and cardiac failures, or by its very scarcity, favoring smaller size and slower growth. So is disease a powerful selective agent, favoring in each generation those with better immunity. The natural world is full of forces that make some individuals, and by inference some populations, better adapted than others because no two individuals or populations have the same capacity of adaptation. The maladapted population will tend to have lower fertility and/or higher mortality than that of the adapted population.

The capacity for adaptation (adaptability) to environmental stress varies between populations and even between individuals. The fitness of an individual or population is determined by its total adaptation to the environment—genetic, physiological, and behavioral (or cultural). Fitness in genetic terms includes more than just the ability to survive and reproduce in a given environment; it must include the capacity for future survival in future environments. The long-range fitness of a population depends on its genetic stability and variability. The greater the adaptation, the longer the individual or population will survive and the greater the advantage in leaving progeny resembling the parents. In a fixed environment, all characteristics could be under rigid genetic control with maximum adaptation to the environment. On the other hand, in a changing environment a certain amount of variability is necessary to ensure that the population will survive environmental change. This requirement for variability can be fulfilled either genetically or phenotypically or both. In most populations a compromise exists between the production of a variety of genotypes and individual flexibility. Extinct populations are those which were unable to meet the challenges of new conditions. Thus, contemporary fitness requires both genetic uniformity and genetic variability.

Therefore contemporary adaptation of human beings is both the result of their past and their present adaptability. It is this capacity to adapt that enables them to be in a dynamic equilibrium in their biological niche. It is the nature of the living organism to be part of an ecosystem whereby it modifies the environment and, in turn, is also affected by such modification. The maintenance of this dynamic equilibrium represents homeostasis, which, in essence, reflects the ability to survive in varying environments.[20,29] The ecosystem is the fundamental biological entity—the living individual satisfying its needs in a dynamic relation to its habitat. In Darwinian terms, the ecosystem is the setting for the struggle for existence, efficiency and survival are the measures of fitness, and natural selection is the process underlying all products.[29]

PURPOSE OF ADAPTATION: HOMEOSTASIS

An environmental stress is defined as any condition that disturbs the normal functioning of the organism. Such interference eventually causes a disturbance of internal homeostasis. *Homeostasis* means the ability of the organism to maintain a stable internal environment despite diverse, disruptive, external environmental influences.[29] On a functional level, all adaptive responses of the organism or the individual are made to restore internal homeostasis. These controls operate in a hierarchy at all levels of biological organization, from a single biochemical pathway, to the mitochondria of a cell, to cells organized into tissues, tissues into organs and systems of organs, to entire organisms.

The maintenance of dynamic equilibrium constitutes the major objective of the various adaptive responses made by organisms. The necessity for the maintenance of homeostasis results from the fact that cellular functions are limited to relatively small variations. For example, the chemical composition of the blood, lymph, and other body fluids varies within relatively narrow limits.

Humans living in hot or cold climates must undergo some functional adjustments to maintain thermal balance; these may comprise the rate of metabolism, avenues of heat loss, heat conservation, respiration, blood circulation, fluid and electrolyte transport, and exchange. In the same manner, persons exposed to high altitudes must adjust through physiological, chemical, and morphological mechanisms, such as increase in ventilation, increase in the oxygen-carrying capacity of the blood resulting from an increased concentration of red blood cells, and increased ability of tissues to utilize oxygen at low pressures. Failure to activate the functional adaptive processes may result in failure to restore homeostasis, which in turn results in maladaptation of the organism and eventual incapacity of the individual.

Therefore homeostasis is a part and function of survival. The continued existence of a biological system implies that the system possesses mechanisms that enable it to maintain its identity, despite the endless pressures of environmental stresses.[29] These complementary concepts of homeostasis and adaptation are valid at all levels of biological organization. They apply to social groups as well as to unicellular or multicellular organisms.[29]

Homeostasis is a function of a dynamic interaction of feedback mechanisms whereby a given stimulus elicits a response aimed at restoring the original equilibrium. Several mathematical models of homeostasis have been proposed. In general, they show (as schematized in Fig. 1-1) that when a primary

stress disturbs the homeostasis that exists between the organism and the environment, to function normally the organism must resort either to biological or cultural-technological responses. Through the biological responses, the organism overcomes the environmental stress and its physiological activities occur either at the same level as before the stress or take place at another level. For example, when faced with heat stress, the organism may simply reduce its metabolic activity so all heat-producing processes are slowed down, or may increase the activity of the heat-loss mechanisms. In either case the organism may maintain homeostasis, but the physiological processes will occur at a different set point. The attainment of full homeostasis or full functional adaptation, depending on the nature of the stress, may require short-term responses such as those acquired during acclimation or acclimatization or may require exposure during the period of growth and development as in developmental acclimatization. In theory the respective contributions of ge-

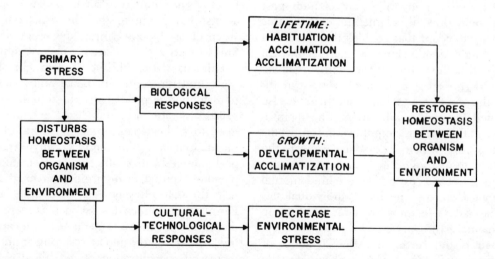

Fig. 1-1. Schematization of adaptation process and mechanisms that enable individual or population to maintain homeostasis in the face of primary disturbing stress.

netic and environmental factors vary with the developmental stage of the organism—the earlier the stage, the greater the influence of the environment and the greater the plasticity of the organism.[23,29,32] However, as will be shown in this book, the principle does not apply to all biological parameters; it depends on the nature of the stress, the developmental stage of the organism, the type of organism, and the particular functional process that is affected. For example, an adult individual exposed to high-altitude hypoxia through prolonged residence may attain a level of adaptation that permits normal functioning in all daily activities and as such we may consider him adapted. However, when exposed to stress that requires increased energy, such as strenuous exercise, this individual may prove to be not fully adapted. On the other hand, humans through cultural and technological adaptation may actually modify and thus decrease the nature of the environmental stresses so that a new microenvironment is created to which the organism does not need to make any physiological responses. For example, cultural and technological responses permit humans to live under extreme conditions of cold stress with the result that some of the physiological processes are not altered. However, on rare occasions humans have been able to completely avoid an environmental stress. Witness the fact that the Eskimos, despite their advanced technological adaptation to cold in their everyday hunting activities, are exposed to periods of cold stress and in response have developed biological processes that enable them to function and be adapted to their environment.

Not all responses made by the organism can be considered adaptive. Although a given response might not be adaptive per se, through its effect on another structure or function it may prove beneficial to the organism's function. Conversely, a given adaptive response may aid the organism in one function but actually have negative effects on other functions or structures. Thus, within all areas of human endeavor a given trait is considered adaptive when its beneficial effects outweigh the negative ones. In theory this is a valid assumption, but in practice, because of the relative nature of adaptation, it is quite difficult to determine the true adaptive value of a given response. Every response must be considered in the context of the environmental conditions in which the response was measured and within the perspective of the length of time of the study and the subject population.

ADAPTATION RESEARCH
Empirical and experimental

The study of human adaptation involves a unique combination of field and laboratory methods, whereby the knowledge of ecologists, physiologists, geneticists, and cultural and physical anthropologists is pooled in an attempt to understand the human-environment relationship. To accomplish this objective, two different but related approaches are employed. The first is the geographical method, which may be called the indirect method. The indirect, or geographical, method attempts to establish the relationship between certain morphological or physiological characteristics and an environmental parameter. For example, anthropologists on a worldwide basis have established the relationship of various morphological features to climatic variables, such as temperature and humidity.[11,12] Because of the complex nature of a given climatic variable, the geographical method does not reveal the cause for the existence of this relationship. The explanation of the observed relationship requires the second, direct or experimental, approach. The experimental method collects and analyzes precise measurable changes in humans under reproducible and controlled experimental conditions, both in the laboratory and in the field. These conditions are the result of measurable environmental factors, which are generally of a chemical, physical, or biological nature and usually enable us to predict the qualitative and quantitative responses to each particular environment. The experimental approach requires a thorough understanding of the physiological and anatomical properties of the organism and the environmental parameters. It is a method designed to test a special theory, hypothesis, or assumption derived from the geographical, or indirect, method. In other words, research in adaptation requires the application of the geographical and experimental methods. The indirect method provides the pathway for experimental research. These methods permit the student of human adaptation to understand the mechanisms whereby a given population survives adverse environmental conditions such as heat, cold, altitude, disease, and malnutrition. The study of human adaptation is not oriented to determining biological or cultural differences among populations; the goal is to identify the sources or causes that resulted in such adaptation and differences.

Individuals vs populations

Whatever the method employed, geographical or experimental research in human adaptation is concerned with populations, not with individuals, although the research itself is based on individuals. There are two related reasons for this.

The first is a practical consideration. Studying all members of a given population, unless its size is small enough, is too difficult to be attempted by any research team. Therefore, according to the objectives of the investigation, the research centers on a sample that is considered representative of the entire population. Based on these studies, the researchers present a picture of the population as a whole, with respect to the problem being investigated.

The second reason is a theoretical one. In the study of adaptation, we usually focus on populations rather than on individuals because it is the population that survives and perpetuates itself. In the investigation of biological evolution, the relevant population is the breeding population because it is a vehicle for the gene pool, which is the means for change and hence evolution. The study of an individual phenomenon is only a means to understand the process. The adaptation of any individual or individuals merely reflects the adaptation that has been achieved by the population of which he is a member.

CONCLUSION

The term *adaptation* encompasses the physiological, cultural, and genetic adaptations that permit individuals and populations to adjust to the environment in which they live. These adjustments are complex, and the concept of adaptation cannot be reduced to a simple rigid definition without oversimplification. The functional approach in using the adaptation concept permits its application to all levels of biological organization from unicellular to multicellular organisms, from early embryonic to adult stages, and from individuals to populations. In this context, human biological responses to environmental stress can be considered as part of a continuous process whereby past adaptations are modified and developed to permit the organism to function and maintain equilibrium within the environment to which it is daily exposed.

The mechanisms for attaining full functional adaptation include acclimation, acclimatization, and habituation. The role played by each of these processes depends on the nature of the stress or stresses, the organ system involved, and the developmental stage of the organism. It is emphasized that the goal of the organism's responses to a given stress is to maintain homeostasis within itself and with respect to other organisms and the environment.

The study of individuals exposed to stressful conditions in natural and laboratory environments is one of the most important

approaches for understanding the mechanisms whereby human populations adapt to a given environment. Knowledge of human adaptation is basic in our endeavors to understand past and present human variation in morphology and physiological performance.

REFERENCES

1. Bateson, G. 1963. The role of somatic change in evolution. Evolution **17**:529-539.
2. Bock, W. J., and G. V. Wahlert. 1965. Adaptation and the form-function complex. Evolution **19**:269-299.
3. Dobzhansky, T. 1968. Adaptedness and fitness. In R. C. Lewontin, ed. Population ecology and evolution. Proceedings of an International Symposium. Syracuse University Press, Syracuse, N.Y.
4. Lewontin, R. C. 1957. The adaptations of populations to varying environments. In Cold Spring Harbor Symposia on Quantitative Biology. vol. 22. Cold Spring Harbor Laboratory of Quantitative Biology, Boston, Mass.
5. Mayr, E. 1956. Geographic character gradients and climatic adaptation. Evolution **10**:105-108.
6. Slobodkin, L. B. 1968. Toward a predictive theory of evolution. In R. C. Lewontin, ed. Population biology and evolution. Proceedings of an International Symposium. Syracuse University Press, Syracuse, N.Y.
7. Livingstone, F. B. 1958. Anthropological implications of sickle-cell gene distribution in West Africa. Am. Anthropol. **60**:533-562.
8. Wallace, B., and A. Sob. 1964. Adaptation. Prentice-Hall, Inc., Englewood Cliffs, N.J.
9. Wright, S. 1949. Adaptation and selection. In E. L. Jepson, E. Mayr, and G. G. Simpson, eds. Genetics, paleontology and evolution. Princeton University Press, Princeton, N.J.
10. Mayr, E. 1966. Animal species and evolution. The Belknap Press of Harvard University Press, Cambridge, Mass.
11. Schreider, E. 1964. Ecological rules, body heat regulation, and human evolution. Evolution **18**:1-9.
12. Roberts, D. F. 1953. Body weight, race and climate. Am. J. Phys. Anthropol. **11**:533-558.
13. Adolf, E. F. 1972. Physiological adaptations: hypertrophies and super functions. Am. Sci. **60**:608-617.
14. Barcroft, J. 1932. La fixité du milieu interieur est la condition de la vie libre. Biol. Rev. **7**:24-87.
15. Bernard, C. 1878. Lecons sur les phenomenes de la vie. Bailliere, Paris.
16. Baker, P. T. 1966. Human biological variation as an adaptive response to the environment. Eugen. Quart. **13**:81-91.
17. Brauer, R. W. 1965. Irreversible effects. In O. G. Edholm and R. Bachrach, eds. The physiology of human survival. Academic Press, Inc. Ltd., London.
18. Cannon, W. B. 1932. The wisdom of the body. W. W. Norton & Co., Inc., N.Y.
19. Cracraft, J. 1966. The concept of adaptation in the study of human populations. Eugen. Quart. **14**:299.
20. Dubos, R. 1965. Man adapting. Yale University Press, New Haven, Conn.
21. Eagan, C. J. 1963. Introduction and terminology. Fed. Proc. **22**:930-932.
22. Folk, G. E., Jr. 1974. Textbook of environmental physiology. Lea & Febiger, Philadelphia.
23. Frisancho, A. R. 1975. Functional adaptation to high altitude hypoxia. Science **187**:313-319.
24. Harrison, G. A. 1966. Human adaptability with reference to IBP proposals for high altitude research. In P. T. Baker and J. S. Weiner, eds. The biology of human adaptability. Clarendon Press, Oxford.
25. Hart, S. J. 1957. Climatic and temperature induced changes in the energetics of homeotherms. Rev. Can. Biol. **16**:133-141.
26. Lasker, G. W. 1969. Human biological adaptability. Science **166**:1480-1486.
27. Mazess, R. B. 1973. Biological adaptation: aptitudes and acclimatization. In E. S. Watts, F. E. Johnston, and G. W. Lasker, eds. Biosocial interrelations in population adaptation. Mouton, the Hague, Paris.
28. McCutcheon, F. H. 1964. Organ systems in adaptation: the respiratory system. In D. B. Dill, E. F.

Adolph, and C. G. Wilber, eds. Handbook of physiology. vol. 4. Adaptation to the environment. American Physiological Society, Washington, D.C.

29. Proser, C. L. 1964. Perspectives of adaptation: theoretical aspects. In D. B. Dill, E. F. Adolph, and C. G. Wilber, eds. Handbook of physiology. vol. 4. Adaptation to the environment. American Physiological Society, Washington, D.C.

30. Selye, H. 1950. The physiology and pathology of exposure to stress. Acta, Montreal.

31. Thomas, R. B. 1975. The ecology of work. In A. Damon, ed. Physiological anthropology. Oxford University Press, Inc., N.Y.

32. Timiras, P. S. 1972. Developmental physiology and aging. Macmillan, Inc., N.Y.

33. Rappaport, R. A. 1976. Maladaptation in social systems. In J. Friedman and M. Rowlands, eds. Evolution in social systems. Gerald Duckworth & Co. Ltd., London.

34. Bligh, J., and K. G. Johnson. 1973. Glossary of terms for thermal physiology. J. Appl. Physiol. **35:**941-961.

2

Thermoregulation and acclimation to heat stress

Environmental factors

Heat exchange and critical air temperature
Radiation (R)
Convection (C)
Conduction (Cd)
Evaporation (E)

General physiological responses to heat stress
Vasodilation and heat conductance
Heat storage
Sweating, dehydration, and circulation

Evaporation and its regulation
Insensible evaporation
Emotional evaporation
Thermal sweating
Thirst
Sodium adjustments

Individual factors and tolerance to heat
Age
Body size and shape
Fatness
Physical fitness and cardiovascular function

Acclimation
General trends
Acclimation of women

Conclusion

Humans, as most mammals, are *homeothermic*, which means they can maintain a relatively constant body temperature independent of environmental temperature. The fundamental problem for humans and all other homeotherms exposed to heat stress is heat dissipation. Therefore, most of the physiological responses to heat stress are aimed at facilitating heat loss. Successful tolerance of heat stress requires the development of synchronized responses that permit the organism to lose heat in an efficient manner and maintain homeostasis. In this chapter we will focus on the basic principles of heat exchange, the immediate physiological responses to heat stress, the individual factors that affect heat tolerance, and the process of acclimation. These will set the stage for a discussion of the process of acclimatization to heat stress of native and non-native populations.

ENVIRONMENTAL FACTORS

Humans encounter heat stress not only in tropical equatorial areas, but also during the summer in many of the vast land areas of the temperate zones. In general, hot climates are classified as either hot-dry or hot-wet. The hot-dry climates are usually found in desert regions such as those in the southwestern United States, the Kalahari, the Sahara of Africa, and other areas of the world. The hot-wet or hot-humid climates are typical of the tropical rain forests usually located within the latitudes of 10° to 20° above or below the equator. Hot-humid climates have the following characteristics: (1) the air temperature does not exceed 35° C (95° F), usually ranging between 26.7° and 32.2° C (80° to 90° F); (2) the average relative humidity exceeds 50%, usually reaching as high as 95%; and (3) there is marked seasonal precipitation. As a result of the high precipitation and hot climate, vegetation is quite abundant and provides ample shade. Because of the combination of moisture and vegetation, much of the solar energy is used to convert liquid water to vapor, which exits into the atmosphere as insensible heat. There is little day-night or seasonal variation in temperature and dew point.

In contrast, a hot-dry climate is characterized by (1) high air temperatures, which during the day range from 32.2° to 51.7° C (90° to 125° F); (2) low humidity, usually from 0% to 10%; (3) intense solar radiation; (4) very little precipitation; (5) little or no vegetation; and (6) marked day-night variation in temperature, often exceeding 50° F. Because of the lack of vegetation the ground absorbs considerable solar energy and may heat to 32.2° C (90° F). When the ground temperature exceeds that of the surrounding environment, the soil acts as a radiator for long-wave (infrared) radiation. Moreover, the terrain may reflect up to 30% of the incident sunlight. The ambient day air temperature is almost always higher than the skin and clothing; therefore this hotter air heats the individual's body instead of cooling it. In other words, in the hot-dry climate, because of the low moisture content, the solar energy either directly or indirectly heats surfaces as well as the ambient air. In this manner, solar energy exists as a sensible heat in contrast to that of the hot-wet climate. Finally, pervasive desert winds, while facilitating evaporative cooling, at the same time may increase the body's heat load by boosting the rate of heat exchange between the hot air and the cooler skin.

HEAT EXCHANGE AND CRITICAL AIR TEMPERATURE

Within a temperature range of 25° to 27° C (77° to 80° F), referred to as the "critical air temperature," an unclothed person at rest can maintain body temperature at the basal metabolic rate as heat production from basic metabolic processes is balanced by heat loss to the air.[1] Beyond this range the individual must resort to both passive and active mechanisms of heat loss to balance heat gain with heat loss and maintain thermal homeostasis. In a warm or hot environment the body may gain heat by the so-called passive mechanisms of radiation (R), convection (C), and conduction (Cd), the efficiency of each depending on the respective temperature gradient between the skin and environment (Fig. 2-1). As external temperatures rise, the gradient works against such passive mechanisms, and the organism must resort to active heat loss, chiefly through evaporation (E) of water from the skin and respiratory air passages and, to a lesser extent, through sweat in a liquid state. The relative amount of heat loss through the skin amounts to an average of 85% of the total body heat loss.

In addition to these external stresses, one must keep in mind that the body constantly produces heat as a by-product of normal metabolic processes. When these processes speed up, as during increased work load, metabolic heat production may become considerable. All these factors exist normally in a complex equilibrium. The interrelation of the principal factors involved in maintenance of a steady thermal state in cold and hot environments was originally expressed in the "Fort Knox Equation"[2]:

$$M \pm R \pm C \pm Cd - E \pm W \pm S = 0$$

$$\text{(all terms in kcal/m}^2\text{/hr)}$$

where M = metabolic heat production; W = heat gained or lost by water taken in or voided; S = stored or lost body heat; and R, C, Cd, and E as previously described. Metabolic heat production (M) is measured directly by calorimetry or indirectly through measurements of respiratory gas exchange. For a complete understanding of these avenues of heat gain and loss, each specific process will be discussed separately.

Radiation (R)

The flow of heat by radiation refers to the heat transfer that occurs when particular electromagnetic waves are emitted by one object and absorbed by another. The organism radiates heat to other objects and receives heat from other warmer objects (thus

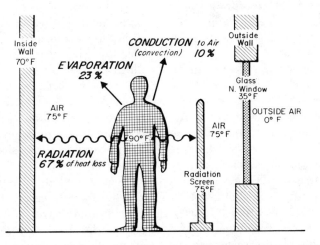

Fig. 2-1. Partitioning of heat exchange avenues from man. At air temperature of 24° C (75.2° F) most heat is lost by radiation and the rest by conduction and evaporation. (From Folk, G. E., Jr. 1974. Textbook of environmental physiology. Lea & Febiger, Philadelphia.)

R is + or −). The length of these waves, called infrared, is greater than that of visible light, from about 0.75 micron to 50 or more.* The radiant energy from mammalian skin varies in wavelength from 5 to 20 μm. Exchanges of heat by radiation between the environment and the body depend on an individual's effective radiating surface area, mean surface temperature, and skin and clothing emissivity and reflecting power in relation to the emissivity and average radiant temperature (infrared) of the environment.

In the infrared range (5 to 20 μm), skin color does not have an effect on reflectance; for this reason it is said that the human skin acts as a black body radiator with a power of emissivity close to 1. However, in the visible and ultraviolet portions of the spectrum, the color of the skin affects the reflectance and absorption of energy. For example, white skin, depending on degree of pigmentation, reflects 30% to 45% of the solar radiation, whereas black skin reflects less than 19% of these same rays.[3] In fact it has been shown that blacks exercising unprotected in the desert had a greater increase in rectal temperatures than did whites.[4] Similarly, white clothing has always been considered more suitable than black, both in the tropics because less heat is absorbed and in the polar regions because less heat is lost.[5]

The amount of heat gained or lost by radiation depends not only on the temperature and color of the object, but also on its surface area (which also includes texture). According to current estimates, the effective radiating surface area of a person standing with arms and legs spread is approximately 85% of the total skin area,[5] whereas for a sitting person it is approximately 70% to 75% of the total body surface area.[6] Indeed, when a person faces the sun rising on the horizon, 24.7% of his body surface receives direct radiation, but when the sun is directly overhead, a standing person receives direct radiation on only 4.4% of the body surface.[7] In other words, vertical posture increases the area available for warming when the sun is low in the morning or evening and minimizes heat load during the middle of the day (Fig. 2-2). The remaining skin surfaces, such as the inner surfaces of legs, arms, and corresponding sites on the trunk of a standing or sitting person, radiate to other skin surfaces and are therefore no considerations in the effective radiating surface area.

Just as variations in posture affect the degree of heat gained or lost by radiation, variations in body surface area have a potential influence on heat exchange by radiation. Body surface area may influence heat exchange in two directions. Under conditions in which the ambient temperature is lower than that of the skin, a large surface area per unit of body weight can be advantageous for facilitating heat loss. However, when the ambient temperature is higher, as is true in the desert, such a ratio can be a disadvantage because it increases the amount of heat that can be gained from the larger surface area exposed.

An increase in absolute size will increase both metabolic heat production and the capacity to store heat, each a function of body volume. This latter phenomenon is easily illustrated by placing two objects made of the same material in direct solar radiation. The smaller object, with less volume to distribute the radiation, will increase its temperature much more than the larger one.[5] Interactions of size, shape, and heat loss will be discussed in more detail later.

Heat gained or lost by radiation is also affected by the degree of insulation. Various investigations have shown that clothed subjects sitting in the sun gain only about half as much heat as when sitting unclothed. However, it must be noted that radiant-heat exchange in persons is complex in natural conditions because of the spectrum of wave-

---

*A micron (=) is one millionth (1×10^{-6}) of a meter.

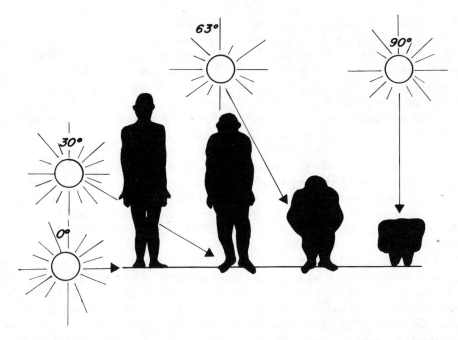

Fig. 2-2. Influence of body posture and surface area on effect of direct sunlight on standing man facing the sun at different solar elevations. Vertical posture increases surface area available for warming when sun is low in morning or evening and minimizes heat load during middle of day when sun is high. (Modified from Underwood, C. R., and E. J. Ward. 1966. Ergonomics **9**:155-168.)

lengths emitted at varying intensities and absorbed by the skin in varying degrees. An additional complicating factor is the fact that the spectrum and intensity of radiation from the terrain are different from those of the sun and sky.

Convection (C)

Convection refers to the transport of heat by a stream of molecules from a warm object toward a cooler object. The most common exchange of heat by convection begins with heat conduction from a warm body to surrounding air molecules. The heated air expands, becomes less dense, and rises, taking the heat with it, to be replaced by cooler, denser air. If the ambient air temperature is lower than that of the body, heat is lost, but if it is higher than that of the body, heat is gained through the reverse process (thus C is + or −). Heat exchange by convection

depends on (1) the difference in temperature between the body surface and the air, which in turn determines the amount of heat gained or lost by a unit mass of air contacting the skin, and (2) the air movements present, which in turn determine the mass of air that will come in contact with the skin surface. In general there are two different forms of convection: (1) natural convection (rising of warm air) and (2) forced convection, caused by the actions of an outside force (e.g., a fan). Natural convection depends on the natural buoyancy of heated material, and forced convection depends on the force of the air current and the movement of heated material within a medium.

Conduction (Cd)

Conduction refers to transfer of heat by direct physical contact. Heat exchange by conduction takes place within and outside the body. Internal conduction occurs from tissue to tissue, especially in the blood, and represents an important force in the distribution of body heat. External conduction occurs through physical contact by the skin with external objects. Conductive heat-loss experiments have usually demonstrated that external conduction represents only a small percentage of total heat exchange. Thus, in studies of adaptation to heat stress, conduction is not usually considered separately, but is discussed with radiation and convection. Furthermore, the areas of skin in contact with surrounding objects are usually small, and direct contact with highly conductive materials is avoided. However, in a clothed individual, conduction of metabolic heat from skin to clothing does take place. When heat reaches the clothing, it is dissipated from the outer clothing surfaces by evaporation and/or convection and radiation, depending on the amount of air movement, the ambient temperature, and the vapor pressure gradients between clothing and environment.

Evaporation (E)

Among the major avenues of heat exchange, only evaporation of water from the skin (in the form of sweat) and respiratory passages will always result in heat loss and never in heat gain. Heat is lost by evaporation because heat is required in the endothermic conversion of water to vapor. This heat is called the *latent heat of evaporation;*

it is estimated that evaporation of 1 ml (or gram) of water requires 0.58 kilocalorie (kcal) (1 L = [liter] or 1000 ml = 580 kcal). Therefore, evaporative heat loss is determined by the rate of water evaporation from the skin and respiratory system multiplied by ($\times$) the latent heat of water evaporation (0.58 kcal).

The relative role played by each of the four avenues of heat loss depends on the interaction of ambient temperature and humidity. Thus, as shown in Table 1, in a comfortable climate with a temperature of 25° C (77° F) an unclothed seated person loses metabolic heat mostly through radiation (67%), and very little heat is lost through evaporation (23%) and convection (10%). At a warm temperature of 30° C (86° F) heat is lost in about equal proportions by radiation (41%), convection (33%), and evaporation (26%). At temperatures higher than 35° C (95° F), 90% of the heat lost is by evaporation, and very little (4% and 6%, respectively) is lost by radiation and convection.[8] As the ambient temperature rises, sweat production is increased to maintain thermal homeostasis. Indeed, the sweat rate increases 20 ml for every 1° C rise in air temperature. Once sweating begins, the skin blood flow must continue to increase as the heat load increases to transfer more heat from the internal body core toward the periphery, where it will be dissipated to the environment by the evaporation of sweat. When evaporation is incomplete because of in-

Table 1. Mechanisms of heat loss from the body (nude) at different room temperatures (at constant low air movement)*

Room temperature	Radiation (%)	Convection (%)	Evaporation (%)
Comfortable = 25° C (77° F)	67	10	23
Warm = 30° C (86° F)	41	33	26
Hot = 35° C (95° F)	4	6	90

*From Folk, G. E., Jr. 1974. Textbook of environmental physiology. Lea & Febiger, Philadelphia.

creased humidity, sweat production is a far less efficient means of heat dissipation. This problem will be considered in detail later.

GENERAL PHYSIOLOGICAL RESPONSES TO HEAT STRESS
Vasodilation and heat conductance

During the first 3 to 5 days of continuous or intermittent exposure to heat stress and work load, the capacity of each avenue of heat loss is maximized. The initial response to this exposure is a reduction in body insulation or an increase in heat conductance. The reduction in body insulation is achieved through an increase in blood flow brought about by vasodilation and a reduction in vasomotor tone. Conspicuous evidence of vasodilation can be seen in the red-faced individual doing work under heat stress. By increasing the blood flow, more heat passes from the core to the shell, so the rate of heat lost by radiation to the environment is enhanced. In this manner, thermoconductance

of peripheral tissues may increase five to six times.

The rate of heat conductance is influenced by the "countercurrent" system of blood flow (Fig. 2-3). In a cold environment most of the venous return from arms and legs is through the deep venae comitantes that receive heat from blood flowing through the arteries and thereby minimize heat loss. Thus heat conductance to the periphery is low, yet actual blood flow to the limbs may be high, protecting tissues of the limbs from cold injury and hypoxia. In a hot environment most of the venous blood flow returns through the peripheral veins, and because these are close to the surface, heat loss to the environment is increased.[9,10] By this pathway external heat loss is maximized with high conductance. Furthermore, blood temperature is directly related to its distance from the body core so, under conditions of heat stress, the temperature of blood in the superficial veins of the fingers is higher than that at the elbow.

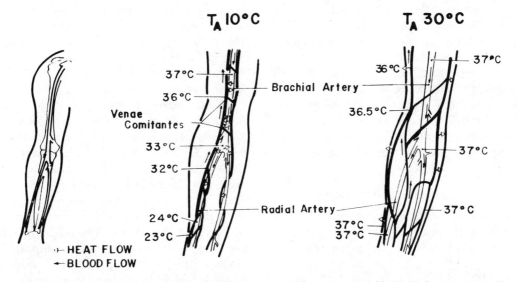

Fig. 2-3. Countercurrent heat exchange in human arm. When room is cold (10° C), heat is given off from veins near skin; as a result radial arterial blood may be 37° C. (Modified from Bullard, R. W., 1971. Temperature regulation. In E. E. Selkurt, ed. Physiology. Little, Brown & Co., Boston.)

As a result of these changes, and in order to compensate for the increased cutaneous blood flow needed for heat dissipation, the organism resorts to a compensatory vasoconstriction of internal vascular beds and to an increase of total circulating blood volume, providing more blood for cutaneous flow. With acclimation evaporative cooling improves, and the blood volume returns to pre-exposure levels.

Heat storage

An individual's mean skin temperature varies with the ambient temperature, whereas the rectal (core) temperature is regulated within narrow limits over a wide range of thermal stresses. However, on initial exposure to work in heat stress, the rectal temperature, especially when associated with body dehydration, rises markedly. The rectal temperature of a man exposed to desert conditions increases in a linear fashion with a progressive water deficit, reaching a 2° C increase at 10% water deficit.[11] This is probably associated with increased viscosity of the blood and the resulting inefficiency of the heart stroke volume during exposure.* On the other hand, the rise in body temperature may be an adaptive response in that it can reduce the heat load in a hot environment because the difference in temperature between the environment and the cooler body is diminished.[12] Since heat flow from the environment is nearly proportional to the temperature gradient, the flow decreases as the difference decreases.

Sweating, dehydration, and circulation

As the ambient temperature and work load increase, nearly all the extra heat produced by the body is lost by evaporation. The

---

*Stroke volume means the amount of blood pumped by the heart with each contraction.

production of thermal sweat, however, is a conspicuous and costly physiological event. On a hot day in the desert most individuals can produce sweat at a rate ranging from 0.5 to 4.2 L/hr. Because of this marked increase in sweat loss, even under conditions of ad libitum water intake, there is always some amount of dehydration, since a person's thirst is not sufficient to stimulate replacement of all the lost body water.

Since dehydration results in weight loss, the physiological effects of dehydration can be evaluated by determining percent changes in body weight. For example, at a 2% weight loss, the immediate response is marked thirst. At 4% the mouth and throat feel quite dry. Between 6% and 8% loss salivary function stops, and speech becomes difficult. At 10% weight loss a person is physically and mentally incapacitated. At a 12% weight loss an individual is no longer able to swallow and cannot recover without assistance; indeed, according to studies of Adolph,[11] an individual who suffers from as much as 12% dehydration must be given water either intravenously or through other invasive means. Finally, if dehydration continues, the organism is not able to maintain internal body temperature, so the rectal temperature increases in a linear fashion with a progressive water deficit.

As the degree of water deficit increases, the heart rate also increases to as much as 40 beats per minute above the normal rate when 8% of the body weight has been lost. Under these conditions the stroke volume decreases although the heart rate increases. Thus, while the pulse rate increases up to 40%, the stroke volume decreases a similar amount, and the amount of blood pumped by the heart per minute (cardiac output) remains nearly the same. Also as a result of marked dehydration, there is a decrease in extracellular fluids such as plasma, resulting in an increased viscosity of the blood and putting an additional load on the heart. Finally, because of the marked sweat or fluid loss, there appears to be a transitory response of reduced excretion of body fluids.

EVAPORATION AND ITS REGULATION

Evaporation of water from the body occurs in three forms: insensible evaporation, emotional evaporation, and thermal sweating.

Insensible evaporation

Insensible evaporation, or perspiration (diffusion of water), leaves the body at all times unless the ambient atmosphere is too humid (100% saturated). This moisture diffuses through the pores of the sweat glands at a rate of approximately 99 ml/24 hr. Similarly, diffusion of water from the lungs occurs at about 400 ml/24 hr. Thus on the average, in temperate zones, insensible perspiration results in a heat loss of 522 kcal from the sweat glands (900 ml × 0.58 kcal = 522 kcal) and 232 kcal from the lungs (400 ml × 0.58 kcal/ml = 232 kcal). This water loss through the skin and lungs may vary with altitude and the general quantity of moisture in the air—the higher the altitude, the greater the insensible moisture loss through the skin.

Emotional evaporation

Emotional evaporation occurs through the skin on the forehead, the eccrine glands (soles of the feet and palms of the hands), and the apocrine glands (axillary and pubic). This nonthermal sweating usually occurs when the individual is under emotional stress rather than physical or thermal stress.

Thermal sweating

The contributions of insensible water loss and emotional perspiration to thermoregulation of heat stress are minimal in contrast to that of thermal sweating. Humans can sweat profusely, and it is this capacity that enables them to adapt to a wide range of heat stresses. Thermal sweating occurs through the eccrine glands located in all body segments (head, face, trunk, arms, and legs). These glands are activated by hypothalamic impulses along sympathetic motor nerve fibers, also termed *cholinergic fibers* because they release acetylcholine. This chemical, usually associated with the parasympathetic nervous system, is a powerful stimulator of the sweat glands.

The reflex control of sweating seems to be partially related to the stimulation occurring from skin receptors and partially from the temperature of the hypothalamus. It has been postulated that the reflex act of sweating is initiated by thermal receptors in the skin, and the degree of activity may be stimulated by a temperature rise in blood passing through the hypothalamus.[5] Another hypothesis maintains that sweating is solely affected by receptors located deep within the skin.[5] Increased temperature of the hypothalamic center appears related to the center's increased responsiveness to incoming impulses from the cutaneous thermoreceptors or to deeper nerve signals.[13] In any event, signals from the cutaneous thermoreceptors seem the first line of defense against environmental heat stress. Heat warms the skin, stimulating these receptors to initiate the reflex arc that elicits sweating and cutaneous vasodilation, thus preventing significant body temperature elevation. However, sweating is initiated not only by a change in skin temperature, but also by an increase in mean body temperature. Even in a cold environment with low skin temperature, a hardworking person sweats profusely. During steady states of work, sweat rate is directly proportional to work rate, metabolic heat production, and the corresponding increase of central body temperature, even without corresponding skin temperature changes.

Whatever mechanisms control sweating, it is clear that water exchange through the kidneys, skin, and respiratory tract may range from 1 to 2 L/24 hr in sedentary conditions and a cool environment, to 10 to 12 L/24 hr for individuals working in a hot environment. Water output from sweat glands increases in proportion to the need for evaporative cooling. The importance of balancing increased output by increasing water input is also clear from the effects of dehydration on blood volume, circulation, sweating, and temperature regulation of individuals working in heat. The regulation of water intake to balance water output in hot climates depends on thirst.

Thirst

There are two traditional theories regarding the mechanisms that control thirst.[5] Cannon[14] postulated that thirst originates locally in receptors in the mouth and pharynx and is stimulated by dryness resulting from decreased salivary secretion as the body becomes dehydrated.[5] On the other hand, Bernard[15] suggested that the sensation of thirst is of diffuse origin and results from general dehydration. Although the sensation of thirst may originate from a mouth and pharynx that are dry from decreased salivary secretion, the regulation of water intake also may depend on other peripheral receptors. Evidence from animal experimentation suggests that a drinking center exists in the hypothalamus, a structure itself sensitive to hypertonic sodium chloride solutions and to differing impulses from peripheral receptors. In one such experiment, the hypothalamus cells were stimulated in goats, and the animals drank large quantities of water and overhydrated themselves up to 40% of their body weight.[16]

Under natural conditions drinking stops before water has been absorbed from the stomach and is capable of diluting the blood. The amount of water passing through the esophagus seems, then, to influence the animal's continued drinking. This mechanism in humans is apparently not sufficient to replace the water lost through evaporated sweat. Even with full access to water, after heavy sweating a human being undergoes a voluntary dehydration that often reaches 2% to 4% of body weight. Thirst is thus satisfied before water intake equals loss.[11] In fact, when volunteers working under heat stress were asked to drink sufficient quantities of water to replace sweat loss, none were able to without reporting abdominal discomfort and nausea.[11,17] Because of this paradoxical drinking behavior, serious dehydration, circulatory strain, and elevated rectal temperature may result when working persons "voluntarily" abstain from water despite a plentiful supply.[11,17] If sodium loss is not replaced, thirst will demand replacement only to restore the isotonic sodium concentrations in the extracellular fluid. If water loss is fully replaced without the corresponding sodium replacement, the plasma sodium concentration will decrease, and diuresis will proceed until the isotonic balance is restored. Thus dehydration is actually secondary to salt deficiency.

Sodium adjustments

Several investigators have demonstrated that sodium loss may be great in unacclimatized individuals, and that with acclimatization the concentration of sodium in the sweat decreases. For example, in an unacclimatized person the sweat contains high concentrations of sodium that may range from 40 to 65 mEq/L. After a 2-week period of acclimatization, the salt concentration in sweat decreases to between 10 and 20 mEq/L. The sweat-salt concentration depends on (1) the presence or absence of a dietary salt deficit along with a water deficit in the extracellular fluid volume and increased mineralocorticoid activity,[18] so as the water and salt deficit increases, the sweat-salt concentration decreases, and (2) the amount of sweating—the greater the sweat output, the greater the concentration of salt.[19]

INDIVIDUAL FACTORS AND TOLERANCE TO HEAT
Age

Age is an important biological factor that affects tolerance to work in heat stress. In general, subjects over the age of 45 are less able to tolerate heat stress than younger subjects.[20,21] However, the relationship between age and tolerance to heat stress is not linear. As shown by studies on men and women,[22,23] preadolescent subjects (less than 11 years old) and older subjects (46 to 67 years) have a lower capacity to sweat and a lesser work capacity than adolescents (15 to 16 years) and adults (20 to 29 years). It is evident, then, that at both extremes of age, the capacity to adjust to heat stress is impaired, probably because of incomplete physiological development in young subjects and onset of thermoregulatory mechanism deterioration among older subjects.

Body size and shape

According to Fourier's Law of Heat Flow, the rate of heat loss per minute is directly proportional to body surface and to the difference between temperature of the body core and that of the environment, and inversely proportional to the thickness of the body shell. In other words, the greater the surface area, the greater the rate at which heat leaves the core toward the surrounding environment. Conversely, the smaller the thickness of the barrier between the core and the exterior, the greater the rate of heat flow. However, the relation of physique to heat tolerance is not a simple one and must be considered in reference to different conditions of heat stress and energy production.

First, heat production during exercise is nearly proportional to body weight, that is, the heavier the subject, the greater the heat production. Second, when body size increases, the increase in surface area does not keep pace with the increase in body weight. Therefore, a tall, heavy subject has a lower surface area:weight ratio than a short, lightweight subject. In the same manner a tall, lean subject has a greater surface area: weight ratio than a short, stocky subject. That is, for a given body weight, a physique that emphasizes linearity increases the surface area:weight ratio.

In theory a tall, heavy or short, stocky subject working under heat stress has greater heat production and smaller ranges of heat loss than a short, lightweight or tall, lean subject. Accordingly, under conditions where the ambient temperature is lower than the skin temperature, a short, lightweight or tall, lean subject with a high surface area: weight ratio would produce less heat and have a greater area for sweat evaporation and for heat loss by radiation and convection than a tall, heavy (large) or short, stocky individual. In contrast, under conditions in which the ambient temperature or effective temperature (either dry or humid heat) is higher than the skin temperature, the subjects with high surface area:weight ratio would have little advantage, since the relatively large surface area providing extensive evaporation of sweat would also result in significant heat gains by radiation and convection, negating the positive effects of the evaporative process.

Experimental studies have confirmed in part these theoretical expectations.[24] These investigations have shown that in humid heat (30° C, 28° C wet bulb) subjects with high surface area:weight ratios produced less heat and lost more heat through radiation and convection and therefore had less heat storage than subjects with low surface area: weight ratios (Fig. 2-4). On the other hand, as the ambient temperature increased to 35°, 45°, or 50° C, the subjects with a high surface area:weight ratio produced less heat,

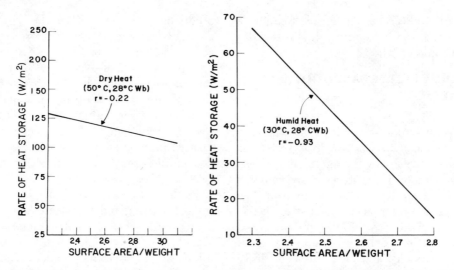

Fig. 2-4. Relationship between surface area:weight ratio and rate of heat storage of twenty-five subjects performing moderate work at dry heat (50° C) and eight subjects performing mild work in humid heat (30° C). Subjects with high surface area:weight ratio in humid heat (30° C) have lower heat storage because of lower heat production and greater area for heat loss than subjects with low surface area:weight ratios. As temperature increases or in dry heat, the high surface area increases heat load and heat storage. (Based on data from Shvartz, E., E. Saavand, and D. Benor. 1973. J. Appl. Physiol. **34:**799-803.)

but because they gained more heat from the ambient temperature through radiation and convection, they had similar heat storage to the subjects with low surface area:weight ratios. Computer simulations indicate that a high surface area:weight ratio is advantageous when evaporative heat loss and radiation-convection heat loss are high.[25] On the other hand, when radiation-convection heat losses are low, a high surface area:weight ratio is not advantageous because rather than increasing heat loss, it may increase heat load. Thus it would appear that the role of body size and shape is dependent on the ambient temperature to which the subjects are exposed.

Fatness

The other component of Fourier's law is that the rate of heat flow from the core to the exterior is greater as the shell thickness decreases. Various investigations have indi-

cated that fat or obese subjects of all ages and both sexes are under greater heat strain while working in heat than their lean counterparts as shown by their higher rectal temperature, higher heart rate, and lower sweat rate.[26,27] These differences, in addition to being related to the insulative effects of subcutaneous fat, are probably related to the fact that overweight or obese subjects have a lower surface area:weight ratio than their lean counterparts. Therefore, the heavier subjects produce more heat and also have less avenues for heat loss by radiation and convection.

Physical fitness and cardiovascular function

Tolerance and acclimation to heat stress are affected by the individual's state of physical fitness, and, in general, the more fit one is, the faster acclimation takes place. It must also be noted that acclimation to heat stress develops when the subject exercises during heat exposure, but will not develop when the subject is exposed to heat stress without any exercise.[28,29]

As measured by maximum oxygen intake (aerobic capacity), tolerance to work in heat stress is related to cardiovascular fitness. Experimental studies have shown that subjects with a high maximum oxygen intake have a greater tolerance to heat stress than those with low oxygen intake.[30] In addition, tolerance to heat stress is affected by the capacity to expand the vascular volume. It has been found that heat-intolerant subjects, even when working at a lower absolute work load with a smaller water deficit, are not able to expand their vascular volume to the same degree as the tolerant subjects, probably because the absolute amount of protein in their extravascular space is markedly less than for the tolerant subjects.[31]

ACCLIMATION

Studies on acclimation involve exposure of physically well-conditioned subjects to work in a wide range of temperatures and humidities under laboratory conditions. The test usually includes 60 to 120 minutes of daily exposure to treadmill or bicycle ergometric work in humid heat (28° to 30° C wet bulbs) or dry heat (50° C dry bulb) for periods of 2 or 4 weeks. During these tests data on rectal temperature, skin temperature, pulse rate, ventilation, oxygen consumption, sweat loss, and other variables are monitored at appropriate intervals. These studies indicate that acclimation to heat stress is attained through adjustments of the cardiovascular system. The mechanism that enables the organism to attain thermal homeostasis during the period of intial acclimation is different from those for full acclimation.

General trends

When exposed to heat stress, the nonacclimated person, because of a poor peripheral heat conductance and a low sweating capacity, exhibits an increased heat and circulatory strain (Fig. 2-5). During the first 4 days of exposure to heat stress, an increase in blood flow from the internal core to the shell may increase the peripheral heat conductance from five to six times its normal value. Simultaneously, there is an excessive increase in sweat rate and sodium loss, which may amount to more than 50% of preacclimation levels. Only a small proportion of this sweat is evaporated; a 10% increase in evaporation is accompanied by a 200% increase in nonevaporated sweat.[33] This means that during acclimation to heat stress the skin and rectal temperatures are lowered through a wasteful overproduction of sweat. During this stage the circulatory strain is decreased as shown by the return of the heart rate to preexposure levels.

With repeated exposure full acclimation to heat stress is attained through the continued maintenance of high peripheral heat conductance. The increase in vasodilation by increased perfusion of the cutaneous interstitial space also results in an increase in plasma volume and total circulating protein.[32,33] The enhanced peripheral heat conductance is also accompanied by a more complete and even distribution of sweat over the skin.[5,28,35]

Furthermore, the skin temperature threshold for the onset of sweating is decreased, which means that an equivalent rate of sweating is achieved at a lower skin temperature.[35-37] As a result of the decrease in skin temperature, the rectal temperature decreases simultaneously and circulatory stability is maintained. During acclimation the renal sodium output is drastically reduced and sweat-sodium concentration is also decreased. However, when considering the total greater sweat loss, even after full acclimation the total loss of sodium exceeds preacclimation levels. Along with an improved physiological response, the disagree-

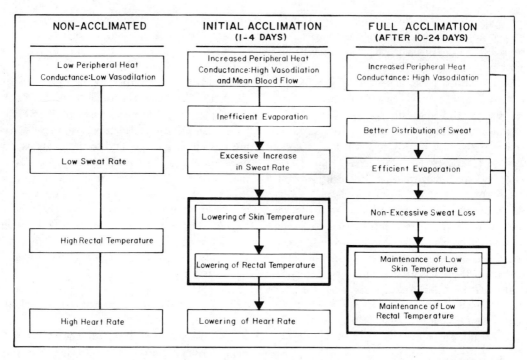

Fig. 2-5. Schematization of mechanism of acclimation to heat stress. During initial acclimation thermal homeostasis is attained through an increased peripheral conductance, but evaporation is inefficient so that sweat rate becomes excessive. In full acclimation thermal homeostasis is achieved through an increased peripheral heat conductance, better distribution of sweat, and efficient evaporation.

able sensations associated with heat exposure are progressively reduced until individuals are able to work without much discomfort.[5]

Acclimation of women

All studies indicate that women, like men, can be artificially acclimated to heat, manifesting similar physiological adjustments. Acclimated women during exposure to work in heat stress show a reduction in heart rate, a lowering of rectal temperature, an increased skin temperature, an onset of sweating at a lower skin temperature, and an increased sweating capacity.[38-42] However, it appears that the limits of endurance under extreme heat stress for women are less than those for men. This difference appears related to a woman's excessively high skin temperature that results in a lower thermal gradient for removing metabolic heat and less reserve capacity for moving blood to the skin.[5]

CONCLUSION

When air temperature exceeds the critical level of 26.7° C (80° F) the organism, to maintain thermal balance, activates its avenues of heat loss. This is accomplished through decreased insulation brought about by increased blood flow and vasodilation, which in turn maximizes heat loss by radiation and convection. If this mechanism is not sufficient, the evaporation of sweat is increased so that heat loss through sweating becomes the major avenue of heat loss under stressful heat conditions.

Onset of sweating appears related to increased skin and internal body temperature. Under extreme heat stress, the rate of sweating can reach as much as 10 to 12 L/24 hr. Along with the increased sweat, the organism loses large amounts of sodium and body fluids. To maintain homeostasis the organism must readjust its excretion. This is what occurs during acclimation and acclimatization, which will be discussed in the next chapter.

Tolerance to heat stress is influenced by age; very young and very old subjects are less tolerant than adolescents and adults. Body size, shape, and subcutaneous fat influence the rate of heat production and heat loss, and their significance depends on the degree of heat intensity and work. In the same manner, cardiovascular function influences both tolerance and acclimation to heat stress; subjects in good health and physical condition are able to tolerate heat stress better than subjects who are not as healthy or physically fit. Acclimation to heat results in an enhanced tolerance to work under heat stress. This is attained through increased peripheral heat conductance in which the rate of heat transfer from the internal body core to the periphery is increased. Along with increased heat conductance, the capacity to sweat increases to as much as four times the preacclimation capacity, and this increase occurs at a lower skin temperature. Although the sweat-sodium concentration decreases with acclimation because of the increase in total sweat output, the sodium loss exceeds preacclimation levels. Concomitant with increased heat conductance and as a result of the improved cooling efficiency of sweat, the rectal temperature and heart rate return to preacclimation levels, and the disagreeable sensations associated with heat exposure are progressively reduced. Although the limits of endurance under extreme heat stress for women are less than those for men, women with acclimation to heat stress show the same thermoregulation responses as men.

REFERENCES

1. Erickson, H., and J. Krog. 1956. Critical temperature for naked man. Acta Physiol. Scand. **37**:35-39.
2. Newburgh, L. H., ed. 1949. Physiology of heat regulation and the science of clothing. W. B. Saunders Co., Philadelphia.
3. Hardy, J. D. 1949. Heat transfer. In L. H. Newman, ed. Physiology of heat regulation. W. B. Saunders Co., Philadelphia.
4. Baker, P. T. 1958. Racial differences in heat tolerance. Am. J. Phys. Anthropol. **16**:287-305.
5. Folk, G. E., Jr. 1974. Textbook of environmental physiology. Lea & Febiger, Philadelphia.
6. Windslow, C. E. A., L. P. Herrington, and A. P. Gagge. 1936. The determination of radiation and convection exchanges by partitional calorimetry. Am. J. Physiol. **116**:669-684.
7. Underwood, C. R., and E. J. Ward. 1966. The solar radiation area of man. Ergonomics **9**:155-168.
8. Hardy, J. D. 1961. The physiology of temperature regulation. Physiol. Rev. **41**:521-606.
9. Bazett, H. C., and B. McGlone. 1927. Temperature gradients in the tissue of man. Am. J. Physiol. **82**:415-451.
10. Gisolfi, C., and S. Robinson. 1970. Central and peripheral stimuli regulating sweating during intermittent work in men. J. Appl. Physiol. **29**:761-768.
11. Adolph, E. F. 1947. Physiology of man in the desert. Interscience, New York.
12. Schmidt-Nielsen, K. 1954. Heat regulation in small and large desert mammals. In J. L. Cloudsley-Thompson, ed. Biology of deserts. Institute of Biology, London.
13. Bazett, H. C. 1949. The regulation of body temperatures. In L. H. Newburgh, ed. Physiology of heat regulation, and the science of clothing. W. B. Saunders Co., Philadelphia.
14. Cannon, W. B. 1918. The physiological basis of thirst. Proc. R. Soc. Lond. **1390**:283-301.
15. Bernard, C. 1850. Lecons de physiologie experi-

mentale appliquée à la medicine. vol. 2. Bailliere, Paris.

16. Andersson, B., and S. M. McCann. 1955. A further study of polydipsia evoked by hypothalamic stimulation in the goat. Acta Physiol. Scand. **33**:333-346.
17. Pitt, G. C., R. E. Johnson, and C. F. Consolazio. 1944. Work in the heat as affected by intake of water, salt and glucose. Am. J. Physiol. **142**:253-259.
18. Smiles, K. A., and S. Robinson. 1971. Sodium ion conservation during acclimatization of men to work in the heat. J. Appl. Physiol. **31**:63-69.
19. Allan, J. R., and C. G. Wilson. 1971. Influence of acclimatization on sweat sodium concentration. J. Appl. Physiol. **30**:708-712.
20. Hellon, R. F., and A. R. Lind. 1958. The influence of age on peripheral vasodilation in a hot environment. J. Physiol. (Lond.) **141**:262-272.
21. Lind, A. R., P. W. Humphreys, K. J. Collins, K. Foster, and K. F. Sweetland. 1970. Influence of age and daily duration of exposure on responses of men to work in the heat. J. Appl. Physiol. **28**:50-56.
22. Wagner, J. A., S. Robinson, S. P. Tzankoff, and R. P. Marino. 1972. Heat tolerance and acclimatization to work in the heat in relation to age. J. Appl. Physiol. **33**:616-622.
23. Lofstedt, B. 1966. Human heat tolerance. Dept. of Hygiene, University of Lund, Lund, Sweden.
24. Shvartz, E., E. Saavand, and D. Benor. 1973. Physique and heat tolerance in hot-dry and hot-humid environments. J. Appl. Physiol. **34**:799-803.
25. Austin, D. M. 1977. Body size and heat tolerance: a computer simulation approach. Am. J. Phys. Anthropol. (Abstract) **47**:116.
26. Bar-or, O., H. M. Lundegren, and E. R. Buskirk. 1969. Heat tolerance of exercising obese and lean women. J. Appl. Physiol. **26**:403-409.
27. Haymes, E. H., R. J. McCormick, and E. R. Buskirk. 1975. Heat tolerance of exercising lean and obese boys. J. Appl. Physiol. **39**:457-461.
28. Gisolfi, C., and S. Robinson. 1969. Relations between physical training, acclimatization and heat tolerance. J. Appl. Physiol. **26**:530-534.
29. Gisolfi, C. 1973. Work-heat tolerance derived from interval training. J. Appl. Physiol. **35**:349-354.
30. Wyndham, C. H., N. B. Strydom, A. J. Von Rensburg, A. J. S. Benade, and A. J. Heyns. 1970. Relation between VO2 max and body temperature in hot humid air conditions. J. Appl. Physiol. **29**:45-50.
31. Senay, L. C., Jr. 1975. Plasma volumes and constituents of heat-exposed men before and after acclimatization. J. Appl. Physiol. **38**:570-575.
32. Senay, L. C., D. Mitchell, and C. H. Wyndham. 1976. Acclimatization in a hot, humid environment: body fluid adjustments. J. Appl. Physiol. **40**:786-796.
33. Mitchell, D., L. C. Senay, C. H. Wyndham, A. J. Van Rensburg, G. G. Rogers, and N. B. Strydom. 1976. Acclimatization in a hot, humid environment: energy exchange, body temperature, and sweating. J. Appl. Physiol. **40**:768-778.
34. Ladell, W. S. S. 1964. Terrestrial animals in humid heat: man. In D. B. Dill, E. F. Adolph, and C. G. Wilber, eds. Handbook of physiology. vol. 4. Adaptation to the environment. American Physiological Society, Washington, D.C.
35. Colin, J., and Y. Houdas. 1965. Initiation of sweating in man after abrupt rise in environmental temperature. J. Appl. Physiol. **20**:984-990.
36. Houdas, Y., J. Colin, J. Timbal, C. Bontelier, and J. D. Guien. 1972. Skin temperatures in warm environments and the control of sweat evaporation. J. Appl. Physiol. **33**:99-104.
37. Wyndham, C. H., G. G. Rogers, L. C. Senay, and D. Mitchell. 1976. Acclimatization in a hot, humid environment: cardiovascular adjustments. J. Appl. Physiol. **40**:779-785.
38. Hertig, B. A., and F. Sargent, II. 1963. Acclimatization of women during work in hot environments. Fed. Proc. **22**:810-813.
39. Wyndham, C. H., J. F. Morrison, and C. G. Williams. 1965. Heat reactions of male and female Caucasians. J. Appl. Physiol. **20**:357-364.
40. Morimoto, T., Z. Slabochova, R. K. Naman, and R. Sargent, II. 1967. Sex differences in physiological reactions to thermal stress. J. Appl. Physiol. **22**:526-532.
41. Kamon. E., and B. Avellini. 1976. Physiologic limits to work in the heat and evaporative coefficient for women. J. Appl. Physiol. **41**:71-76.
42. Dill, D. B., M. K. Yousef, and J. D. Nelson. 1973. Responses of men and women to two-hour walks in desert heat. J. Appl. Physiol. **35**:231-235.

3 Acclimatization to heat stress: native and non-native populations

Since the 1950s several reports have appeared on indigenous adaptations in Mauritania,[1] Nigeria,[2] and Singapore.[1] However, the only detailed studies have been those conducted among whites and Bantus prior to and after acclimation to work in heat stress.[3] In addition, the thermoregulatory responses to work in heat stress of Bushmen from the Kalahari Desert,[4] Arabs from the Sahara Desert,[5] and aborigines from central Australia[6] have also been evaluated. Because these investigations were all conducted under the same thermal and work conditions, they provide an excellent opportunity for evaluating the quality and functional significance of population differences in adaptation to work in heat stress. The following discussion is based on the results of these studies.

One of the difficulties in evaluating population differences in heat acclimatization is the diversity of techniques and reference populations. For this reason, researchers of the Human Science Laboratory of South Africa have evaluated the thermoregulatory responses to work in heat stress of whites and Bantus before and after acclimation, and Bushmen, Arabs, and Australian aborigines all under the same standard conditions of temperature and workload. The experimental routine consisted of having the subjects step up and down on a bench with the height adjusted to give a work load of 216 kg-m/min (1560 foot-pounds/min) at a rate of 12 steps per minute. The external work was set to require an oxygen consumption of about 1 L/min. The experiment lasted for 4 hours and was conducted at 33.9° C (93° F) dry bulb and 32.2° C (90° F) wet bulb temperatures, with 24 m/min (80 feet/min) air movement.

ACCLIMATED AND NONACCLIMATED BANTUS AND WHITES

The Bantus of South Africa, like those of central Africa, are both agriculturalists and

Table 2. Anthropometric characteristics of adult nonacclimated and acclimated whites, Bantus, Bushmen, Chaamba Arabs, and Australian aborigines tested in studies of heat stress*

	Whites				Bantus				Bushmen				Chaamba Arabs		Australian aborigines	
	Non-acclimated		Acclimated		Non-acclimated		Acclimated		Desert		River					
	N = 20		N = 10		N = 22		N = 20		N = 8		N = 10		N = 15		N = 31	
	Mean	SD	Mean	SD	Mean	SD	Mean	SD	Mean	SD	Mean	SD	Mean	SD	Mean	SD
Height (cm)	175.9	7.71	174.6	6.54	165.9	6.13	166.8	5.87	160.5	6.08	171.3	6.73	105.4	5.51	172.0	5.25
Weight (kg)	70.24	7.02	69.34	6.97	59.1	6.18	60.5	5.92	47.5	5.18	61.22	4.89	55.18	5.47	56.48	6.47
Surface area (m²)	1.86	0.13	1.84	0.12	1.66	0.11	1.68	0.10	1.47	0.11	1.74	0.09	1.60	0.09	1.67	0.10
Surface area : weight ratio (cm²/kg)	2.65	0.12	2.65	0.25	2.82	0.42	2.78	0.14	3.11	0.03	2.85	0.14	2.91	0.16	2.97	0.16
Skinfold (mm)	8.09	2.99	8.27	2.62	5.45	1.05	5.95	1.64	4.75	1.99	4.73	0.04	6.15	3.35	6.63	1.12

*Modified from Wyndham, C. H. 1966. In P. T. Baker and J. S. Weiner, eds. The biology of human adaptability. Clarendon Press, Oxford.

pastoralists, living in a moderately hot environment. The mean daily maximum temperature for January (summer) ranges from 25° C (77° F) to 31.1° C (88° F). The relative humidity ranges from 44% to 68%; the wet bulb temperature ranges from 18.1° C (65° F) to 25.1° C (77° F). The effective general temperature, then, falls within the range of 22° C (71° F) to 25.1° C (79° F).[7]

To evaluate the degree of acclimatization of the Bantus, a sample of twenty male Bantus and twenty white male subjects was acclimated to work in heat stress. The white subjects were second-year medical students. The Bantus were all recruits for work in the South African mines. The acclimation procedure included 12 days of work, 4 hours per day, at an air temperature of 36° C (96° F) dry bulb and 33.8° C (93° F) wet bulb, with 24 m/min air movement. The external work was the same as indicated before.

All twenty nonacclimated Bantus completed the 4-hour experiment, but only ten of the twenty nonacclimated whites were able to do so. Although both the nonacclimated and acclimated Bantus were shorter, lighter in weight, and leaner than the whites, they had a greater surface area per unit of body weight. The mean surface area:weight ratio for the nonacclimated Bantus equaled 2.82 cm^2/kg and 2.78 cm^2/kg for the acclimated Bantus, whereas for the nonacclimated and acclimated whites it equaled 2.65 cm^2/kg (Table 2). The nonacclimated Bantus sweated at a lower rate ($ml/m^2/hr$) during most of the test while maintaining a lower rectal temperature and a lower heart rate than the nonacclimated whites (Fig. 3-1). Furthermore, as

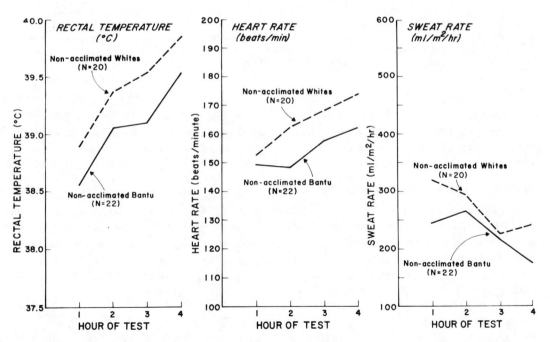

Fig. 3-1. Physiological responses to standardized heat stress test of nonacclimated Bantus and nonacclimated whites. The Bantus respond to heat stress with lower increase in rectal temperature and heart rate while maintaining a lower sweat rate than the nonacclimated whites. (Based on data from Wyndham, C. H. 1966. Southern African ethnic adaptation to temperature and exercise. In P. T. Baker and J. S. Weiner, eds. The biology of human adaptability. Clarendon Press, Oxford.)

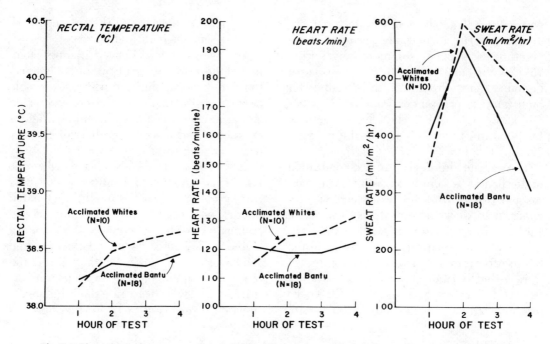

Fig. 3-2. Physiological responses to standardized heat stress test of acclimated Bantus and acclimated whites. The Bantus, as those in the nonacclimated state, are able to maintain thermal homeostasis with lower sweat rate and lower heart rate than the acclimated whites. (Based on data from Wyndham, C. H. 1966. Southern African ethnic adaptation to temperature and exercise. In P. T. Baker and J. S. Weiner, eds. The biology of human adaptability. Clarendon Press, Oxford.)

illustrated in Fig. 3-2, the acclimated Bantus, during the last 3 hours of the test, had a systematically lower rectal temperature and lower heart and sweat rates than the whites.

BANTUS: INTERTRIBAL COMPARISON

An evaluation of a total of 120 nonacclimated male Bantu subjects belonging to six Bantu tribes was made when they arrived (within 1 week) in Johannesburg.[7,8] No significant intertribal differences in terms of work performance or thermoregulatory responses were revealed. An outstanding observation of this study was that only three of the 120 Bantu subjects developed rectal temperatures above 40° C (104° F), and only one individual collapsed, with a rectal temperature of 38.9° C (102° F). This finding contrasts markedly with the fact that 50% of the twenty nonacclimated young whites in the aforementioned study failed to complete the 4-hour test, five with a rectal temperature of 40° C (104° F), and five either collapsed or were exhausted. These findings clearly document the fact that when exposed to heat the nonacclimated Bantus are less liable to heat collapse and have greater cardiovascular stability than do Caucasians. These Bantu subjects also had lower sweat rates than the nonacclimated whites.

The Bantus, then, whether nonacclimated or acclimated, maintain thermal homeostasis with a generally lower sweat rate while working in heat stress than both the nonacclimated and acclimated whites. The fact that the rectal temperatures of the acclimated

Bantus were not higher than those of the acclimated Caucasians indicates that the Bantus were losing heat through channels other than sweat evaporation alone.

BUSHMEN

The Bushmen are divided into several tribal groups, some of which live along with the Bantus in pastoral tribes. Ethnographic sources indicate that the Bushmen have lived in the Kalahari Desert for at least a hundred years.[9,10] The Kalahari Desert is characterized by three seasons: a hot summer with a 5-month rainy season from November to March; a cool, dry winter from April to August; and a hot, dry spring in September and October. The daily mean maximum temperature for the midwinter month of July ranges from 20° C (68° F) to 22.5° C (72.5° F). The minimum daily temperature is about 3.2° C (37.8° F). Dry bulb temperatures, for the summer only, rise above 32° C (89.6° F), and black globe thermometer readings in direct sunlight sometimes rise to 60° C (140° F).[4,7,9,10] In the summer the mean maximum and minimum air temperatures for January equaled 30° C (86° F) to 32.5° C (90.5° F) and 18° C (64.4° F), respectively. The annual rainfall varies from 400 to 600 mm.

Despite the high temperatures the loose sandy soil supports abundant vegetation, and underlying limestone strata allow for the formation of water holes. Because of these geological factors the distribution of water sources is by far the most important ecological determinant of Bushman subsistence. The Bushmen camps are anchored to water sources, and the Bushmen exploit only vegetable foods and game within a reasonable walking distance from water; yet their food resources are varied and abundant. Lee[9] indicates that the Bushmen know over 200 plant and 220 animal species; of these, 85% of the plants and 54% of the animals are edible. The predominant staple is the mongongo (mangetti) nut, which is found in abundant quantities and gives an energy yield of 600 cal/100 g. The major constituents of the diet by weight are 33% mongongo nuts, 37% meat, and 30% vegetable matter.[9]

In addition to desert environments, Bushmen also inhabit river areas; these are the so-called river Bushmen, whose economy is a mixture of horticulture, hunting, and gathering. They have a more settled existence than the desert Bushmen, living in fixed villages, sowing crops, and raising domestic animals. These Bushmen are said to be somewhat hybridized with the neighboring Bantu tribes, which would then be reflected in their genetic constitution.

During the summer of 1962 the physiological responses to work in heat stress of a sample of eleven desert Bushmen of the Maxqong tribe and ten river Bushmen of the Makanchwe tribe were studied.[4,7] The thermoregulatory responses of these Bushmen were compared to those of nonacclimated and acclimated whites studied using the same procedures. The desert Bushmen were shorter and lighter in weight, but they had a greater surface area:weight ratio than the river Bushmen. The mean surface area: weight ratio for the desert Bushmen equaled 3.11 cm²/kg and 2.85 for the river Bushmen (Table 2). Rectal temperatures and sweat rates of both Bushmen samples were similar, but the heart rates of the desert Bushmen were lower than those of the river Bushmen (Fig. 3-3). The rectal temperatures and heart rates of the two Bushmen groups were intermediate between the nonacclimated and acclimated whites, but their sweat rates were lower than the acclimated whites. From these data the investigators determined that the Bushmen are only partially acclimatized to work in heat stress.[4,7] This conclusion is surprising in view of the fact that in their everyday activities the Bushmen are continuously exposed to environmental heat stress and

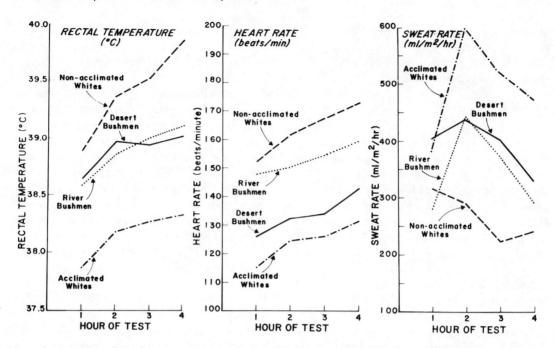

Fig. 3-3. Physiological responses to standardized heat stress test of nonacclimated whites, desert Bushmen, river Bushmen, and acclimated whites. Bushmen, like the Bantus, perform work under stress with a lower sweat rate. (Based on data from Wyndham, C. H. 1966. Southern African ethnic adaptation to temperature and exercise. In P. T. Baker and J. S. Weiner, eds. The biology of human adaptability. Clarendon Press, Oxford.)

strenuous physical work; therefore, one would expect a full adaptation. It must be noted that although the Bushmen had higher rectal temperatures and heart rates than the acclimated whites, their performance (all completed the 4-hour experiment, and none had rectal temperatures above 40° C) was equal to that of the acclimated whites. This exceptional performance was attained despite their lower sweat rates, suggesting that the Bushmen, like the Bantus, are less susceptible to heat collapse and have greater cardiovascular stability than the whites when exposed to work in heat stress.[4,7]

CHAAMBA ARABS

The climate of the Sahara Desert is characterized by higher temperatures and lower humidity than that of the Kalahari. The mean

maximum temperature for the midsummer month of July is between 35° and 37.5° C (95° and 99.5° F), and the mean minimum temperature is about 26° C (78.8° F). The annual rainfall is less than 100 mm. Because of the higher temperatures and lower moisture of the Sahara, the direct and reflected solar radiation from bare sand is greater than in the Kalahari.

Following the same procedures as in the previous studies described, the thermoregulatory reactions to work in heat stress of fifteen Arabs from the Chaamba tribe, as well as fifteen whites were evaluated.[5,7] The Chaamba tribesmen are of Arab origin; in the past they were pastoral nomads, but at the time of the study they were working as laborers in Hassi-Messaoud. The white subjects were French soldiers who had come from metropolitan France to serve at the garrison in Hassi-Messaoud.

The performances in heat of both Arabs and white French soldiers were comparable. Compared to the South African acclimated whites, the Arabs and Frenchmen had higher rectal temperatures and higher heart rates. Although the Arabs had, during the last 2 hours of the experiment, lower sweat rates than the French soldiers, the fact that their rectal temperatures and heart rates were higher than those of the South African whites indicates that the thermoregulatory responses to heat stress of the Arabs were inferior to those of the whites (Fig. 3-4).

This paradoxical finding may be caused by several factors. First, the increased heart rates of the Arabs are indicative of their poor physical conditioning. Second, without exception the Arabs wear clothing that in a hot-dry environment minimizes conductive and radiant energy gains from the environment. Arab clothing reduces heat stress by trapping a boundary of stale air between the skin and the cloth, which serves to insulate the skin from the ambient temperature and solar radiation.[11] Thus it is likely that the Arabs have succeeded in protecting themselves so effectively that in their normal state they are seldom exposed to temperatures conducive to heat stress or prolonged dehydration. Therefore, their adaptation to heat stress is probably more cultural than physiological.

AUSTRALIAN ABORIGINES

Central Australia is also characterized by a hot-dry climate. The mean maximum daily temperature for the summer months of January through March is 37° C (98.6° F), and the daily minimum temperature is 22° C (71.6° F). In the winter month of July, the mean maximum daily temperature is 21° C (69.8° F), and the minimum is 4° C (39.2° F), with an average annual rainfall of 260 mm. The native flora and fauna of central Australia are quite limited. The subsistence economy of the aborigines is therefore based on the capture of small, slow game and the gathering of wild roots and fruit plants. Compared to the Bushmen, the Australian aborigines live in a more stressful environment in terms of natural nutritional resources, availability of water holes, and presence of high temperatures.[7]

Two groups of aborigines were studied, fourteen men from Weipa Mission Station and another seventeen men from Aurukun Mission Station.[6,7] In terms of the ratio of surface area to weight the Australian aborigines (2.97) are similar to the Bantus (2.85) and Bushmen (2.80 to 3.10) (Table 2). As shown in Fig. 3-5, compared to the South African nonacclimated and acclimated whites, throughout the heat stress test the Australian aborigines maintained lower rectal temperatures and lower heart rates associated with lower sweat rates than the nonacclimated whites. On the other hand, compared to the acclimated whites, they maintained higher rectal temperatures and higher heart rates but lower sweat rates. In other words, the thermoregulatory responses to heat stress of the aborigines, like the Bantus and Bushmen, are intermediate between that of the nonacclimated and acclimated whites. Furthermore, the performance of the aborigines in heat stress was superior to that of nonacclimated South African whites tested under the same conditions in that none of the aborigines collapsed. In this respect the aborigines are like the nonacclimated South African Bantus. The aborigines, therefore, appear to have a more stable circulatory system under hot conditions than the nonacclimated South African whites.

CONCLUSION

In summary, the Bantus, Bushmen, and Australian aborigines, when compared to both acclimated and nonacclimated whites,

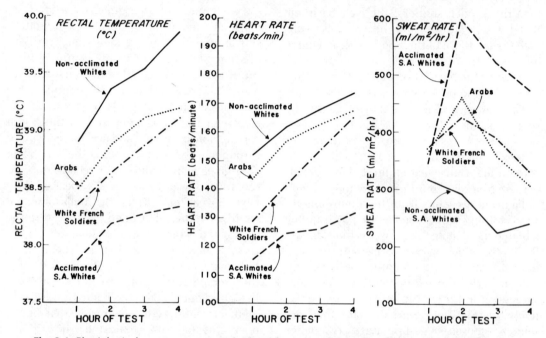

Fig. 3-4. Physiological responses to standardized heat stress test of nonacclimated South African whites, Chaamba Arabs, white French soldiers, and acclimated whites. Judging by their high rectal temperatures, high heart rates, and completion of tests, the Arabs are only partially acclimatized to work in heat stress. (Based on data from Wyndham, C. H. 1966. Southern African ethnic adaptation to temperature and exercise. In P. T. Baker and J. S. Weiner, eds. The biology of human adaptability. Clarendon Press, Oxford.)

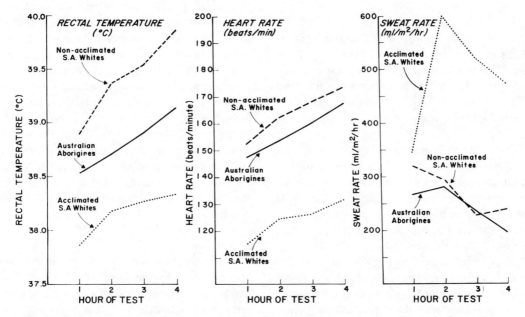

Fig. 3-5. Physiological responses to standardized heat stress test of nonacclimated whites, Australian aborigines, and acclimated whites. The Australian aborigines show lower increase in rectal temperatures and heart rates than nonacclimated whites but have lower sweat rates than both nonacclimated and acclimated whites. (Based on data from Wyndham, C. H. 1966. Southern African ethnic adaptation to temperature and exercise. In P. T. Baker and J. S. Weiner, eds. The biology of human adaptability. Clarendon Press, Oxford.)

experience lower sweat rates when working in heat stress. All three groups sweat at a lower rate, yet they maintain a similar core temperature to that of the nonacclimated whites and a slightly higher core temperature than the acclimated whites. Furthermore, their individual performances in heat were better than the nonacclimated whites, since nearly all these men completed the 4-hour experiment, and less than 3% had a rectal temperature above 40° C (104° F). This finding means that these populations have been able to maintain thermal homeostasis in heat stress with a lower body fluid loss. The implication is that in these populations heat dissipation is not simply a function of sweat evaporation, but probably of other physiologically less expensive avenues of heat loss as well, such as radiation and convection. These populations, when compared to the whites, are leaner and have a higher ratio of surface area to weight, thus having the appropriate morphology to facilitate heat loss through radiation and convection.

As shown by experimental studies and computer simulations (Chapter 2), heat loss though radiation and convection in subjects with high surface area:weight ratio is maximized in moderate heat stress. The temperature in which the Bantus, Bushmen, and Australian aborigines were tested (32.9° C dry bulb and 32.2° C wet bulb) is appropriate for a maximization of heat loss through radiation and evaporation. In these circumstances these populations would not need to produce as much sweat as the whites. As indicated by recent investigations (p. 26), maintenance of a high sweat rate during acclimation to heat stress is not an efficient mechanism for maintaining thermal homeostasis. Indeed, with continuous exposure to heat stress the sweat rate does decline, and the skin temperature is maintained at the level necessary to evaporate just the amount of sweat sufficient to maintain thermal balance. For this reason, and given the fact that these populations have been exposed continuously to heat stress during daily activities, they have probably developed a much more sensitively adjusted thermoregulatory control channel between rectal temperature and sweat rate than the whites. Thus, with an increase in rectal temperature, the Bantus, Bushmen, and aborigines sweat just enough to maintain thermal equilibrium, whereas the white person sweats excessively. This lower sweat rate could then be regarded as advantageous for surviving longer in hot environments where no water is available, since the rate of dehydration would be slower. In view of the limited natural nutritional resources that these populations have, a lower sweat rate would also have an additional adaptive significance in that they would lose less salt, iron, and other minerals than the Caucasians. The sweat loss of Indians, Nigerians, and Papago Indians has also been found to be less than that of either residentially or artificially acclimated Europeans exposed to the same standardized conditions.[12-14]

Presently, however, we do not know how or by what mechanisms populations that live in tropical, stressful climates acquire the capacity to maintain thermal homeostasis with a lower sweat rate. There are, however, several possible explanations.

First, this capacity may be acquired through long-term residence in tropical climates. It has been shown that the water intake of persons acclimatized to heat is lower than that of nonacclimatized persons.[5] Furthermore, this investigation indicates that restricting the water intake of nonacclimatized persons hastens their acclimation process and that long-term residence and work in a hot climate is not necessarily accompanied by a dramatic increase in sweat loss so commonly observed when nonacclimatized persons are first exposed to heat stress. How-

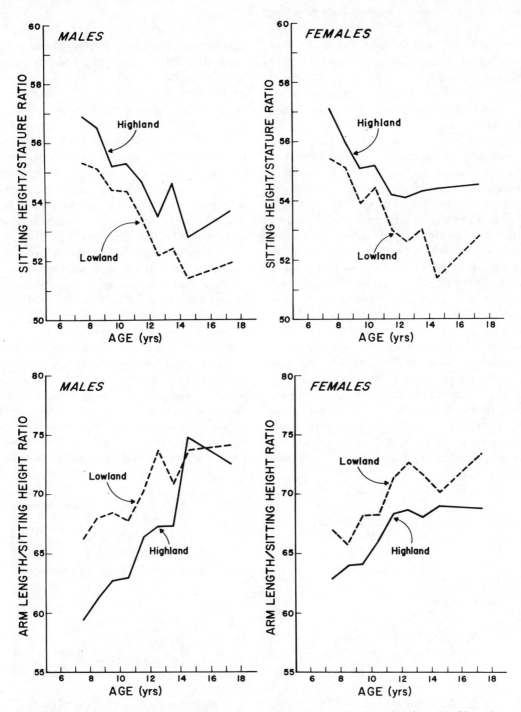

Fig. 3-6. Comparison of sitting height : stature ratio and arm length : sitting height ratio of Peruvian highland and lowland tropical Quechua samples. (Modified from Stinson, S., and A. R. Frisancho. 1978. Hum. Biol. **50:**57-68.)

ever, persons acclimatized by living and working in a hot climate for as long as 9 months do not have lower water intakes or sweat rates than similar, nonacclimatized persons.[16] Therefore, it is doubtful that a low sweat rate can be acquired simply by long-term residence in a hot climate.

Second, this capacity may be acquired through morphological changes oriented toward the maximization of sweat evaporation. In general, the extremities, because of enhanced potential for convective heat loss from their relative larger surface areas, are the most effective areas for sweat evaporation from the body. As revealed by a growth study of American white children of good nutritional status, acclimatization to the tropical climate of Rio de Janeiro of Brazil results in development of smaller calf girts as compared to non–heat-stressed controls.[17] Similarly, as illustrated in Fig. 3-6, Quechua children acclimatized to the tropical climate of the Peruvian lowlands have a proportionally smaller trunk (low sitting height: stature ratio) and greater arm length (high arm length:sitting height ratio) than their Quechua counterparts of the same genetic

composition living in the cold climate of the Peruvian Highlands.[18] Since the extremities have a greater density of functional sweat glands than the trunk and the distal parts of the limbs have greater density of functional sweat glands than the proximal parts,[19-21] the development of leaner extremities would contribute to a better sweat evaporation. Furthermore, the reduction in trunk size and increase in relative arm length would result in an increase in the surface area:weight ratio, which would facilitate radiative and convective heat loss. It is likely, then, that populations who have been raised in tropical climates do have a more efficient sweat evaporation and, therefore, do not have to sweat as excessively as those non–heat-acclimatized populations.

Finally, the lower sweat rate may be a developmental response to heat stress mediated by nutritional factors. Almost all minerals and vitamins are excreted in the sweat, the principal components being iron, calcium, zinc, and especially sodium chloride. It has been demonstrated that the concentration of sodium chloride in sweat decreases with continuous exposure and acclimatization to heat

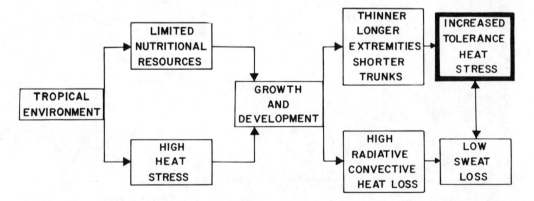

Fig. 3-7. Schematization of interaction of tropical environmental stresses influencing adaptation to heat stress. Joint influences of limited nutritional stress and heat stress growth and development in tropical environment result in development of adaptive morphology and increase in heat tolerance capacity.

stress. However, it has also been shown that even in acclimatized subjects there is a positive relationship between sweat output and total sweat-sodium loss.[22] This means that when the sweat losses are high, total sodium losses will also tend to be high. In addition, when the sweat rate and the state of acclimatization are held constant, sweat-salt loss is mediated by dietary salt intake. For example, when men worked in a room at 38° C (100.4° F) and 80% relative humidity, the sweat loss in 162 minutes was 25 g, which amounts to approximately 15% of the total estimated body salt.[22] Thus, if a high sweat rate is maintained, the salt output must be replaced through the diet if an adequate electrolyte balance is to continue. In view of the limited availability of salt to most tropical, indigenous populations,[23] it is likely that the low sweat rate is a developmental response that prevents excessive loss of body fluids and salt.

In summary, major population differences in adaptation to heat stress are reflected in high tolerance to heat stress and low sweat loss of indigenous populations. At the present stage of knowledge, these differences can be explained as a result of interaction of limited nutritional resources and high heat stress associated with a tropical environment operating during the period of growth and development (Fig. 3-7). Thus, populations inhabiting tropical climates during growth develop proportionally thinner, longer extremities and shorter trunks than those raised in temperate climates. In turn, this development affects the rate of radiative and convective heat loss. As a result, tropical native populations demonstrate an enhanced tolerance to heat stress and a low sweat rate.

Similarly, viewed in this context, the relationship between body weight and mean annual temperature observed among world populations[24,25] would reflect a developmental response to the joint effects of heat and nutritional stress associated with tropical climates. Whether the same conclusion is applicable to the observed relationship between head form and climate remains to be determined.[27]

REFERENCES

1. Pales, L. 1950. Les sels alimentaires: sels mineraux. Gouvern. Gen. de L'A. O. F., Dakar.
2. Ladell, W. S. S. 1957. Disorders due to the heat. Trans. R. Soc. Trop. Med. Hyg. **51**:189-207.
3. Wyndham, C. H., J. F. Morrison, C. G. Williams, G. A. G. Bredell, M. J. E. Von Raliden, L. D. Holdsworth, C. H. Van Graan, A. J. Van Rensburg, and A. Munro. 1964. Heat reactions of caucasians and Bantu in South Africa. J. Appl. Physiol. **19**:598-606.
4. Wyndham, C. H., N. B. Strydom, J. S. Ward, J. F. Morrison, C. G. Williams, G. A. G. Bredell, M. J. E. Von Raliden, L. D. Holdsworth, C. H. Van Graan, A. J. Van Rensburg, and A. Munro. 1964. Physiological reactions to heat of Bushmen and of unacclimatized and acclimatized Bantu. J. Appl. Physiol. **19**:885-888.
5. Wyndham, C. H., B. Metz, and A. Munro. 1964. Reactions to heat of Arabs and caucasians. J. Appl. Physiol. **19**:1951-1954.
6. Wyndham, C. H., R. K. McPherson, and A. Munro. 1964. Reactions to heat of aborigines and Caucasians. J. Appl. Physiol. **19**:1055-1058.
7. Wyndham, C. H. 1966. Southern African ethnic adaptation to temperature and exercise. In, P. T. Baker and J. S. Weiner, eds. The biology of human adaptability. Clarendon Press, Oxford.
8. Wyndham, C. H., N. B. Strydom, C. G. Williams, J. F. Morrison, G. A. G. Bredell, J. Peter, C. H. Van Graan, L. D. Holdsworth, A. J. Van Rensburg, and A. Munro. 1964. Heat reactions of some Bantu tribesmen in southern Africa. J. Appl. Physiol. **19**:881-884.
9. Lee, R. B. 1969. !Kung bushman subsistence: an input-output analysis. In A. P. Vayda, ed. Environment and cultural behavior: ecological studies in cultural anthropology. Natural History Press, New York.
10. Truswell, A. S., and J. D. L. Hansen. 1976. Medical research among the Kung. In R. B. Lee and I.

DeVore, eds. Kalahari hunters-gatherers. Harvard University Press, Cambridge, Mass.

11. Briggs, L. C. 1975. Environment and human adaptation in the Sahara. In A. Damon, ed. Physiological anthropology. Oxford University Press, Oxford.

12. Edholm, O. G. 1966. Acclimatization to heat in a group of Indian subjects. In M. S. Malhatra, ed. Human adaptability to environments and physical fitness. Madras Defense Institute of Physiology and Allied Sciences, India.

13. Ladell, W. S. S. 1955. Physiological observations on men working in supposedly limiting environments in a West African gold-mine. Br. Med. J. **12:**111-125.

14. Hanna, J. M. 1970. Responses of native and migrant desert residents to arid heat. Am. J. Phys. Anthropol. **32:**187-196.

15. Yunusov, A. Y. 1970. In Proceedings of a Symposium on Adaptation of Man and of Animals to Extreme Natural Environments, pp. 12-17. Siberian Branch of the Academy of the USSR, Novosibirsk.

16. Edholm, O. G. 1972. The effect in man of acclimatization to heat on water intake, sweat rate and water balance. In S. Itoh, K. Ogata, and H. Yoshimura, eds. Advances in climatic physiology. Springer-Verlag New York, Inc., Heidelberg, N.Y.

17. Eveleth, P. B. 1965. The effects of climate on growth. Ann. N.Y. Acad. Sci. **134:**750-755.

18. Stinson, S., and A. R. Frisancho. 1978. Body proportions of highland and lowland Peruvian Quechua children. Hum. Biol. **50:**57-68.

19. Randall, W. C., and A. B. Hertzman. 1953. Dermal recruitment of sweating. J. Appl. Physiol. **5:**399-409.

20. Hofler, W. 1968. Changes in the regional distribution of sweating during acclimatization to heat. J. Appl. Physiol. **25:**503-506.

21. Ogawa, T. 1972. Local determinants of sweat gland activity. In S. Itoh, K. Ogata, and H. Yoshimura, eds. Advances in climatic physiology. Springer-Verlag New York, Inc., Heidelberg, N.Y.

22. Ladell, W. S. S. 1964. Terrestrial animals in humid heat: man. In D. B. Dill, E. F. Adolph, and C. G. Wilber, eds. Handbook of physiology. vol 4. Adaptation to the environment. American Physiological Society, Washington, D.C.

23. Gleibermann, L. 1973. Blood pressure and dietary salt in human populations. Ecology of Food and Nutrition **2:**83-90.

24. Roberts, D. F. 1953. Body weight, race and climate. Am. J. Phys. Anthropol. **11:**533-558.

25. Schreider, E. 1964. Ecological rules, body heat regulation, and human evolution. Evolution **18:**1-9.

26. Mitchell, D., L. C. Senay, C. H. Wyndham, A. J. Van Rensburg, G. G. Rogers, and N. B. Strydom. 1976. Acclimatization in a hot, humid environment: energy exchange, body temperature, and sweating. J. Appl. Physiol. **40:**768-778.

27. Beals, K. 1972. Head form and climatic stress. Am. J. Phys. Anthropol. **37:**85-92.

4 Thermoregulation and acclimation to cold stress

Environmental factors

General responses to cold stress
Vasoconstriction
Countercurrent
Hunting response or cold-induced vasodilation
Sympathetic action
Sympathetic and vagal reflex
Food consumption
Metabolic rate and shivering

Individual factors and tolerance to cold
Surface area
Insulation of fat
Physical fitness
Age

Acclimation to cold stress
Experimental animals
Nonshivering thermogenesis
Hormonal effects
Morphological changes
Lipid changes
Brown adipose tissue
Humans

Conclusion

Biological responses to cold stress involve mechanisms of heat production and conservation. These adaptive mechanisms to cold stress are more complex than those of heat adaptation. Successful responses to cold stress require the synchronization of cardiovascular and circulatory systems and, most important, the activation of the metabolic process. In this chapter the basic physiological responses with which organisms counteract cold stress, the individual factors that modify and affect these responses, and the process of acclimation to cold stress will be discussed. In subsequent chapters the process of acclimatization of native and non-native populations is discussed to illustrate the variety of characteristics of human adaptation to cold stress.

ENVIRONMENTAL FACTORS

Besides low temperatures, there are several other environmental factors that must be taken into account when considering human responses to cold stress. Among these, the most important are wind velocity, humidity, and duration of exposure to cold. In general, it is assumed that a low temperature, usually around 0° C (32° F), with high humidity results in greater cold sensation than with low humidity. However, these assumptions have not been confirmed by experimental studies.

Heat loss is strongly affected by wind velocity; a given temperature and a rapid wind result in greater cold stress than the same temperature with slow wind. Accordingly an index for deriving the equivalent temperature that results from the actual (or total) temperature and wind velocity has been devised and is shown in Table 3. For example, if the local temperature is 0° C (32° F) and wind velocity is 25 mph, the person loses heat as if the dry bulb temperature were $-38.9°$ C ($-38°$ F). Therefore, the chilling power of the wind can produce an almost supercooling effect on exposed skin.

In general, the degree of cold stress to which a person is exposed is classified as either *acute* or *chronic* cold. *Acute cold stress* refers to severe cold stress for short periods of time. *Chronic cold stress* refers to moderate cold stress experienced for prolonged periods of time, either seasonally or throughout the year. Obviously, the degree of cold stress depends on the amount of insulation. To quantify the amount of thermal insulation

Table 3. Wind chill effect: equivalent effective temperature*

Wind speed (mph)	Actual air temperature (° F)											
	50	40	30	20	10	0	−10	−20	−30	−40	−50	−60
	Equivalent temperature (° F)											
5	48	36	27	17	−5	−5	−15	−25	−35	−46	−56	−66
10	40	29	18	5	−8	−20	−30	−43	−55	−68	−80	−93
15	35	23	10	−5	−18	−29	−42	−55	−70	−83	−97	−112
20	32	18	4	−10	−23	−34	−50	−64	−79	−94	−108	−121
25	30	15	−1	−15	−28	−38	−55	−72	−88	−105	−118	−130
30	28	13	−5	−18	−33	−44	−60	−76	−92	−109	−124	−134
35	27	11	−6	−20	−35	−48	−65	−80	−96	−113	−130	−137
40	26	10	−7	−21	−37	−52	−68	−83	−100	−117	−135	−140
45	25	9	−8	−22	−39	−54	−70	−86	−103	−120	−139	−143
50	25	8	−9	−23	−40	−55	−72	−88	−105	−123	−142	−145

*Modified from Ward, M. 1975. Mountain medicine: a clinical study of cold and high altitude. Crosby Lockwood Staples Ltd., London.

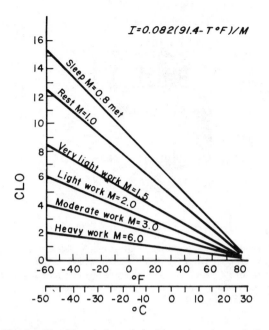

$$I = 0.082(91.4 - T°F)/M$$

Sleep M=0.8 met
Rest M=1.0
Very light work M=1.5
Light work M=2.0
Moderate work M=3.0
Heavy work M=6.0

CLO

°F
°C

Fig. 4-1. Total insulation of clothing plus air needed for different metabolic rates. (Modified from Burton, A. C., and O. G. Edholm. 1955. Man in a cold environment. Edward Arnold [Publishers] Ltd., London.)

and heat exchange the index called *clo* has been devised.[1] One clo of thermal insulation will maintain a resting-sitting person with a metabolic rate of 50 kcal/m²/hr comfortably in an environment of 21° C (70° F) with relative humidity less than 50% and air movement of 6 m/min (20 feet/min). In these basal conditions 1 clo is equivalent to a business suit or 0.64 cm (¼ inch) of clothing. A heavy article of arctic clothing provides about 5 clo units. Fig. 4-1 presents a series of curves for an estimation of clo requirements at various environmental temperatures and metabolic activities.

GENERAL RESPONSES TO COLD STRESS

As previously indicated, within the thermoneutral temperature range of 25° to 27° C (77° to 80° F) the individual is in thermal equilibrium, but below this range the nude individual responds immediately through mechanisms that permit both the conservation of heat and an increase in heat production. The major mechanism concerned with heat conservation is vasoconstriction, alternated with vasodilation and synchronized with the countercurrent system; the major mechanism concerned with heat production is shivering. As a side effect of cold stress, changes occur in the activities of the sympathetic nervous system and vagal reflex. Since each mechanism is multifaceted and in order to have a broader view of the general responses to cold stress, each response will be discussed and illustrated with representative research data dealing with various temperature conditions in cold water and cold air.

Vasoconstriction

On exposure to cold stress, such as a temperature of 0° C (32° F) or even 15° C (60° F), the cold receptors in the skin of a nude individual are activated to initiate those reflexes involved in conserving heat. This is accomplished through a constriction of the subcutaneous blood vessels (vasoconstriction), which limits the flow of warm blood from the core to the shell (skin). The result of this lower blood flow is a decrease in skin temperature, a reduction of the temperature gradient between the skin surface and the environment, and, consequently, a reduction in the rate of heat loss (Fig. 4-2). As a result of vasoconstriction, heat conductivity of the blood is also reduced.* For example, at a temperature of 35° C (95° F), the conduction of blood flow amounts to 20.3 cal/m²/° C, whereas during vasoconstriction at 15° C the heat conductance is reduced to 12.6 cal/m²/° C.[2] Concomitant with decreased blood flow to the skin, the blood flow to the viscera

---

*The conductivity of the blood is measured in terms of cal/m²/° C.

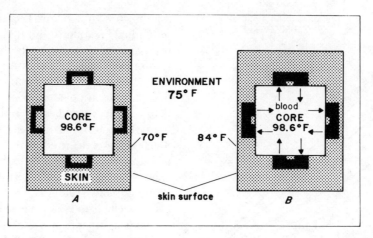

Fig. 4-2. Schematization of relationship of skin's insulating capacity to its blood flow. **A,** Skin acts as good insulator, that is, with minimal blood flow temperature of skin surface approaches that of external environment. When skin blood vessels dilate, **B,** the increased blood flow carries heat to body surface, that is, reduces insulating capacity of skin, and surface temperature becomes intermediate between that of core and external environment.

and internal organs is augmented. This shift in blood flow is probably responsible for increased blood pressure and heart rate under severe cold stress.

Countercurrent

As shown in Fig. 4-3, the temperature of the blood varies both with the depth and location of the superficial venous plexuses and superficial arteriolar plexus. The temperature is highest at a depth of about 0.8 mm and lowest both above and below this point. The abrupt drop in temperature beyond a depth of 0.8 mm is caused by the returning venous blood being cooler than the arterial blood; thus some heat from the arterioles is given off to the venous blood. These fluctuations in temperature are controlled by the arteriovenous anastomoses, which connect the arterioles to the superficial plexuses. The opening of these anastomoses results in shunting of blood from the arterioles to the superficial veins, bringing heat closer to the surface for dissipation to the environment.[3]

Countercurrent heat exchange occurs because each outgoing artery is always surrounded by two incoming and returning veins. Because the outgoing arterial blood is always warmer than the incoming venous blood, there is continuous heat exchange; therefore, even within the arteries of the human arm there is a longitudinal temperature gradient.[4] For example, at an ambient temperature of 30° C this gradient was about 0.03° C/cm, but when the arm was exposed to 4° C, the gradient was about 0.35° C/cm. As shown in Fig. 2-3, when the room is cold (10° C), heat is given off from the brachial artery to veins around the artery, and the blood's temperature is about 37° C. By the time the blood reaches the wrist, its temperature may decrease to about 23° C. On the other hand, when the room is warm (30° C), heat is given off from the veins near the skin, and as a result the radial artery may be 37° C, hence facilitating heat loss.

Hunting response or cold-induced vasodilation

A typical response to immersion of the finger in cold water is the spontaneous, semirhythmic changes in temperature. As shown

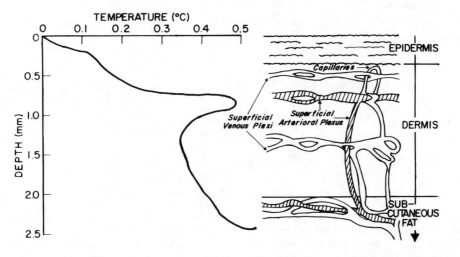

Fig. 4-3. Temperature gradient from surface of skin to depth of 2.5 mm in relation to approximate position of superficial blood vessels. In the subcutaneous layer arteries and veins follow a similar course. (Modified from Bazett, H. C. 1941. Temperature sense in man. In H. C. Bazett, Temperature, its measurement and control in science and industry. Reinhold Publishing Co.)

in Fig. 4-4, on immersion digital temperature drops for about 15 minutes until the temperature is about 2.5° C above the ice water temperature. After about 16 minutes, digital temperature rises by some 6° to 8° C and fluctuates thereafter between 4° and 6° C. These fluctuations in temperature are caused by fluctuations in the blood flow and have been termed the Lewis "hunting" phenomenon.[5] Further studies were made showing that this cold-induced vasodilation results from an increase in blood flow because of the sudden opening of the arteriovenous anastomoses.[6] This in turn produces the marked variation in temperature. Similar responses to cold were noted in the skin of the ear, cheek, nose, chin, and toes. This mechanism may have importance in cold water conditions for protecting exposed parts of the skin from excessive cooling and injury.[5] However, current research has not demonstrated a relationship between this type of response and individual susceptibility to cold injury.[7]

Another effect of cold stress is that pain sensation increases with falling skin tem-

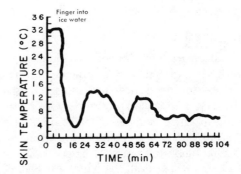

Fig. 4-4. Cold vasodilation of finger immersed in crushed ice. Curve shows large, prolonged temperature oscillations finally giving way to smaller, more rapid ones—Lewis' hunting phenomenon. (Modified from Lewis, T. 1930. Heart **15:**177-181.)

peratures; with rewarming of the skin by cold-induced vasodilation (CIVD), this sensation disappears, giving the sensation that the hand is being immersed in lukewarm water. Recurrence of vasoconstriction coincides with an elevation in the pain sensation. However, pain is observed not only when skin temperature cools, but also when the skin warms up after cooling. Indeed, fre-

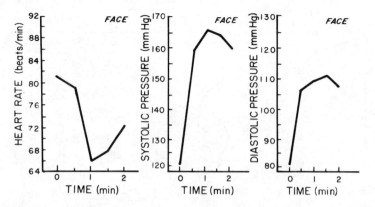

Fig. 4-5. Effects of immersion of face in water at 4° C for 2 minutes on heart rate and systolic and diastolic pressure. Decreased heart rate but increased blood pressure during immersion in cold water suggest activation of both vagal reflex and sympathetic nervous system. (Modified from LeBlanc, J. 1975. Man in the cold. Charles C Thomas, Publisher, Springfield, Ill.)

quently rewarming of the hand or face at room temperature produces a marked pain sensation. This increase in pain occurs when skin temperature increases rapidly.

Sympathetic action

Vasoconstriction induced by cold stress on the face (water at 4° C) coincides with an increase in blood pressure, suggesting an activation of the sympathetic nervous system in these circumstances. Concomitant with vasoconstriction is an increase in systolic and diastolic blood pressures.[8,9] There is also an increase in heart rate.[8,9] All these changes are indicative of increased sympathetic activity (Fig. 4-5).

Sympathetic and vagal reflex

Exposure of the face to cold stress (water at 4° C) for 2 minutes causes a decrease in heart rate (bradycardia) and an increase in blood pressure, but exposure of the hand to the same stress causes an increase in heart rate and blood pressure (Fig. 4-6). These findings suggest that exposure of the face to cold causes an increased activity of the vagal reflex and sympathetic system, but exposure of the hand results only in activation of the

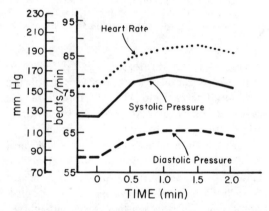

Fig. 4-6. Increase in blood pressure and heart rate during immersion of one hand into cold water (4° C) for 2 minutes. The increase in heart rate and blood pressure associated with vasoconstriction suggest activation of sympathetic nervous system. (Modified from LeBlanc, J. 1975. Man in the cold. Charles C Thomas, Publisher, Springfield, Ill.)

sympathetic system.[8] It has been suggested that pain experienced by angina pectoris patients when their faces are exposed to cold winds may be the result of a decreased heart rate.[8] Furthermore, the cold-induced increase in blood pressure along with bradycardia may impose additional stress on the hearts of the subjects. Perhaps, then, the higher cardiovascular mortality that occurs in winter in the United States[10] may have a thermoregulatory cause.

Food consumption

Early investigations suggested an inverse relationship between temperature and food intake.[11] However, subsequent studies have not substantiated this conclusion, and the present consensus is that at comparable levels of activity, environmental temperature has no effect on food intake in arctic regions.[8]

Metabolic rate and shivering

Humans, like all animals, obtain energy from oxidation of foodstuffs such as carbohydrates, fats, and protein. The energy content of food is normally measured in kilocalories, or large calories. On the average, about 4, 9, and 4 calories are derived from each gram of carbohydrate, fat, and protein, respectively.

Despite variability in the amount of energy available in food, the energy generated by a person does not vary a great deal according to the kind of food eaten. Thus, a subject at rest in a steady state, oxidizing an average diet, generates about 4.83 calories for every liter of oxygen he consumes. The metabolic rate (MR) in calories equals the volume of oxygen in liters consumed each minute multiplied by 4.83.

$$MR = 4.83 \times VO_2$$

Assuming a basal oxygen consumption of 250 ml/min, in 24 hours the total oxygen intake will equal 360 L (250 × 60 min × 24 hr = 360,000 ml), which equals 1800 kcal/24 hr. This is the amount of energy the body needs to maintain its function in absolute resting basal conditions, hence, the name *basal metabolic rate*. Since individuals vary in body proportions and weight and energy use varies in proportion to body size and surface area, the metabolic rate is usually expressed in terms of energy output per unit area per unit time or cal/m²/hr.

When the vasoregulatory mechanisms of heat conservation are not sufficient to counteract heat loss, the organism adjusts by increasing the rate of heat production. For an unclothed man an increase in heat production usually occurs when the ambient temperature falls below 25° C. The most rapid and efficient way to increase heat production is by voluntary exercise, such as running, which may increase the metabolic rate from a basal value of 1.17 cal/min to 37.94 cal/min.[12] However, such high rates of activity cannot be maintained for prolonged periods. Thus, in the absence of voluntary exercise, shivering of the skeletal muscle is the main source of increased heat production. As shown by experimental studies, shivering requires the activation of skin receptors through the lowering of skin temperature.[13] The major function of shivering is to increase the rate of heat production (but it also adds to heat loss). In addition, shivering provides improved protection of core heat by enlarging the thermogenesis of the muscle mass. Through this mechanism the temperature of muscle is raised to approach that of the core, thus eliminating the temperature gradient heat loss.

As a result of shivering the metabolic rate may be increased two to three times the basal value. This increase in heat production is progressive throughout the cold stress. For example, during intense cold, heat production increases from a basal level at preexposure of 35.4 cal/m²/hr to 54 cal/m²/hr by the end of the first hour. By the end of the second, third, and fourth hours production had risen to 72, 92, and 96 cal/m²/hr, respectively.[14]

Along with shivering, subcutaneous blood vessels dilate (vasodilation) to keep the skin warm and prevent tissue injury from frostbite. Thus, adjustment to cold stress is an interplay between mechanisms to conserve heat and mechanisms to produce and dissipate heat. In terms of energy expenditure, defense against cold is achieved more economically by increasing body heat conservation than by increasing heat production. However, the extent to which these mechanisms are operative in humans depends on the degree of cold stress experienced and on technological and cultural adaptation, as will be shown in later chapters.

INDIVIDUAL FACTORS AND TOLERANCE TO COLD

As indicated in Chapter 2, heat flow follows Fourier's Law which indicates that heat loss per minute is directly proportional to body surface and the difference between the temperature of the body and of the environment. It is also inversely proportional to thickness of the body shell. When considering the sources of individual variability in cold tolerance, the most important factors include surface area and insulation.

Surface area

Tolerance to cold stress is affected by the size and shape of the individual. When expressed as per unit of body weight, the heat required to maintain a constant internal body temperature will be greater in a small rather than a large individual.[1,8,9,15] This is because surface area exposed to the environment, all other factors being constant, is greater per unit of body weight if the total body is smaller. For this reason, in a cold environment, all factors being constant, a small individual would be expected to produce relatively more heat than a large individual to maintain homeostasis. The same principle applies to children who, when compared to adults, have a high surface area:weight ratio (SA/weight). Analyses of the thermoregulatory characteristics of highland Peruvian Quechua

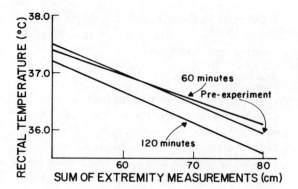

Fig. 4-7. Relationship between rectal temperature and sum of hand and foot size measurements on Quechua Indians during exposure to 10° C. The higher the available surface area of extremities, the lower the rectal temperature. (From Weitz, C. A. 1969. Morphological factors affecting responses to total body cooling among three human populations at high altitude. M. A. Thesis. Pennsylvania State University, University Park, Pa.)

Indians[16] revealed a significant negative correlation between rectal temperatures and the measurements of hand and foot size when hands and feet were exposed for 2 hours at 10° C (Fig. 4-7). In the same manner, among Japanese and European white subjects born and raised in Hawaii, a positive correlation between the measurements of trunk size and mean finger temperatures was found when the hands were exposed to 0° C moving air temperatures.[17]

Insulation of fat

One of the most important factors affecting heat loss is the degree of artificial or natural insulation. In humans, subcutaneous fat represents the most important form of natural insulation. Because the subcutaneous fat layer is not very well vascularized, the thermal conductivity of fat is much less than that of muscle. For this reason, the greater the fat layer, the lower the skin temperature, and, consequently, the smaller the gradient between the body's surface temperature and

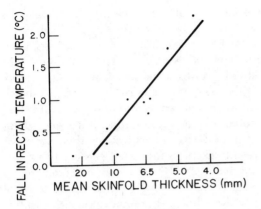

Fig. 4-8. Relationship of subcutaneous fat thickness and heat loss in cold water. The lower the mean skinfold thickness, the greater the fall in rectal temperature. (Modified from Keatinge, W. R. 1969. Survival in cold water: the physiology and treatment of immersion hypothermia and of drowning. Blackwell Scientific Publications Ltd., Oxford.)

that of the environment.[8,9,18-22] As a result of these interactions, the greater the fat layer, the lower the total heat loss. As shown in Fig. 4-8, when men were exposed to water at 15° C for 30 minutes, the higher the skinfold thickness, the smaller the drop in rectal temperature.[18] For the same reason, the frequency and intensity of shivering is more pronounced in thin persons than in fat ones.[8] Increased heat production as a result of cold immersion is also much greater in thin subjects because of less tissue insulation.[8,18,19]

For human survival in cold water, the amount of subcutaneous fat, along with the amount of artificial insulation such as clothing, is the most important consideration.[8,18,19] However, the insulative effectiveness of subcutaneous fat during immersion in cold water is affected by the degree of physical activity. At a given fat thickness the subjects who were at rest experienced a lower fall in rectal temperature than those who were swimming.[18] Thus, because cold water facilitates heat loss by convection,

movements associated with swimming, while increasing heat production, also accentuate heat loss. For human survival in cold water this heat loss from activity could be detrimental even for subjects with a high fat layer.

Physical fitness

Some of the major adaptive effects of physical training include increased vascularization, increased size of the striated and cardiac muscles, and increased maximum aerobic capacity. Although the influence of training has not been documented, one would expect that degree of physical fitness would affect degree of tolerance and rate of acclimatization to cold stress. Fit individuals would be able to attain a higher heat production than those with low fitness; this could be important for survival during severe cold stress. However, in view of the lack of research in this area, any conclusion is only speculative.

Age

As measured by peripheral responses of the hand, thermoregulatory responses are better in young adulthood than during old age. During immersion in 10° C water (with normal room temperatures) cold-induced vasodilation of the fingers was more frequent and the "hunting waves" more rapid during shorter periods in the nonadult and adult subjects than in the older adult subjects over 70 years.[23] These differences are probably caused by the effects of aging—decreased vascularization and peripheral blood flow and diminished heat conductivity. Obviously, there is a critical need for further research in this area.

ACCLIMATION TO COLD STRESS
Experimental animals

Information on the process of acclimation to cold stress has been derived mainly from studies with animals, specifically rats. These studies have been concerned with the mechanisms that enable an animal to survive severe cold stress. Studies have emphasized energy sources for heat production; this approach involves evaluations and identification of thermogenic hormones, morphological changes, and the role of lipids.

Nonshivering thermogenesis. When rats are continuously exposed to temperatures of 5° C (41° F) for 2 or 3 weeks, they are able to maintain a high metabolism (elevated about 80%) and normal temperature, without resorting to shivering. This increase in heat production without muscular movement is referred to as nonshivering thermogenesis.[8,9] That the increased heat production associated with continuous cold exposure is the result of shivering is indicated by experiments showing that cold-acclimated rats whose shivering was blocked by curare increased their metabolic rates and their rectal and skin temperatures more effectively when exposed to cold stress than did nonacclimated rats (Fig. 4-9). The increased metabolism of the cold-acclimated rats persisted even after the animals had been transferred to warmer climates (30° C).

Hormonal effects. An important factor as-

sociated with nonshivering thermogenesis appears to be noradrenaline, which is released from sympathetic nerve endings. Continuous exposure to cold, like any other stress, causes a marked increase in activity of the sympathetic nervous system, as shown by the enhanced secretion of adrenaline and noradrenaline in the urine. It has been demonstrated that nonshivering thermogenesis results from an increased sensitivity to noradrenaline.[8,9,24-26] Animals injected for 3 weeks with relatively small daily doses of noradrenaline became more sensitive to this amine and at the same time were made more resistant to the cold.[8] This change in the calorigenic effect of noradrenaline has been confirmed in studies of men who were cold-acclimated.[7,8] For this reason, noradrenaline (or norepinephrine) is considered the hormone of cold acclimation. Daily injections for 3 weeks of isoproterenol also produced a thermogenic sensitivity that appeared as important as noradrenaline's effect in both heat production and cold resistance.[8,27] However, noradrenaline and isoproterenol are not the only factors in cold acclimation because repeated injections of these hormones, although they produce as much sensitization to catecholamines as cold exposure does, do not elevate the threshold of tolerance as much as actual exposure of the animal to a cold environment.[8,9,27]

Thyroxine, because of its importance in calorigenesis, is another hormone that plays a significant role in cold acclimation. Various studies have shown that exposure for several weeks to cold stress increased the output of thyroxine by as much as 100%, an amount that can increase heat production of an animal as much as 20% to 30%.[9] Furthermore, continuous treatment of normal animals with relatively small doses of thyroxine (10 ml/24 hr) enhances cold tolerance.[8] For these reasons, it is assumed that the most important control components of nonshivering

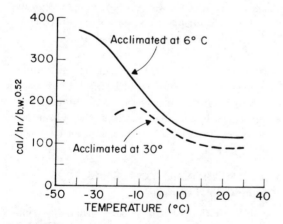

Fig. 4-9. Effects of cold acclimation at 6° C on metabolic rate of rats. (Modified from Depocas, F. 1960. Fed. Proc. **19** [Suppl. 5]:19-24.)

thermogenesis are the combined effects of noradrenaline and thyroxine. However, these hormones are not the only factors in cold acclimation. Experiments have demonstrated that thyroxine- and noradrenaline-treated rats exposed for 3 hours to severe cold stress ($-25°$ C) maintained high colonic temperatures but experienced frostbite of the tail and extremities, whereas naturally cold-acclimated rats maintained a warm and flexible tail even after 6 hours of exposure to the same cold stress.[8,9,27] All this evidence together suggests, again, that acclimation to cold stress involves more than just sensitization to and activation of calorigenic hormones.

Morphological changes. Along with increases in nonshivering thermogenesis, total daily food consumption increases. Similarly, continuous exposure of rats to cold stress is associated with hypertrophy of the thyroid, adrenal cortex, heart, kidney, liver, and digestive tract as compared to non–cold-exposed controls.[28] When oxygen consumption of each of these tissues is measured, total oxygen consumption, expressed per unit tissue weight, is greater for the visceral regions than those of the shell, such as the muscle and skin. Thus, with acclimation heat production by the core region becomes more important than that of the surrounding shell.[28]

Lipid changes. Nonshivering thermogenesis requires rapid mobilization of energy. Because of its abundance fat appears to be the most important source of fuel. With continuous exposure to cold stress, the triglycerides of depot fat, influenced by noradrenaline, are mobilized and split into free fatty acids and glycerol. Subsequently, the free fatty acids are broken down into two carbon fragments called acetyl-CoA, which in turn are used to liberate energy in the tricarboxylic acid cycle. Also continuous exposure to cold stress causes the lipoprotein lipase ac-

tivity to decrease in white adipose tissue, while markedly increasing it in brown adipose tissue and cardiac and skeletal muscles.[29] Based on this information, it has been postulated that with acclimation to cold the triglycerides of the very low density lipoproteins are directed as an energy source to those tissues involved in thermogenesis, such as brown adipose tissue and muscle, but are withheld from white adipose tissue, which under nonacclimated conditions is the usual site of storage.[30] Recent investigations indicate that, like the free fatty acids, the ketone bodies found in the urine are an important source of energy for rats acclimated to cold.[31]

Brown adipose tissue. Animals exposed to cold stress exhibit a marked increase in brown adipose tissue. This tissue's importance in cold acclimation is inferred from evidence that (1) the fall in body temperature of animals exposed to $-25°$ C for 3 hours was inversely related to the weight of brown adipose tissue,[27] (2) hypertrophy of brown adipose tissue through treatments with thyroxine and noradrenaline was associated with cold tolerance,[8] and (3) removal of brown adipose tissue in cold-acclimated rats significantly reduced the animals' response to the sensitization of noradrenaline and their tolerance to cold.[30,32]

Several hypotheses have been postulated to explain the mechanisms of brown adipose tissue and its actual contribution to nonshivering thermogenesis. First, brown adipose tissue's thermogenic capacity and its special vascularization (the positions of arteries and veins are closely juxtaposed in both cervical brown fat pads and in the interscapular pad) return metabolically warmed blood to the thorax through its venous drainage. This arrangement results in a bathing of thoracic and cervical spinal cord areas with warmed blood and adequate heat to supply the heart and sympathetic chain.[28,33] This "metabolic warming blanket" protects the central body core from the peripheral cooling effects of a cold environment.[8,9] Second, brown adipose tissue is an important source of noradrenaline for the organism. The brown fat of cold-acclimated animals has been found to contain three times more noradrenaline than that of nonacclimated controls.[8] Third, because of its special anatomical location combined with its high calorigenic properties, brown adipose tissue controls shivering.[34] This is supported by evidence that local heating of cervical, but not lumbar vertebral, canals suppresses shivering and diminishes heat production. Fourth, brown adipose tissue contributes to nonshivering thermogenesis by releasing into the circulation a hormonal factor such as noradrenaline.[30] Removal of the interscapular brown fat reduces noradrenaline sensitivity by 40% and significantly reduces cold tolerance even in cold-acclimated animals.[30,32]

Humans

In contrast to the many animal studies, investigations of human acclimation have been limited both in scope and quantity. Studies that have been done with humans have been concerned mostly with the occurrence of nonshivering thermogenesis and the maintenance of core and skin temperatures.

In one experiment five subjects were placed in a 15° C room for 2 weeks, with the subjects nude 24 hours a day. By the second week their metabolic rates were higher than the controls, whereas skin temperatures showed no decline at all.[35] In another experiment thirty-six subjects dressed in shorts

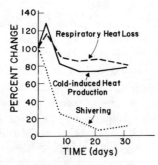

Fig. 4-10. Human acclimation within 20 days. After 20 days (except nights) of exposure to cold chamber (12° C) shivering declines whereas heat production continues to increase. (Modified from Davis, T. R. A. 1961. J. Appl. Physiol. **16:**1011-1015.)

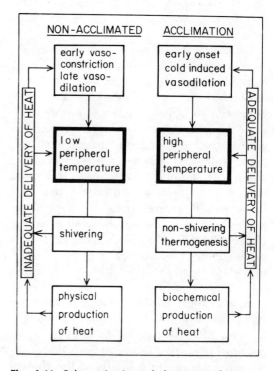

Fig. 4-11. Schematization of thermoregulatory responses to cold before and after acclimation. Before acclimation onset of cold-induced vasodilation is delayed and increase in heat production is attained through shivering, but delivery of heat is still inadequate, resulting in low peripheral temperature. After acclimation cold-induced vasodilation occurs earlier, heat production is increased through nonshivering thermogenesis, and peripheral temperature is higher.

only were exposed for 4 weeks for daily 8-hour periods to temperatures of 5° to 11° C.[36] In this experiment there was a decrease in shivering, an increase in nonshivering thermogenesis, and later initiation of shivering (Fig. 4-10). Therefore when sufficiently exposed to cold stress, a human behaves like other species and can acclimate to cold through similar metabolic changes. However, a recent study of the thermoregulatory responses of seventeen black American soldiers who underwent 4-hour daily exposures at 5° C (41° F) for 8 weeks (5-day work weeks) wearing minimal clothing indicates that after this period of acclimation, although there was a significant reduction in shivering activity and warmer skin temperatures, the rectal temperatures and heat production were not affected by these daily exposures.[37]

CONCLUSION

Initial responses to cold stress are oriented to conserving heat through vasoconstriction alternated with vasodilation. These responses appear to be mediated through the activity of the central nervous system as demonstrated by the action of the sympathetic system and vagal reflex.

As schematized in Fig. 4-11, when ex-posure to cold stress is severe, before acclimation the organism increases its rate of heat production through shivering. As a result of shivering the metabolic rate increases two to three times the normal rate; thus the rate of heat production is increased; however, because of inefficient delivery of heat the peripheral temperature is cold. On the other hand, acclimation to cold stress appears linked to maintenance of warm skin temperatures, made possible by an increased ability to produce heat. Increased heat production is achieved without shivering. The source of energy for nonshivering thermogenesis appears to be white and brown adipose tissue depots converted into free fatty acids. Lipid sources of energy appear to be mediated through the increased activity of calorigenic hormones such as noradrenaline (norepinephrine) and thyroxine.

Limited studies with humans suggest that acclimation to cold stress is associated with increased ability to tolerate low temperatures. This is attained through a maintenance of warmer skin temperatures and increased heat production. However, at present it is not clear to what extent acclimation leads to an increased metabolic rate without shivering.

REFERENCES

1. Burton, A. C., and O. G. Edholm. 1955. Man in a cold environment. Edward Arnold (Publishers) Ltd., London.
2. Winslow, C. E. A., and L. P. Harrington. 1949. Temperature and human life. Princeton University Press, Princeton, N.J.
3. Bazett, H. G., and B. McGlone. 1927. Temperature gradients in the tissue of man. Am. J. Physiol. 82:415-451.
4. Bazett, H. G. 1949. The regulation of body temperature. In L. H. Newburgh, ed. The physiology of temperature regulation and the science of clothing. W. B. Saunders Co., Philadelphia.
5. Lewis, T. 1930. Vasodilation in response to strong cooling. Heart 15:177-181.

6. Grant, R. T., and E. F. Bland. 1931. Observations on arterio-venous anastomoses in human skin and in bird's foot with special reference to reaction to cold. Heart 15:385-407.
7. Carlson, L. D., and A. C. L. Hsieh. 1965. Cold. In O. G. Edholm, and A. L. Bacharach, eds. The physiology of human survival. Academic Press, Inc., New York.
8. LeBlanc, J. 1975. Man in the cold. Charles C Thomas, Publisher, Springfield, Ill.
9. Folk, G. E. 1974. Textbook of environmental physiology. Lea & Febiger, Philadelphia.
10. Smolensky, M., F. Halberg, and F. Sargent. 1972. Chronobiology of the life sequence. In S. Itoh, K. Ogata, and H. Yoshimura, eds. Advances in climatic

physiology. Springer-Verlag New York, Inc., Heidelberg, N.Y.

11. Johnson, R. E., and R. M. Kark. 1947. Environment and food intake in man. Science **105**:378-379.

12. Consolazio, C. F., R. E. Johnson, and L. J. Pecora. 1963. Physiological measurements of metabolic functions in man. McGraw-Hill, Inc., N.Y.

13. Benzinger, T. H. 1959. On physical heat regulation and the sense of temperature in man. Proc. Natl. Acad. Sci. U.S.A. **45**:645-659.

14. Glickman, N., H. Mitchell, R. Keeton, and E. Lambert. 1967. Shivering and heat production in men exposed to intense cold. J. Appl. Physiol. **22**:1-8.

15. Pugh, L. G. C., and Edholm, O. G. 1955. The physiology of channel swimmers. Lancet **2**:761-768.

16. Weitz, C. A. 1969. Morphological factors affecting responses to total body cooling among three human populations tested at high altitude. M.A. Thesis. Pennsylvania State University, University Park, Pa.

17. Steegman, A. T. 1974. Ethnic and anthropometric factors in finger cooling: Japanese and Europeans of Hawaii. Hum. Biol. **46**:621-631.

18. Keatinge, W. R. 1969. Survival in cold water: the physiology and treatment of immersion hypothermia and of drowning. Blackwell Scientific Publications Ltd., Oxford.

19. Buskirk, E. R., R. H. Thompson, and G. D. Whedon. 1963. Metabolic response to cold air in men and women in relation to total body fat content. J. Appl. Physiol. **18**:603-612.

20. Rennie, D. W., B. G. Covino, B. J. Howell, S. H. Song, B. S. Kang, and S. K. Hong. 1962. Physical insulation of Korean diving women. J. Appl. Physiol. **17**:961-966.

21. Hanna, J. A., and S. K. Hong. 1972. Critical water temperature and effective insulation in scuba divers in Hawaii. J. Appl. Physiol. **33**:770-773.

22. Daniels, F., and P. T. Baker. 1961. Relationship between body fat and shivering in air at 15° C. J. Appl. Physiol. **16**:421-425.

23. Spurr, G. B., B. K. Hutt, and S. M. Horratt. 1955. The effects of age on finger temperature responses to local cooling. Am. Heart J. **50**:551-555.

24. Hsieh, A. C. L., and L. D. Carlson. 1957. Role of the thyroid in metabolic response to low temperature. Am. J. Physiol. **188**:40-44.

25. Depocas, F. 1960. Calorigenesis from various organ systems in the whole animal. Fed. Proc. **19** (Suppl. 5):19-24.

26. Jansky, L. 1966. Body organ thermogenesis of the rat during exposure to cold and at maximal metabolic rate. Fed. Proc. **25**:1297-1302.

27. LeBlanc, J., and A. Villemaire. 1970. Thyroxine and noradrenaline or noradrenaline sensitivity, cold resistance, and brown fat. Am. J. Physiol. **218**:1742-1745.

28. Smith, R. E., and D. J. Hoijer. 1962. Metabolism and cellular function in cold acclimatization. Physiol. Rev. **42**:60-142.

29. Radomski, M. W., and T. Orme. 1971. Responses of liproprotein lipase in various tissues to cold exposure. Am. J. Physiol. **220**:1852-1856.

30. Himms-Hagen, J. 1969. The role of brown adipose tissue in the calorigenic effect of adrenaline and noradrenaline in cold-acclimated rats. J. Physiol. (Lond.) **205**:393-403.

31. Hiroshige, T., K. Yoshimura, and S. Itoh. 1972. Mechanisms involved in thermoregulatory heat production in brown adipose tissue. In S. Itoh, K. Ogata, and H. Yoshimura, eds. Advances in climatic physiology. Springer-Verlag New York, Inc., Heidelberg, N.Y.

32. Leduc, J., and P. Rivest. 1969. Effets de l'ablation de la graisse brune interscapulaire sur l'acclimatation au froid chez le rat. Rev. Can. Biol. **28**:49-66.

33. Smith, R. E., and J. C. Roberts. 1964. Thermogenesis of brown adipose tissue in cold-acclimated rats. Am. J. Physiol. **206**:143-148.

34. Bruck, K. 1970. Brown adipose tissue. L. O. Lindberg, New York.

35. Iampietro, P. F., D. E. Bass, and E. R. Buskirk. 1957. Diurnal oxygen consumption and rectal temperature of men during cold exposure. J. Appl. Physiol. **10**:398-400.

36. Davis, T. R. A. 1961. Chamber cold acclimatization in man. J. Appl. Physiol. **16**:1011-1015.

37. Newman, R. W. 1969. Cold acclimation in Negro Americans. J. Appl. Physiol. **37**:316-319.

5 | Acclimatization to cold environments: native populations

Investigators concerned with human acclimatization and adaptation to cold have centered their investigations on the study of indigenous populations who live and work in the cold. In general, the methodology employed in these studies can be classified into three major types: (1) the night-long cold-bag technique, which has been used to study the thermoregulatory characteristics of Australian aborigines, Kalahari Bushmen, Alacaluf Indians, Norwegian Lapps, Eskimos, Athapascan Indians, and Peruvian Quechuas; (2) the short-period laboratory whole-body-cooling technique, which has been used to evaluate the thermoregulatory characteristics of Eskimos, Asiatic divers, Peruvian Quechuas, and European whites; (3) the short-period laboratory extremity-cooling technique, which complements the whole-body–cooling technique. These approaches, although their results are not strictly comparable and they have produced contradictory results within the same population, provide valuable information about human adaptation.

In this chapter the thermoregulatory responses to cold of Australian aborigines, Kalahari Bushmen, Alacaluf Indians, Norwegian Lapps, Eskimos, Athapascan Indians, and Peruvian Quechuas will be discussed separately. The aim is not to determine populational differences in cold adaptation, but to ascertain the mechanisms that enable a given population to overcome cold stress. Most studies of adaptation to cold have been concerned with measurements of metabolic rates and rectal and skin temperatures; little attention has been given to technological adaptations. The exceptions are those studies conducted among Eskimos and Peruvian Quechua Indians, both of which have been extensively studied for technological and physiological adaptation to cold. For this reason, the Eskimos and especially the Quechuas, because of my research experience, will be discussed in more detail than the other populations. Furthermore, the climatic conditions in which a given population lives will always be presented before summarizing their adaptations to cold.

AUSTRALIAN ABORIGINES
Environment

The aborigines of central Australia are exposed during the day to heat stress and during the night to moderate cold stress, as a result of a great diurnal-nocturnal variation in temperature. In the summer months of January through March the normal maximum temperature is 37° C (98.6° F), and the minimum is 22° C (71.6° F). In the winter months, such as July, the mean daily maximum and minimum temperatures are 21° C and 4° C (69.8° and 39.2° F).[1] Given the fact that Australian aborigines do not wear clothing and have no adequate housing during either the winter or summer nights, they are exposed to moderate cold stress.

Although by gathering wild foods and hunting small game (Kangurus, opossum, lizards, etc.) the aborigines of central Australia are able to attain an adequate dietary intake,[2] they are subjected to frequent seasonal food shortages.

Physiological adaptation

The thermoregulatory characteristics of the aborigines from central and northern Australia have been studied both in winter and summer.[3,4] The test consisted of the subjects sleeping overnight (8 hours) in an air temperature ranging from 3° to 5° C (37.4° to 41° F), with an insulation ranging from 2.9 to 3.4 clo units (1 clo = 38 cal/m²/hr).

As shown in Fig. 5-1, the aborigines compared to white control subjects studied under the same conditions tolerated a greater lowering of the skin and rectal temperatures, resulting in a 30% reduction in heat conductance from core to shell. Hence, metabolic

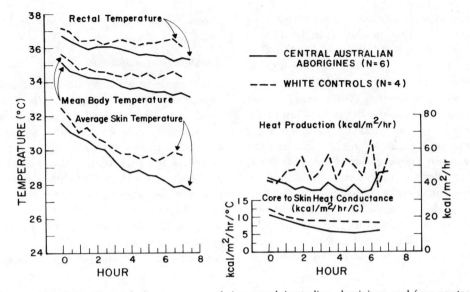

Fig. 5-1. Thermal and metabolic responses of six central Australian aborigines and four control whites during a night of moderate cold exposure in winter. For the Australian aborigines, adaptation to the moderate night cold temperatures (about 3° C) involves a decrease in skin temperature and metabolic rate. (Modified from Scholander, P. F., H. T. Hammel, J. S. Hart, D. H. LeMessurier, and J. Steen. 1958. J. Appl. Physiol. **13:**211-218.)

heat production was also lower. The aborigines appear to oppose cold stress by both decreasing insulation of the body shell through vasoconstriction and by tolerating moderate hypothermia without metabolic compensation. The same pattern of body cooling without metabolic compensation during moderate cold exposure was found among seven aborigines studied in the summer.[4] Furthermore, the aborigines living in the northern tropical less cold-stressed region of Australia exhibited a metabolic and thermoregulatory response that was intermediate between the aborigines of central Australia and the control whites.[1]

Cultural adaptation

The Australian aborigines do not wear clothing except for a genital covering. During the night they do not shield themselves from the cold air, and they sleep on the lee-

ward side of a windbreak hastily made from brush and between small fires. Field studies indicate that the glowing embers of the fire, if attended frequently, would provide sufficient radiant heat to the body through the exposed side to balance heat loss, but the Australian aborigines do not do so. Thus, the degree of cold exposure in the sleeping microenvironment is below the thermoneutral temperature. Despite this cold stress the Australian aborigines were able to sleep comfortably without shivering, whereas the white controls studied under the same conditions shivered continuously without being able to sleep.

KALAHARI BUSHMEN
Environment

The Bushmen of the Kalahari Desert, like the Australian aborigines, are exposed during the night to moderate chronic cold stress.

The average daily minimum temperatures for the month of July in the Kalahari Desert range from 3° to 5° C, the same as found in central Australia. Also like the aborigines, the Bushmen do not wear clothing except for a genital covering. Most field reports agree that the Bushmen have an abundant variety of flora and fauna and given their excellent skills in gathering and hunting are able to attain a good dietary intake.[5] Indeed, the evaluations of nutritional status indicate that the Bushmen maintain good health and nutrition. However, as shown by the changes in body weight and subcutaneous fat,[6] the Bushmen are periodically subjected to restrictions in their dietary intakes, which at times reach levels of chronic undernutrition.[6]

Physiological adaptation

A sample of Kalahari Bushmen, using the same night-long cold exposure tests as those used with the Australian aborigines, was evaluated by Hammel et al.[7] As shown in Fig. 5-2, the Bushmen after the second hour had lower rectal temperatures and lower metabolic rates than the white controls, but skin temperatures and heat conductivity were higher. The increased heat conductivity of the Bushmen has been attributed to their small amount of subcutaneous fat.[1] Although rectal temperatures and metabolic

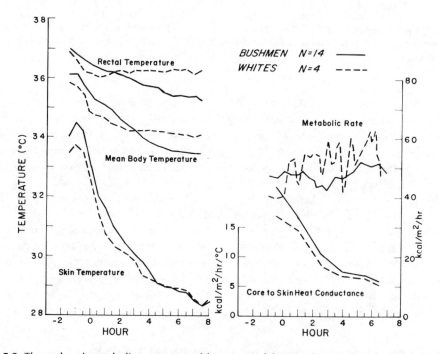

Fig. 5-2. Thermal and metabolic responses of fourteen Kalahari Bushmen and four control whites during a night of moderate cold exposure in winter. Adaptation to moderate night cold temperatures (3° to 8° C) for Bushmen involves greater body cooling than for whites, but unlike the Australian aborigines their excessive heat loss (conductance) is compensated for by increased metabolic rate. (Modified from Hammel, H. T. 1962. Tech. Rep. 62-44. Arctic Aeromedical Laboratory, Fort Wainwright, Alaska.)

rates were lower than those of the whites, the Bushmen, like the Australian aborigines, experienced a higher grade of sleep throughout the entire night of the test. However, other investigations indicate that Bushmen subjects, when exposed to air temperatures of 5°, 10°, 15°, and 20° C for 2 hours, each maintained a lower skin temperature with a marked increase in metabolic rate.[8,9] In other words, according to this study the thermoregulatory responses of the Bushmen were different from those of the aborigines in that their lower skin temperatures were caused by a smaller skinfold thickness, which resulted in an enhanced rate of heat loss, in turn eliciting an increase in metabolic rates. It must be noted that this cold test is not comparable to that given the Australian aborigines, since it was given in four sequential 2-hour night exposures rather than 8-hour night-long exposures. In these studies the Bushmen were awakened and moved from their shelters near the fires to the test site and there exposed for 1½ to 2 hours on a stretcher, naked except for the genital covers. It is quite possible that these conditions could have caused an increase in the subjects' anxiety levels, which may have increased their metabolic rates.

Cultural adaptation

Field investigations indicate that the Bushmen through efficient use of fires and skin cloaks during cold nights have been able to create a microclimate around their bodies that is close to the thermoneutral temperature of 25° C.[10] These investigations indicate that Bushmen employ the following techniques. First, in the early part of the evening large fires are built around which the Bushmen sit huddled in their skin cloaks. Second, they sleep in groups, three or four to a group, in families or in single-sex groups. Third, when they retire, they lie with their feet to the fire and have their blankets (skin cloaks) tucked in around their bodies and over their heads. When the fires die down on cold nights, they wake up and stoke the fires. Fifth, their huts of grass and boughs are used as a windbreak, and for this purpose the huts are placed in a half-circle.

ALACALUF INDIANS
Environment

The Alacaluf Indians of Tierra del Fuego in southern Chile numbered only fifty as of 1960. These Indians have little protection from the wind and rain other than crude huts and are poorly clothed. As shown by temperature recordings at Puerto Eden on Wellington Island, the Indians are exposed to moderate, chronic cold stress. The mean maximum temperature for the summer month of January is 13.1° C (55.6° F), and the mean minimum temperature is 7° C (44.6° F). In the winter month of July, the mean maximum and minimum temperatures are 5.3° C (41.5° F) and −0.3° C (31.5° F), respectively.[1] The area of Tierra del Fuego is also characterized by high precipitation and high winds.

Physiological adaptation

Using the night-long cold-exposure tests, like those employed in the aborigine and Bushmen studies, a sample of Alacaluf Indians was studied.[11] As shown in Fig. 5-3, the thermoregulatory responses of the Alacaluf Indians are similar to those of whites studied under equal conditions of humidity and temperature. However, during the entire test the foot temperatures of the Indians were maintained at about 2° to 3° C higher than those of the whites. Furthermore, evaluations of foot temperatures after immersion in water at 5° C for 30 minutes showed that the Alacaluf Indians sustained the stress without any signs of pain from cold, whereas the whites tested under the same conditions were in great agony.[11]

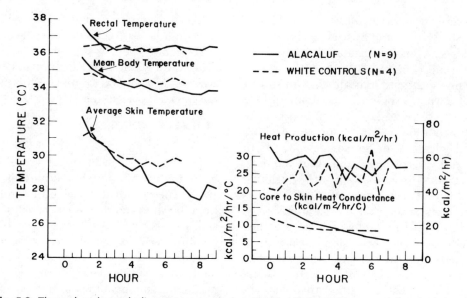

Fig. 5-3. Thermal and metabolic responses of nine Alacaluf Indians during a night of moderate cold exposure and four control whites studied in central Australia under similar conditions in winter. The Alacaluf respond to night cold temperatures (3° C) in a manner similar to control whites, but they begin with high metabolic rates, which are maintained throughout night. (Modified from Hammel, H. T. 1960. Tech. Rep. 60-633. Wright Air Development Division.)

In summary, the Alacaluf Indians respond to the humid cold stress of Tierra del Fuego with the maintenance of high metabolic rates and high extremity temperatures. Furthermore, they appear to exhibit the ability to tolerate cold stress without pain.

NORWEGIAN LAPPS
Environment

The Lapp shepherds from Norway, because of their nomadic life-style, have not developed formal housing and thus are continuously exposed to cold stress. They are reindeer hunters and herders who spend most of the daylight hours outdoors and sleep in poorly heated tents at night. During the night the outdoor temperature usually falls from −25° C (−13° F) to −30° C (−22° F).[12] The inside tent temperature, initially at a comfortable level, by morning is the same as outdoors because of the dying fire. The underblanket consists of a single reindeer hide, and the top blanket is made of skins of long-haired sheep. In contrast to the nomadic shepherds, there are also village Lapps who are farmers living in formal modern houses that provide adequate protection against the cold.

Physiological adaptation

Fig. 5-4 shows that the metabolic responses and rectal temperatures of the Lapp villagers and white controls during night-long cold exposure were comparable.[13] In contrast, the shepherds experienced a substantially smaller metabolic response accompanied by a 1° C greater drop in rectal temperature (down to 35.8° C by the fifth hour of testing). However, the foot temperatures of the shepherds were maintained at a higher level than those of the villagers or controls. The shepherds also slept more comfortably than the other two groups. Furthermore, Norwegian and Finnish Lapps exhibited an

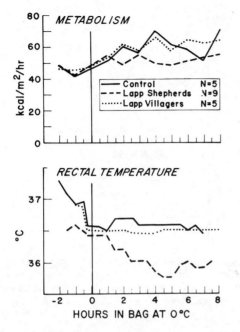

Fig. 5-4. Thermal and metabolic responses of nine nomadic Lapp shepherds, five Lapp villagers, and five control whites during night of moderate cold exposure in winter. The Lapp shepherds during the cold night (0° C) sleep had a lower metabolic rate and rectal temperature than control whites and Lapp villagers. (Modified from Andersen, K. L., Y. Loyning, J. D. Nelms, O. Wilson, R. H. Fox, and A. Bolstad. 1960. J. Appl. Physiol. **15**:649-653.)

earlier onset of cold-induced vasodilation and less pain than the white controls when immersing their hands in ice water for 15 minutes.[14,15]

In summary, the Norwegian Lapp shepherds respond to cold stress with a lower metabolic rate increase and higher peripheral temperatures than white controls.

ESKIMOS
Environment

The world's population of Eskimos, numbering 50,000 to 60,000, occupies the northwestern coast of America and across the Bering Strait into Asia. The Eskimo culture is most characteristically found around the shores of Baffin Island and the northern parts of Hudson Bay, in latitudes 69° to 70° N. In this central area, as throughout the arctic zone, the principal factors that distinguish the seasons are length of daylight and temperature. In the arctic archipelago the average winter temperature ranges from −46° C (−50° F) to −31° C (−35° F); in the summer the temperature rarely goes above 46° F. Equally important is the drastic change in sunlight hours. During the brief arctic summer the sun shines almost continually for 2 months; in the fall there is a maximum of 12 hours of sunshine per day, followed by a complete absence of sun in midwinter. With the coming of spring the sun again shines for increasing periods each day until the annual cycle is complete. It is quite evident that such an inhospitable environment requires thorough technological and physiological adaptation.

Technological adaptation

Housing. The native Eskimo housing, whether permanent, temporary, or "igloo" type is well-insulated. The walls made of whale rib rafters are covered with a double layer of seal skin alternated with moss. This design permits trapping considerable air which, in turn, acts as further insulation. In addition, through efficient use of underground tunnels and by placing the source of heat, usually an oil, blubber, or coal lamp, at a lower level than the main floor the Eskimos have produced a useful system of heat exchange whereby cold air is warmed before it reaches the area where the people live.[16-18] Thus, despite subzero outside temperatures the indoor night and day temperatures average between 10° and 21° C for the coastal Eskimos and around 0° C for the Baffin Island Eskimos.[12-17]

Clothing. In most areas the Eskimo clothing is made of caribou. This is the preferred skin because of its high-quality insulation, its light weight, and its suppleness compared to seal skin. When caribou is not available, as among the polar Eskimos, polar bear skins are the replacement.[19] It has been determined that Eskimo clothing, which consists of caribou fur in thicknesses of 1½ to 3 inches, provides insulation equivalent to 7 to 12 clo units.[20] That is, the insulative efficiency of Eskimo clothing ranges from 266 to 456 cal/m²/hr.

Although it is evident that this type of clothing has succeeded in creating a comfortable microclimate, it has by no means removed cold stress, especially for the extremities. Although Eskimos wear snowshoes and short skin mittens at times, during their daily activities such as fishing their hands and feet are continuously subject to cold stress. As indicated by ethnographic accounts,[18,19,21] during hunting and fishing the Eskimos continually dip their hands in cold water and expose their feet to severe cold; occasionally they experience whole-body chilling while waiting motionless at a fishing hole. In fact, some hunters have been known to sit over the breathing holes of seals for up to 72 hours at a time in subzero temperatures.[22] Thus, despite their efficient technological adaptations, the Eskimos are not always "tropical men in arctic clothing" since the subsistence activities of the coastal and inland Eskimos induce conditions of prolonged extremity chilling and, at times, body chilling. In response to this cold stress, the Eskimos have developed specialized thermoregulatory characteristics.

Physiological adaptation

Metabolic rate. Most studies agree that the Eskimos' metabolic rates during warm and cold conditions are between 13% and 45% higher than that of white controls or expected standards (Fig. 5-5).[23-35] However, there is disagreement as to the source of increased heat production. Investigations of thyroid function have not shown any major relation-

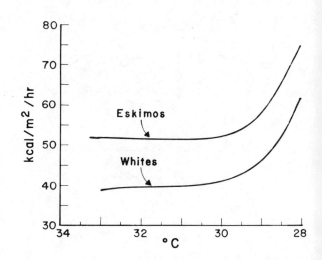

Fig. 5-5. Relationship between skin temperature and metabolic rate during cold exposure of Eskimos and whites. At given temperature Eskimos respond with greater metabolic rate. (Modified from Adams, T., and B. G. Covino. 1958. J. Appl. Physiol. **12:**9-12.)

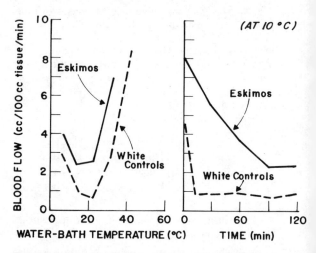

Fig. 5-6. Hand blood flow during different water bath temperatures and immersion of hand in water bath at 10°C. Eskimos respond to cold temperatures with greater blood flow than white controls. (Modified from Brown, G. M., and J. Page. 1953. J. Appl. Physiol. **5:**221-227.)

ship between thyroid levels and increased metabolic rates in Eskimos. Nutritional studies have indicated, on the other hand, that the higher metabolic rates may be related in part to the Eskimos' dietary habits. Earlier investigations in East Greenland described the Eskimos as "the most exquisitely carnivorous people on earth."[23] The Eskimos' daily diet was reported to contain an excessive amount of animal protein (280 g), a great deal of fat (135 g), and a small amount of carbohydrates (54 g), of which more than one half was glycogen derived from meat. Controlled dietary studies and metabolic measurements of Eskimos from four localities in northern Alaska during the summer and winter concluded that the dynamic action of a protein diet was the main source of high metabolism.[17] On the other hand, other studies indicate that the Eskimos' elevated

metabolism during sleep was not correlated with either protein or fat energy fractions in the diet.[36] Furthermore, the more cold-stressed inland Eskimos have been found to have a greater metabolic rate than the lesser cold-stressed coastal Eskimos, who were studied under similar dietary conditions.[37,38] Thus, it would appear that the Eskimos' elevated metabolism is not caused only by high protein intake.

Peripheral temperature. All studies indicate that when either the feet or hands of Eskimos are cooled in water or air at any temperature, peripheral temperatures and degree of spontaneous fluctuations in blood flow are greater among Eskimos than among

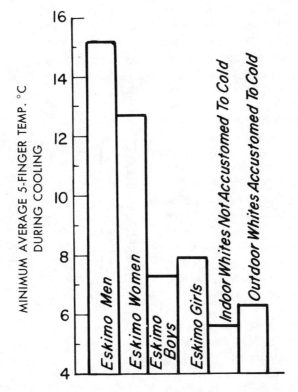

Fig. 5-7. Peripheral temperature of left middle finger of Eskimo men, boys, outdoor whites, and indoor whites during cold air exposure (−3° to −7° C). Eskimo men maintain higher skin temperatures than both outdoor and indoor whites, and Eskimo children, in spite of smaller hand volumes, maintain temperatures equal to adult indoor whites. (Modified from Miller, L. K., and L. Irving. 1962. J. Appl. Physiol. **17**:449-465.)

white controls (Fig. 5-6).[27,30,39,40] This response results in improved performance and reduced cold sensation for the Eskimo, which is reflected in the Eskimos' remarkable ability to work with bare hands and to continue to perform fine movements in the winter cold.[27] Furthermore, when the subjects' hands were exposed to a 10° C waterbath for 2 hours, the Eskimos experienced only a mild cold sensation during immersion but did not exhibit signs of pain, whereas the white controls experienced first the sensation of severe cold in the immersed hand and then a deep aching pain. Similarly, all the Eskimos sustained exposure of fingers to water baths at 0° C, but 75% of the white controls could not finish the test either because of frostbite or intense pain.[41] The Eskimos' higher peripheral temperature is also associated with greater amounts of red blood cells, higher plasma volumes, and more globulins.[28,42,43] Since the increase in red blood cells requires a greater vascular bed, it is very plausible that the Eskimos' high peripheral temperature is maintained through an enhanced vascularization.

In summary, the climatic conditions in which Eskimos live provide severe acute and chronic cold stress. The Eskimos' material culture, in the form of housing and clothing, represents one of the most important adaptations to cold stress. However, because of their subsistence economy, the Eskimos are still exposed to prolonged extremity, and at times, whole-body chilling. The Eskimo diet is based on a high fat and protein intake that provides calorigenic effects and, in view of their natural resources, is an adaptive response to cold stress by its contribution to the maintenance of high metabolic rates. All evidence confirms the Eskimos' increased metabolic rates, high peripheral temperatures, and remarkable tolerance to cold exposure of the extremities. As shown in Fig. 5-7, the minimum finger temperature of Eskimo children and

women when exposed to air temperatures between −3° and −7° C, despite their smaller hand volumes, are as high or higher than those of white men accustomed to outdoor cold.[44] Thus the Eskimos' ability to maintain high extremity temperatures and their ability to tolerate cold appear to be acquired during growth. That is, the thermoregulatory characteristics of Eskimos reflect the influence of developmental adaptation (or developmental acclimatization). The thermoregulatory characteristics of Eskimos from the village of Igloolik were recently studied.[45] The population of this community is in a period of rapid acculturation and is adopting some of the eating and cultural habits of whites. Furthermore, the women and children who attend comfortably heated schools are less cold-exposed than the adult males who still make their living by hunting. As shown in

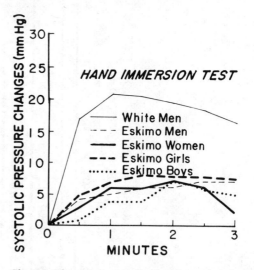

Fig. 5-8. Changes in systolic blood pressure in white male subjects, Eskimo men and women, and Eskimo boys and girls during immersion of hand in water at 4° C for 3 minutes. Eskimo women and children, despite the fact that they lived in comfortably heated houses, tolerate cold stress as well as adult Eskimo hunters and better than whites. (Modified from LeBlanc, J. 1975. Man in the cold. Charles C Thomas, Publisher, Springfield, Ill.)

Fig. 5-8, the Eskimo women and children during immersion of the hand in cold water are as tolerant as the Eskimo adult male hunters and more tolerant than the whites. These findings suggest that the Eskimos' developmental response to cold is probably mediated by genetic factors.

ATHAPASCAN INDIANS
Environment

The Athapascan Indians neighbor the Eskimos in Northern Canada. The climatic conditions of this area are very similar to those for the Eskimos; however, the cold is not as intense as that encountered in northern Alaska or on Baffin Island. Among Athapascan-speaking people, the Indians from Old Crow have been studied most extensively by physiologists.[39,46,47] Based on climatological data collected in Fort Yukon in 1958, the mean temperature for January was $-28°$ C, and for September the mean maximum temperature was $21°$ C. These temperatures are made more severe by high winds, especially in winter. The short summer has both warm and chilly days, but frost is so frequent that vegetables are not grown.

The subsistence economy of the Athapascan people is based on hunting, trapping, and fishing. As with the Eskimos, the subsistence activities of the Athapascan people involve severe cold stress for the extremities as well as severe whole-body cooling.

Technological adaptation

Housing. Aboriginal housing consists of excavated caves or inverted V-shaped houses whose sides and roofs are covered with moss to retain heat. A fire is also maintained in the center of the dwelling. Other housing forms are simple bivouacs and cabins that are not as well insulated as those of the Eskimos.

Clothing. The clothing of the Old Crow people consists of a duffed parka (blanket cloth), wool underclothing, flannel shirt, wool or cotton trousers, moosehide mitts, and wool-duffed socks under smoke-tanned moosehide moccasins.

Physiological adaptation

Whole-body cooling. The basal metabolic rates of the Athapascan Indians, when expressed per kilogram of body weight, were about 10% to 14% higher than expected on the basis of white standards.[46] Evaluations using the night-long exposure technique indicated that these Indians exhibit the same metabolic responses as white controls (Fig. 5-9).[39,46,47] However, even though the Athapascan Indians' rectal temperatures declined at a faster rate than those of the white controls, their foot temperatures were always maintained at a higher level. Myographic records indicate that although the Athapascan Indians exhibited the same frequency of shivering bouts as the white controls, they were able to sleep better and for longer periods than whites tested under the same conditions.[46,47]

Extremity cooling. Temperature evaluations of hands exposed to either cold water ($5°$ C) or ice water indicate that the Athapascan Indians had warmer hand temperatures than white controls.[39,46] Furthermore, the Indians had a more rapid rewarming and suffered less pain than the whites.

In summary, the Athapascan Indians differ from whites in their ability to distribute heat toward the extremities and tolerate cold stress. However, these differences are less well defined than those observed between Eskimos and Europeans, suggesting that the adaptation to cold stress of Athapascan Indians and other subarctic populations is based on both physiological mechanisms and behavioral and cultural responses as well.[48,57]

PERUVIAN QUECHUAS

The highland Quechua populations from the Peruvian Andes and other mountain

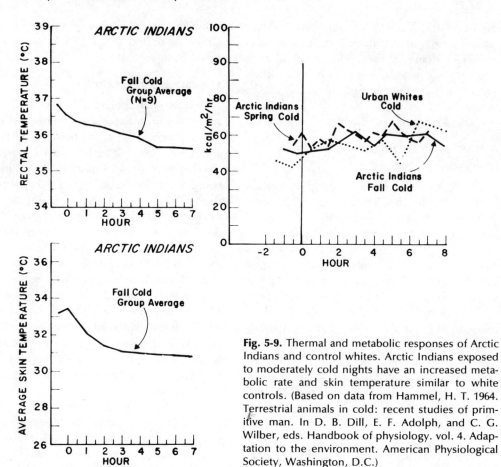

Fig. 5-9. Thermal and metabolic responses of Arctic Indians and control whites. Arctic Indians exposed to moderately cold nights have an increased metabolic rate and skin temperature similar to white controls. (Based on data from Hammel, H. T. 1964. Terrestrial animals in cold: recent studies of primitive man. In D. B. Dill, E. F. Adolph, and C. G. Wilber, eds. Handbook of physiology. vol. 4. Adaptation to the environment. American Physiological Society, Washington, D.C.)

areas of South America are exposed to a variety of stresses including hypoxia, cold, low humidity, and high levels of solar radiation. These climatic stresses interact with other stresses such as limited energy and food resources and disease. The pattern of adaptation to each of these stresses depends on the interaction of environmental, cultural, and human biological parameters. For this reason, interpretation of the cold adaptation of the highland populations requires a synergic interpretation of all stresses, since any adaptive pattern developed by a population represents a compromise to often conflicting and antagonistic stresses.

This discussion is based on the multidisciplinary research centered in the Altiplano population of the district of Nuñoa situated at a mean altitude of 4150 m in southern Peru.[49]

Environment

The economic focus of the highland region is herding sheep, llamas, and alpacas, the major domestic animals of the altiplano. However, the subsistence pattern of much of the indigenous population between 3000 and 4000 m is based on a mixed economy of corn, potatoes, barley, wheat, and native chenopodium (canihua and quinua) cultivation and the herding of sheep and llamas. On the other hand, at elevations above 4000 m, such as those of the altiplano region, agriculture is not practiced because of severe cold and frost, and the subsistence pattern is primarily pastoral. The sheep, llama, and alpaca skins are used for bedding, the sheep and alpaca wool is used for clothing, the dung is used for fuel and fertilizer, and the meat is used for private consumption as well as for trade. The hides and animals are also often traded for cash, although the greater part of the family income is derived from the sale of wool. With this income cereal foods, additional clothing, yarn dyes, coca leaves, alcohol, and other small luxuries can be purchased. All the meat and the wool for basic clothing is provided by herding. Every Indian owns some of these domestic animals, and many own highland ponies as well. Llamas and horses are used as pack animals, whereas sheep and alpacas are raised solely for their wool and meat.

By most standards the altiplano of the Nuñoa region is cold. The mean annual temperature is 8.3° C (47° F), which is well below the thermoneutral zone for humans. The mean monthly temperature ranges from 10° C in the warmest month of November to 5.5° C in the coldest month of June. Daily temperatures throughout the year are lower than those considered comfortable for most populations. Seasonal variation in temperature in the highlands is primarily the result of the monsoon pattern in the Pacific, which creates dry and wet seasons.

The dry season extends from April to September. About 50% of the days are free of cloud cover. As a result, daytime temperatures, especially outdoors, are pleasant with high solar radiation, but the afternoons and nights are very cold because the clear sky increases heat loss through long-wave radiation. Most of the nights have temperatures below freezing, and a low of −8° C has been

recorded for this period. The wet season extends from October to March and is characterized by almost daily thunderstorm activity producing heavy local precipitation. The precipitation most often occurs as sleet, rain, hail, or snow and is accompanied by high winds. The daytime cloud cover usually reduces solar radiation and causes a drop in temperature to about 5° C. Snow may accumulate up to 4 cm but is frequently melted by sunshine. Because the heavy cloud cover reduces solar radiation, the daytime outdoor climate is less pleasant than during the dry season, but since sunlight hits at a greater angle at this time of year, the temperatures are actually higher. Furthermore, because the cloud cover reduces heat loss through long-wave radiation, the nights are warmer than in the dry season. Both in the dry and wet seasons the varying temperatures are accompanied by gusty winds that add to the cold stress when temperatures are low. The coolness is accentuated by the lack of internal heating in houses.

Observation in the natural state

Evaluations of the thermoregulatory responses of individuals in their natural state were obtained during both the dry and wet seasons.[50]

Cold stress in the dry season. The greatest cold stress in the dry season is nighttime.[50-52] As shown in Fig. 5-10, even though the interior house temperatures averaged only 3.6° C (38.5° F), the subjects were not greatly cold stressed. The severity of the ambient cold stress is ameliorated by the fact that the subjects usually sleep clothed and in groups of two to four.

Cold stress in the wet season. During the wet season because the rain, snow, sleet, and hail fall daily and are driven by high winds the potential for cold stress is rather high. Since this season coincides with the time of planting and cultivation as well as

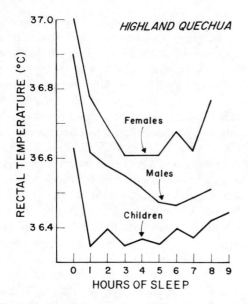

Fig. 5-10. Rectal temperature of Quechua females, males, and children while sleeping in their own houses. Rectal temperatures did not decrease to initial low levels even though interior house temperatures were only 3.6° C. The children show a rapid fall in rectal temperature for the first hour and then attain a certain equilibrium for remainder of night. (Modified from Hanna, J. M. 1976. Natural exposure to cold. In P. T. Baker and M. A. Little, eds. Man in the Andes: a multidisciplinary study of high-altitude Quechua. Dowden, Hutchinson & Ross, Inc., Stroudsburg, Pa.)

herding, exposure of the entire body, and extremities in particular, to cold stress cannot be avoided. However, the body surface temperatures of fifty-eight individuals ranging in age from 3 to 80 years were not very low and in fact approximated the thermoneutral zone, despite the fact that ambient temperatures were 11° C.[51] This adequate temperature regulation was maintained even during the coldest days of the rainy season.

In summary, although the climatic conditions are severe and provide potential cold stress, evaluations of peripheral and rectal temperatures indicate that both at night during the dry season and by day during the

wet season the Quechua Indians live within tolerable limits.

Technological adaptation

The success of the Quechua populations in preventing severe body cold stress reflects the effectiveness of their technological adaptations, the most important of which are housing, bedding, and clothing.

Housing. The housing of the highland natives differs with variations in altitude and subsistence pattern. A distinct advantage of the more sedentary, mixed economy populations living below 4000 m is individual or community ownership of land. In higher regions of the altiplano the large herds make individual ownership of pasture land impractical. Personal ownership provides for a greater economic investment in the land itself. Thus, at elevations of 4000 m the houses are built of adobe and are permanent. These adobe houses seem quite effective in protecting against cold stress in that they maintained the indoor temperatures more than 10° C above outdoor temperatures.[53]

On the other hand, the housing at those elevations above 4300 m, because of a pastoral economy requiring high mobility, is more temporary. It usually consists of two or three circular dwellings, about 30 square feet in area, constructed of piled stones and roofed with straw. These houses have the advantage of minimal economic investment and may be abandoned without great economic loss each time the family moves on to new grazing lands (Fig. 5-11). The insulative effectiveness of this type of housing, however, is very inadequate, as shown by the fact that the average indoor-outdoor differential temperature of twenty-one houses equaled only 3.7° C.[52] In many cases, especially above 4500 m, the inside temperature nearly equalled the outside one.

In summary, housing at around 3500 to 4000 m provides adequate protection against

Fig. 5-11. Natural cold exposure and circular house of pastoral Quechuas living above 4500 m in district of Nuñoa in southern Peruvian highlands.

cold stress; however, at higher elevations, because the housing is very temporary, it has only a minimal effect on the severity of cold stress. Nevertheless, it does provide protection against wind and rain and consequently helps reduce heat loss through conduction and radiation.

Bedding. The adaptive significance of Nuñoa Quechua bedding has been studied by comparing thermoregulatory characteristics while the subjects were sleeping overnight (8 hours) under three different conditions: (1) in light woolen sleeping bags at 23° C, (2) in light woolen sleeping bags at 4° C, and (3) in their own bedding at 4° C. The results of this study indicate that when native bedding was used at 4° C, the skin temperatures of Quechua men throughout the night were comparable to those attained when sleeping in the thermoneutral conditions of 23° C.[51] However, the metabolic

rate showed cyclic variations indicating bouts of shivering but not so severe as to disturb the sleeping subjects. The authors point out that if clothing was used, as is the native practice, a shiver-free sleep would be maintained. Thus, it would appear that native bedding provides adequate thermal protection against cold stress.

Clothing. The effectiveness of the Nuñoa Quechua clothing has been studied by comparing the thermoregulatory responses of men and women to a standard cold stress of 10° C for 2 hours with and without clothing.[54] This study indicated that the insulative value of the men's clothing without poncho and hat equaled 1.21 clo units and 1.43 clo units for women without shawls and hats. With clothing the metabolic heat production was lower than without. Furthermore, the skin temperatures, including hands and feet uncovered, were maintained at higher levels than without clothing. Use of clothing resulted in a 4° C increase in microclimate temperature (temperature of the skin under clothing), and the resulting caloric saving equaled 139 kcal for men and 107 kcal for women. Although there was no sex difference in skin temperature when exposed nude, when clothing was used, men maintained lower hand temperatures than women, but higher foot temperatures. This sex difference reflects differences in the pattern of local acclimatization.[54] Men experience greater cold exposure of the foot than women because of their daily herding and agricultural activities, whereas women experience more daily cold exposure to the hand from cooking, washing, and weaving. These daily exposure differences become evident when the stress is milder (10° C wearing clothing) and body heat content is not a major problem, so local vascular adaptations are more operative.

In summary, the most singly important technological adaptation to cold stress is clothing. However, the use of gloves and socks for protection of the hands and feet of adults and children is not normally practiced.

Observation under laboratory conditions

Whole-body cold exposure. Studies of whole-body cooling, including nude exposures of 2 hours at 10° C, were conducted in a laboratory built especially for this purpose

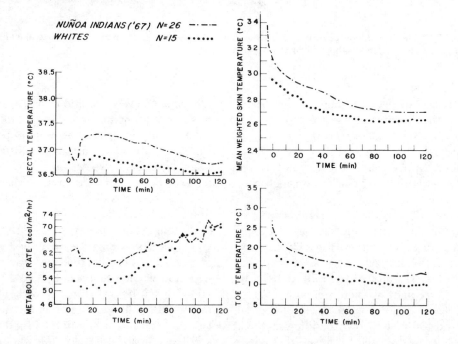

Fig. 5-12. Thermal and metabolic responses of highland Quechua Indians from Nuñoa and control whites during 2-hour exposure at 10° C at 4150 m altitude. Highland Quechuas maintain higher rectal and peripheral temperatures, especially of the toe, than white controls, whereas metabolic rate during the first 1½ hour is higher than that of whites. (Modified from Little, M. A. 1976. Natural exposure to cold. In P. T. Baker and M. A. Little, eds. Man in the Andes: a multidisciplinary study of high-altitude Quechua. Dowden, Hutchinson & Ross, Inc., Stroudsburg, Pa.)

at 4150 m in the town of Nuñoa.[49] As illustrated in Fig. 5-12, the highland Nuñoa Quechua maintained higher foot temperatures and hence higher mean-weighted skin temperatures than the sea level United States whites. Associated with increased peripheral extremity temperatures, the Quechuas had higher rectal temperatures. Furthermore, although metabolic heat production during the first hour of the test was higher for the Quechuas than for sea level whites, the rest of the test results were comparable for the two groups. In other words, the central highland Quechuas, when compared to sea level controls, showed a metabolic compensation that enabled them to maintain warmer skin temperatures.[58]

Extremity cooling. Tests of extremity cooling were done under a variety of conditions including exposure of the hand and foot to air temperatures of $0°$ C; exposure of the foot in water at $4°$, $10°$, and $15°$ C; and exposure of the hand in water at $4°$ C.[55,56] These studies indicate that in each test the highland Nuñoa Quechuas displayed warmer skin temperatures and hence greater blood flow to the surface of the extremities than white subjects who were tested at sea level and after a residency of 14 months at high altitude (Fig. 5-13). It must be noted that the

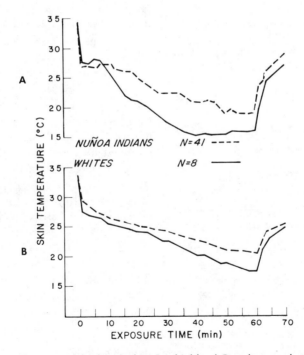

Fig. 5-13. Skin temperature of the hand of Nuñoa highland Quechuas and white controls during 1-hour exposure to $0°$ C air at 4150 m. **A,** Comparison of temperature of subjects' third finger. **B,** comparison of temperature of subjects' dorsum hand. The highland Nuñoa Quechuas had warmer peripheral temperatures than white controls who resided 14 months at high altitude. (Modified from Little, M. A. 1976. Physiological responses to cold. In P. T. Baker and M. A. Little, eds. Man in the Andes: a multidisciplinary study of high-altitude Quechua. Dowden, Hutchinson & Ross, Inc., Stroudsburg, Pa.)

greatest highland Quechua-white differences occurred at a water temperature of 10° to 15° C. This finding suggests that the peripheral vasomotor system of the highland Quechuas operates more effectively in moderate cold stress.[55,56]

Fig. 5-14 compares the responses of 1-hour exposure of the foot to 0° C air tempera-

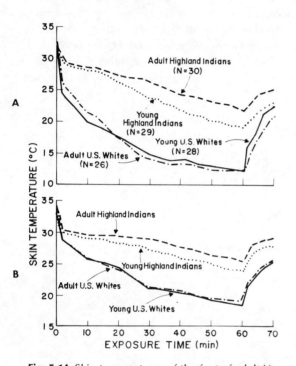

Fig. 5-14. Skin temperatures of the foot of adult Nuñoa highland Quechuas, young highland Quechuas, adult lowland whites, and young lowland whites during 1-hour exposure to 0° C air tested at 4150 m. **A,** Temperature comparison of subjects' first toe. **B,** Temperature comparison of dorsum foot of subjects. Both adult and young highland Quechuas had higher peripheral temperature than white controls, suggesting that developmental acclimatization influences high peripheral temperatures of Andean Indians. (Modified from Little, M. A. 1976. Physiological responses to cold. In P. T. Baker and M. A. Little, eds. Man in the Andes: a multidisciplinary study of high-altitude Quechua. Dowden, Hutchinson & Ross, Inc., Stroudsburg, Pa.)

tures of thirty Nuñoa Quechua adults, twenty-nine young Quechuas aged 7 to 19 years, twenty-six adult whites, and twenty-eight young whites aged 7 to 18 years. These data demonstrate that the adult and nonadult whites maintained the same low peripheral temperatures. In contrast, the adult Quechuas maintained higher temperatures than the nonadults, but both groups had systematically warmer foot temperatures than the whites. The fact that there were no young adult differences among the whites suggests that developmental acclimatization is one factor contributing to the elevated extremity temperatures of Andean Indians.[55,56] In other words, the existence of a relationship between age and foot temperatures of the Quechuas indicates that cold stress is present during the developmental period and that some acclimatization to this stress has taken place.

In summary, the environmental conditions in which the highland Quechua Indians live provide potential cold stress. The Quechua Indians, through the use of clothing, sleeping patterns, and housing, have successfully modified and ameliorated the severity of cold stress. Evaluations of the thermoregulatory characteristics in natural and laboratory settings demonstrate that the Quechua Indians respond to cold stress with metabolic compensation and great heat flow to the extremities. The fact that maintenance of high peripheral temperatures characterizes both children and adult Quechua Indians suggests that the thermoregulatory characteristics of the Indian native are acquired through developmental acclimatization to cold.[55,56]

CONCLUSION

The major conclusion derived from these studies is that humans have developed a great capacity to tolerate varying degrees of cold stress. Using the ability to sleep comfortably in the cold as an index of adaptation,

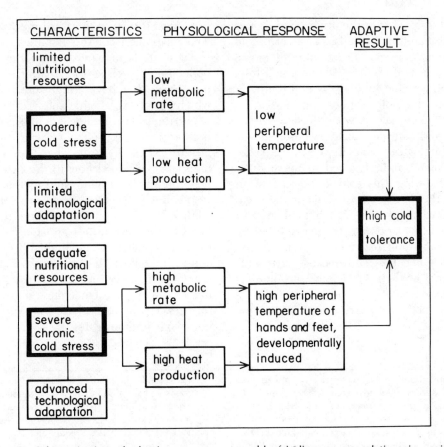

Fig. 5-15. Schematization of adaptive responses to cold of indigenous populations in environments of moderate and severe cold stress. Populations inhabiting environments of moderate and severe cold stress through specialized thermoregulatory responses, which are intimately related to degree of access to nutritional resources and technological adaptation, have attained high degree of cold tolerance.

all indigenous populations exhibit a high degree of adjustment to cold stress, but they differ in manner of attaining the adaptation (Fig. 5-15). The Australian aborigines inhabiting the deserts of Central Australia sleep well by tolerating colder peripheral temperatures. In contrast, populations inhabiting the colder regions of the world appear to sleep well because they can keep their peripheral and especially their extremity temperatures high. Considering that the desert, both in duration and intensity of cold,

provides conditions of moderate cold stress and adds no risk of frostbite, letting the body shell cool is an excellent response. In contrast, the arctic, subarctic, and Andean regions are characterized by severe cold stress and letting the body shell cool would lead to considerable body injury and frostbite. Furthermore, maintaining a low metabolic rate and low peripheral temperature is very economical from the energy standpoint and may be adaptive under conditions of limited nutritional resources as occurs among the Australian aborigines. On the other hand, populations inhabiting regions of severe cold stress do have access to adequate nutritional resources, and therefore maintaining a high metabolic rate and high peripheral temperature is an affordable response.

As expected, along with these environmental and thermoregulatory differences, the technological adaptations to cold are more efficient and advanced in the populations inhabiting the cold regions than in those in the deserts of Australia or the Kalahari. However, despite the high degree of technological adaptation that is exhibited by the Eskimos, and to a lesser extent by the Peruvian Quechuas, and because of the requirements of their subsistence economies, their environments provide conditions of moderate body cold stress and severe extremity cold stress.

At least three physiological mechanisms of cold adaptation set the Eskimos and Quechuas apart from white controls or tropical populations, such as the Australian aborigines. First, they have a high metabolic rate, which is not explainable solely on the basis of nutritional factors. Second, a test of whole-body exposure as well as local extremity exposure to cold indicates that they maintain high levels of blood flow to the extremities, resulting in warm hands and feet and a correspondingly greater heat loss than for whites. Third, the high peripheral temperatures of the extremities and high tolerance to cold of Eskimos and highland Quechuas appear to reflect the influence of developmental acclimatization. Among the Eskimos, but not among the Quechuas, these characteristics appear to be based on specific genetic contribution.

REFERENCES

1. Hammel, H. T. 1964. Terrestrial animals in cold: recent studies of primitive man. In D. B. Dill, E. F. Adolph, and C. G. Wilber, eds. Handbook of physiology. vol. 4. Adaptation to the environment. American Physiological Society, Washington, D.C.
2. McArthur, M. 1960. Food consumption and dietary levels of groups of aborigines living on naturally occurring foods. In C. P. Mountford, ed. Anthropology and nutrition. Cambridge University Press, N.Y.
3. Scholander, P. F., H. T. Hammel, J. S. Hart, D. H. LeMessurier, and J. Steen. 1958. Cold adaptation in Australian aborigines. J. Appl. Physiol. 13:211-218.
4. Hammel, H. T., R. W. Elsner, D. H. LeMessurier, H. T. Anderson, and F. A. Milan. 1959. Thermal and metabolic responses of the Australian aborigine exposed to moderate cold in summer. J. Appl. Physiol. 14:605-615.
5. Lee, R. B. 1969. !Kung bushman subsistence: an input-output analysis. In A. P. Vayda, ed. Environment and cultural behavior: ecological studies in cultural anthropology. Natural History Press, New York.
6. Wilmsen, E. 1978. Seasonal effects of dietary intake on Kalahari san. Fed. Proc. 37:65-72.
7. Hammel, H. T., J. S. Hildes, D. C. Jackson, and H. T. Anderson. 1962. Thermal and metabolic responses of the Kalahari Bushmen to moderate cold exposure at night. Tech. Rep. 62-44. Arctic Aeromedical Laboratory, Fort Wainwright, Alaska.
8. Ward. J. S., G. A. C. Bredell, and H. G. Wenzel. 1960. Responses of Bushmen and Europeans on exposure to winter night temperatures in the Kalahari. J. Appl. Physiol. 15:667-670.
9. Wyndham, C. H., and J. F. Morrison. 1958. Adjustment to cold of Bushmen in the Kalahari Desert. J. Appl. Physiol. 13:219-225.
10. Wyndham, C. H. 1964. Southern African ethnic adaptation to temperature and exercise. In P. T. Baker, and J. S. Weiner, eds. The biology of human adaptability. Clarendon Press, Oxford.
11. Elsner, R. W. 1963. Comparison of Australian Aborigines, Alacaluf Indians, and Andean Indians. Fed. Proc. 22:840-843.
12. Milan, F. A. 1962. Racial variations in human response to low temperature. In L. P. Hannon, and E. Viereck, eds. Comparative physiology of temperature regulation. Arctic Aeromedical Laboratory, Fort Wainwright, Alaska.
13. Andersen, K. L., Y. Loyning, J. D. Nelms, O. Wilson, R. H. Fox, and A. Bolstad. 1960. Metabolic and thermal response to a moderate cold exposure in nomadic Lapps. J. Appl. Physiol. 15:649-653.

14. Krog, J., B. Folkow, R. H. Fox, and K. L. Andersen. 1960. Hand circulation in the cold of Lapps and North Norwegian fishermen. J. Appl. Physiol. **15**:654-658.

15. Krog, J., M. Alvik, and K. Lund-Larsen. 1969. Investigations of the circulatory effects of submersion of the hand in the water in Finnish Lapps, the "Skolts." Fed. Proc. **28**:1135-1137.

16. Jenness, D. 1928. People of the twilight. Macmillan, Inc. N.Y.

17. Rodahl, K. 1952. Basal metabolism of the Eskimo. J. Nutr. **48**:359-368.

18. Murdock, G. P. 1964. Our primitive contemporaries. Macmillan, Inc., New York.

19. Nelson, R. K. 1966. Literature review of Eskimo knowledge of the sea ice environment. Tech. Rep. AAL-TR-65-7. Arctic Aeromedical Laboratory, Fort Wainwright, Alaska.

20. Scholander, P. F., V. Walters, R. Hock, and L. Irving. 1950. Body insulation of some arctic and tropical mammals and birds. Biol. Bull. **99**:225-236.

21. Forde, C. D. 1963. Habitat, economy and society. E. P. Dutton & Co., Inc., New York.

22. Perry, R. 1966. The world of the polar bear. University of Washington Press, Seattle.

23. Krough, A., and M. Krogh. 1913. A study of the diet and metabolism of Eskimos. Bianco Lund, Copenhagen.

24. Heinbecker, P. 1928. Studies on the metabolism of Eskimos. J. Biol. Chem. **80**:461-475.

25. Rabinowitch, I. M., and F. C. Smith. 1936. Metabolic studies of Eskimos in Canadian Eastern Arctic. J. Nutr. **12**:337-356.

26. Høygarrd, A. 1941. Studies on the nutrition and physiopathology of Eskimo. Skrifter 9. Norske Videnskaps Akademi, Oslo.

27. Brown, G. M., and J. Page. 1953. The effect of chronic exposure to cold on temperature and blood flow of the hand. J. Appl. Physiol. **5**:221-227.

28. Brown, G., J. Malcom, J. D. Hatcher, and J. Page. 1953. Temperature and blood flow in the forearm of the Eskimo. J. Appl. Physiol. **5**:410-420.

29. Brown, G. M., G. S. Bird, L. M. Boag, D. J. Delahaye, J. E. Green, J. D. Hatcher, and J. Page. 1954. Blood volume and basal metabolic rate of Eskimos. Metabolism **3**:247-254.

30. Adams, T., and B. G. Covino. 1958. Racial variations to a standardized cold stress. J. Appl. Physiol. **12**:9-12.

31. Rennie, D. W., and T. Adams. 1957. Comparative thermoregulatory responses of Negroes and white persons to acute cold stress. J. Appl. Physiol. **11**:201-204.

32. Rennie, D. W., B. G. Covino, M. R. Blair, and K. Rodahl. 1962. Physical regulation of temperature in Eskimos. J. Appl. Physiol. **17**:326-332.

33. Hart, J. S., H. B. Sabean, J. A. Hildes, F. Depocas, H. T. Hammel, K. L. Andersen, L. Irving, and G. Foy. 1962. Thermal and metabolic responses of coastal Eskimos during a cold night. J. Appl. Physiol. **17**:953-960.

34. Milan, F. W., and E. Evonuk. 1966. Oxygen consumption and body temperature of Eskimos during sleep. Tech. Rep. AAL-TR-66-10. Arctic Aeromedical Laboratory, Fort Wainwright, Alaska.

35. Rodahl, K., and B. Issekutz. 1965. Nutritonal requirements in the cold. Symposia on Arctic Biology and Medicine. Arctic Aeromedical Laboratory, Fort Wainwright, Alaska.

36. MacHattie, L., P. Haab, and D. W. Rennie. 1960. Eskimo metabolism as measured by the technique of 24-hour indirect calorimetry and graphic analysis. Tech. Rep. AAL-TR-60-43. Arctic Aeromedical Laboratory, Fort Wainwright, Alaska.

37. Milan, F. A., J. P. Hannon, and E. Evonuk. 1963. Temperature regulation of Eskimos, Indians and Caucasians in a bath calorimeter. J. Appl. Physiol. **18**:378-382.

38. Milan, F. A., R. W. Elsner, and K. Rodahl. 1961. Thermal and metabolic responses of men in the Antarctic to a standard cold stress. J. Appl. Physiol. **16**:401-404.

39. Meehan, J. P. 1955. Individual and racial variations in a vascular response to a cold stimulus. Milit. Med. **116**:330-334.

40. Page, J., and G. M. Brown. 1953. Effect of heating and cooling the legs on hand and forearm blood flow in the Eskimo. J. Appl. Physiol. **5**:753-758.

41. Eagan, C. J. 1963. Introduction and terminology: habituation and peripheral tissue adaptation. Fed. Proc. **22**:930-933.

42. Paul, J. R., J. T. Riordan, and L. M. Kraft. 1951. Serological epidemiology. Antibody patterns in North Alaskan Eskimos. Immunology **66**:695-713.

43. Luzzio, A. J. 1966. Comparison of serum proteins in Americans and Eskimos. J. Appl. Physiol. **21**:685-688.

44. Miller, L., and L. Irving. 1962. Local reactions to air cooling in an Eskimo population. J. Appl. Physiol. **17**:449-455.

45. LeBlanc, J. 1975. Man in the cold. Charles C Thomas, Publisher, Springfield, Ill.

46. Elsner, R. W., J. D. Nelms, and L. Irving. 1960. Circulation of heat to the hands of Arctic Indians. J. Appl. Physiol. **15**:662-666.

47. Irving, L., K. L. Andersen, A. Bolstad, R. W. Elsner, J. A. Hildes, Y. Loyning, J. D. Nelms, L. J. Peyton, and R. D. Whaley. 1960. Metabo-

lism and temperature of Arctic Indian men during a cold night. J. Appl. Physiol. **15:**635-644.

48. Steegman, A. T. 1977. Finger temperatures during work in natural cold: the Northern Ojibwa. Hum. Biol. **49:**349-374.

49. Baker, P. T., and M. A. Little, eds. 1976. Man in the Andes: a multidisciplinary study of high-altitude Quechua. Dowden, Hutchinson & Ross, Inc., Stroudsburg, Pa.

50. Hanna, J. M. 1976. Natural exposure to cold. In P. T. Baker, and M. A. Little, eds. Man in the Andes: a multidisciplinary study of high-altitude Quechua. Dowden, Hutchinson & Ross, Inc., Stroudsburg, Pa.

51. Mazess, R. B., and R. Larsen. 1972. Responses of Andean highlanders to night cold. Int. J. Biometeorol. **16:**181-192.

52. Baker, P. T. 1966. Micro-environment cold in a high altitude Peruvian population. In H. Yoshimura, and J. S. Weiner, eds. Human adaptability and its methodology. Japanese Society for the Promotion of Sciences, Tokyo.

53. Baker, P. T. 1966. Ecological and physiological adaptation in indigenous South Americans with spe-cial reference to the physical environment. In P. T. Baker, and J. S. Weiner, eds. The biology of human adaptability. Clarendon Press, Oxford.

54. Hanna, J. M. 1970. A comparison of laboratory and field studies of cold response. Am. J. Phys. Anthropol. **32:**227-232.

55. Little, M. A. 1976. Physiological responses to cold. In P. T. Baker, and M. A. Little, eds. Man in the Andes: a multidisciplinary study of high-altitude Quechua. Dowden, Hutchinson & Ross, Inc., Stroudsburg, Pa.

56. Little, M. A., and J. M. Hanna. 1978. The responses of high-altitude populations to cold and other stresses. In P. T. Baker, ed. The biology of high-altitude peoples. Cambridge University Press, N.Y.

57. Hurlich, M. G. 1978. Comparison of children's and adults' response to laboratory CIVD testing in a Cree Indian village. Am. J. Phys. Anthropol. (Abstract) **48:**407.

58. Blatteis, C. M., and L. O. Lutherer. 1976. Effect of altitude exposure on thermal regulatory response of man to cold. J. Appl. Physiol. **41:**848-858.

6 | Acclimatization and habituation to severe cold stress: Asiatic divers and whites

Asiatic divers
  Ama women from Korea
  Ainu from Hokkaido

Whites

Conclusion

The previous chapters show that humans when exposed to cold stress respond with a wide spectrum of physiological, cultural, and technological adaptations. In general, populations inhabiting regions of moderate cold stress, such as those of the desert, have developed physiological mechanisms oriented toward conserving body heat. On the other hand, populations living in the regions of severe cold stress, such as the Arctic and Andes, have developed efficient technological and cultural adaptations that ameliorate the cold stress to which they are exposed for short periods of time. Because of this dual response it is difficult to determine the extent to which cold stress can modify human thermoregulatory characteristics. To do so one needs to study individuals or populations who are periodically and voluntarily exposed to cold stress. For this reason, the purpose of this chapter is to discuss the thermoregulatory characteristics of Asiatic divers, who periodically are exposed to cold stress, and of European whites, who because of their economic activities or for investigative purposes were exposed to cold stress.

ASIATIC DIVERS
Ama women from Korea

Nearly 30,000 women from the Korean peninsula of Ama make their living by diving for plant and animal food. They are initiated into their profession by the age of 12 years and continue it for most of their lives. The diving water temperature falls to 10° C (46° F) in the winter and rises to 27° C (80.6° F) in the summer, yet the women continue to dive throughout the year.[1] They dive as deep

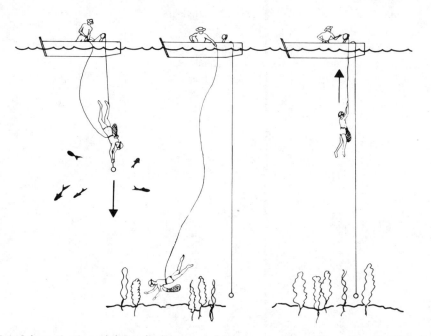

Fig. 6-1. Schematization of diving by Korean and Japanese women. (From Kita, H. 1965. Review of activities: harvest, seasons, and diving patterns. In H. Rahn and T. Yokoyama, eds. Physiology of breath-hold diving and the Ama of Japan. National Research Council Publication 1341, Washington, D.C.)

as 20 m while tied to a heavy ballast belt and holding on to another weight of up to 15 g (Fig. 6-1). After the dive is completed, the boatman quickly pulls the diver to the surface.[2] The women wear only lightweight cotton clothing and face masks for underwater vision. Depending on the temperature, they engage in diving for periods of 1 to 5 hours daily, rewarming themselves at open fires during the winter.[1-4] In the course of a dive, their oral temperatures routinely fall between 33° and 35° C (91.4° and 95° F). This degree of chronic, intermittent cold exposure is perhaps the most severe form of cold stress to which humans voluntarily submit.[1]

As shown in Fig. 6-2, the basal metabolic rate of the Ama women was greater in the winter,[1,5] whereas that of the nondiving controls continued at a constant level. Furthermore, the basal metabolic rate (BMR) of the Ama varied as an inverse function of the water temperature at diving; BMRs of 35% above normal were observed in the winter

when the water temperature fell to 10° C.[1] Daily urine samples indicated that excretion of nitrogen was the same in the Ama and in the control subjects. For this reason, the increased metabolic rate of the Ama must reflect the influence of the acclimatization response to cold and cannot be caused by differences in diet.[1,5]

Using as a criterion the diving water temperature at which 50% of the women shivered, it was found that among Ama women exposed to sequentially colder water baths, the shivering threshold occurred at 28.2° C (82.8° F), whereas for the controls it occurred at 29.9° C (87.8° F) (Fig. 6-3). In other words, among the Ama the shivering threshold is lower, allowing them to tolerate a reduced core temperature without shivering.[1,3,4] Although continuous exposure to cold enhances the mechanism of heat production, it also leads to a lower threshold at which heat production starts. The lowering of the threshold for initiation of shivering may be interpreted as habituation, another

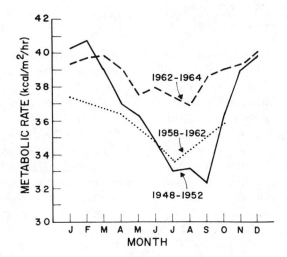

Fig. 6-2. Seasonal changes of basal metabolic rate of Ama women from Korea. For all years metabolic rate is higher in winter (December, January through March). (Modified from Sasaki, T. 1966. Fed. Proc. **25**:1163-1168.)

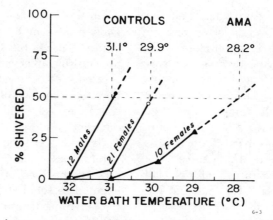

Fig. 6-3. Relationship between water temperature and shivering threshold among Korean Ama diving women and controls. The winter cold-acclimatized Ama women shiver at lower temperature than controls. (Modified from Hong, S. K. 1963. Fed. Proc. **22**:831-833.)

facet of acclimatization. The effects of acclimatization also are reflected in the elevated tissue insulation of Ama and other Asiatic divers.[3,4]

Ainu from Hokkaido

The Ainu men and women from Hokkaido Island of Japan, like the Ama women from Korea, make their living by diving into the cold waters for animal and plant food. The lipid metabolism of this population has been extensively studied.[6] Investigators found that in the cold-acclimatized Ainu a small dose of noradrenaline produced a greater elevation in metabolic rate and plasma levels of free fatty acids and ketone bodies than in the non-cold–acclimatized Japanese. Since more adrenaline elicits an increase in oxygen consumption by enhancing the oxidation of fatty acids, these findings suggest that as a result of cold acclimatization, the calorigenic effects of noradrenaline are increased and free fatty acids are oxidized faster in the Ainu than in nonacclimatized Japanese (Fig. 6-4).

In summary, continuous exposure to cold stress, as experienced by the Ainu and Ama divers, results in maintenance of high metabolic rates and higher tolerance to cold stress as indicated by shivering thresholds. As learned from studies of the Ainu, maintenance of high metabolic rates appears related to the fact that chronic exposure to cold stress leads to faster oxidation of free fatty acids.

WHITES

Studies on acclimatization and habituation of whites have been conducted among populations who live in cold areas in northern Canada, the antarctic region, and in the fishing areas of the Gaspe Peninsula of Canada and England.

Studies of the thermoregulatory responses of Canadian soldiers who were transferred from Winnipeg to northern Manitoba in November and remained there until the following spring have provided valuable information on habituation to cold.[7] Because of their duties, these soldiers spent from 8 to 10 hours a day outdoors, 6 days a week, throughout the winter. The average air temperature was −24° C (−20° F). These subjects were exposed for 1 hour at 9.5° C (49°

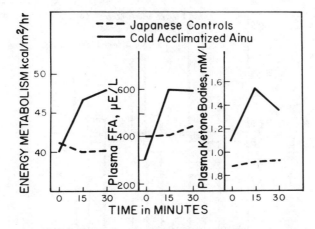

Fig. 6-4. Comparison of effects of noradrenaline on metabolism, plasma free-fatty acid concentration, and plasma ketone bodies among cold-acclimatized Ainu and control Japanese. Acclimatization to cold is associated with increased calorigenic effects of noradrenaline and faster mobilization of plasma free fatty acids and ketone bodies. (Modified from Itoh, S., and A. Kuroshima. 1972. Lipid metabolism is cold-adapted man. In S. Itoh, K. Ogata, and H. Yoshimura, eds. Advances in climatic physiology. Springer-Verlag New York, Inc., New York.)

F) immediately after their arrival in Manitoba and then again in January and March. Compared to the values measured in November and to basal levels, the metabolic rates showed a marked reduction throughout the winter while the skin temperatures remained constant (Fig. 6-5).

Similarly, on comparing the characteristics of eight subjects after 5 weeks' residence in Antarctica in the autumn and again in the winter and the spring, a reduction in metabolic rates was observed only in the winter, but the rectal and skin temperatures were not changed.[8] The most consistent change from autumn to spring was a continuous increase in body weight. On the other hand, when five men who resided for 12 months in Antarctica were compared to the controls (their metabolic rates were measured before the move to Antarctica), their response to cold (5° C) was characterized by lower metabolic rates and lower rectal temperatures. At a given skin temperature the increase in metabolic rate was lower after 6 months

in Antarctica. The skin temperatures, except for the toes which were higher, were also lowered. The subjective reactions indicated that with continued residence in the cold, most of the subjects found they were comfortable with ever decreasing amounts of heavy arctic clothing.

From these studies it can be inferred that prolonged residence of European whites in cold climates is associated with a reduction in metabolic rate and a lowering of skin temperature, which exemplify habituation to cold. On the other hand, fishermen accustomed to fishing in cold water (approximately 9.4° C) maintained higher hand temperatures when the hands were immersed in cold water (2.5° C) for 10 minutes and higher blood flow than did white controls. Thus the fishermen's response is an example of local acclimatization to cold and not of habituation in that they were able to tolerate cold through a physiological process. In fact, the fishermen, when exposed naked to 15° C air, shivered more than the controls.[9,10]

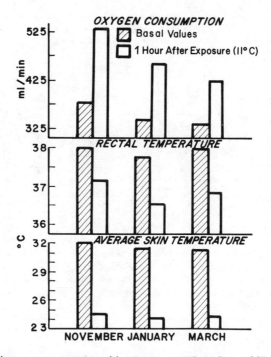

Fig. 6-5. Thermoregulatory responses to cold stress among Canadian soldiers who lived outdoors all winter (January, February, and March). Habituation to cold resulted in reduced oxygen consumption (metabolic rate) and rectal temperature but no change in skin temperature. (Modified from LeBlanc, J. 1975. Man in the cold. Charles C Thomas, Publisher, Springfield, Ill.)

CONCLUSION

Studies of Korean and Japanese divers provide conclusive evidence that chronic exposure to cold stress increases the metabolic rate. These findings are in marked contrast to those of European whites living in cold climates, which indicate a lowering of metabolic rates and concomitant decreases in rectal and skin temperatures. The cause of these differences can be explained by the severity of cold stress experienced by each population. The divers are exposed to severe cold stress for prolonged periods throughout the year and for most of their lives. In contrast, the whites, although they have lived for prolonged periods in cold climates, because of their use of clothing do not have comparable severity and length of exposure

to cold. In fact, whites who exposed themselves to cold in the Norwegian mountains as much as possible did show increased metabolic rates.[20] For this reason, it can be concluded that when sufficiently exposed to cold, all humans adapt to cold through increased metabolic rates and with an attendant increase in peripheral temperature. The high metabolic rates observed among Eskimos, the Ama women from Korea, and divers from Hokkaido, and to a lesser extent among Peruvian Quechuas and Alacaluf Indians may be viewed as examples of acclimatization to cold stress. In the same manner, maintenance of high finger temperatures and decreased pain sensation exhibited by the Gaspe and British Isles fishermen reflect their acclimatization to the chronic cold stress to which their daily activities exposed them.

On the other hand, studies of European whites suggest that when exposed to relatively moderate cold stress, the organism can adapt without metabolic compensation. This kind of adaptation is attained through continuous exposure leading to habituation, whereby the organism becomes accustomed to sustaining some degree of hypothermia. As indicated by LeBlanc,[7] if life is not endangered, the responses of the body seem oriented to retaining individual identity and preserving homeostasis, avoiding unnecessary challenges, etc. In a sense one can say that the thermostat is lowered to a more economical level. The fact that adaptation to moderate cold stress is attained through habituation suggests involvement of the central nervous system.[7,8] Along with reduced cold sensation, habituation to cold brings

a reduced activation of the sympathetic nervous system as shown by decreased changes in blood pressure with exposure to cold. The fact that northern Japanese have a higher finger vasodilation and earlier onset of cold-induced vasodilation than those of southern origin[11-13] may be explained on the basis of local acclimatization to cold stress rather than habituation. There is conclusive evidence that blacks have lower finger temperatures when exposed to ice water than whites and that in Korea and Alaska cold injury to the hands occurs with greater frequency.[14-17] Based on the similarities between South African blacks and whites[18] and thermoregulatory responses to whole-body exposure to cold between United States' blacks and whites,[19] it would not be surprising if the observed differences in responses to hand cooling and cold injury were proved to reflect different degrees of acclimatization.

REFERENCES

1. Hong, S. K. 1963. Comparison of diving and non-diving women of Korea. Fed. Proc. **22**:831-833.
2. Kita, H. 1965. Review of activities: harvest, seasons, and diving patterns. In H. Rahn, and T. Yokoyama, eds. Physiology of breath-hold diving and the Ama of Japan. National Research Council Publication 1341, Washington, D.C.
3. Rennie, D. W., B. G. Covino, B. J. Howell, S. H. Song, B. S. Kang, and S. K. Hong. 1962. Physical insulation of Korean diving women. J. Appl. Physiol. **17**:961-966.
4. Rennie, D. W. 1965. Thermal insulation of Korean diving women and nondivers in water. In H. Rahn, and T. Yokoyama, eds. Physiology of breath-hold diving and the Ama of Japan. National Research Council Publication 1341, Washington, D.C.
5. Sasaki, T. 1966. Relation of basal metabolism to changes in food composition and body composition. Fed. Proc. **25**:1163-1168.
6. Itoh, S., and A. Kuroshima. 1972. Lipid metabolism of cold-adapted man. In S. Itoh, K. Ogata, and H. Yoshimura, eds. Advances in climatic physiology. Springer-Verlag New York, Inc., Heidelberg, N.Y.
7. LeBlanc, J. 1975. Man in the cold. Charles C Thomas, Publisher, Springfield, Ill.

8. Wyndham, C. H., R. Plotkin, and A. Munro. 1964. Physiological reactions to cold of men in the Antarctic. J. Appl. Physiol. **19**:593-597.
9. LeBlanc, J., J. A. Hildes, and O. Heroux. 1960. Tolerance of Gaspe fishermen to cold water. J. Appl. Physiol. **15**:1031-1034.
10. LeBlanc, J. 1962. Local adaptation to cold of Gaspe fishermen. J. Appl. Physiol. **17**:950-952.
11. Kondo, S. 1969. A study on the acclimatization of the Ainu and the Japanese with reference to hunting temperature reaction. J. Faculty Science, Tokyo University, Sect. V, 3-4:253-265.
12. Yoshimura, H., and T. Iida. 1952. Studies on the reactivity of skin vessels to extreme cold. Part 2. Factors governing the individual difference of the reactivity or the resistance against frostbite. Jpn. J. Physiol. **2**:177-185.
13. Yoshimura, H., and T. Iida. 1950. Studies in the reactivity of skin vessels to extreme cold. Part I. A point test on the resistance to frostbite. Jpn. J. Physiol. **1**:147-159.
14. Schuman, L. M. 1953. Epidemiology of frostbite, Korea, 1951-1952. Pages 205-568 in Cold injury-Korea, 1951-1952. Rep. 113. (U.S. Army Medical Research Laboratory, Ft. Knox, Ky.)
15. Meehan, J. P. 1955. Individual and racial variations

in a vascular response to a cold stimulus. Milit. Med. **116**:330-334.

16. Iampietro, P. F., R. F. Goldman, E. R. Buskirk, and D. E. Bass. 1959. Response of Negro and white males to cold. J. Appl. Physiol. **14**:798-800.

17. Rennie, D. W., and T. Adams. 1957. Comparative thermoregulatory responses of Negro and white persons to acute cold stress. J. Appl. Physiol. **11**: 201-204.

18. Wyndham, C. H. 1964. Southern African ethnic adaptation to temperature and exercise. In P. T. Baker, and J. S. Weiner, eds. The biology of human adaptability. Clarendon Press, Oxford.

19. Newman, R. W. 1969. Cold acclimation in Negro Americans. J. Appl. Physiol. **37**:316-319.

20. Scholander, P. F., H. T. Hammel, K. L. Andersen, and Y. Loyning. 1958. Metabolic acclimation to cold in man. J. Appl. Physiol. **12**:1-8.

7

Biological responses, acclimatization to solar radiation, and evolution of population skin color differences

NATURE OF SOLAR ENERGY

Every second inside the sun thermonuclear reactions convert approximately 564 million tons of hydrogen into 560 million tons of helium. During this process, large quantities of matter are destroyed and released from the sun's surface in the form of radiant energy. This radiant energy spreads in every direction at the speed of light and arrives at the outer limits of the earth's atmosphere at an intensity of 135.30 mW/cm^2 or slightly less than 2 gcal $\times$ min^{-1}. This value is called the *solar constant*. In ascending order the solar spectrum includes (1) short-wave, high-energy x rays, (2) ultraviolet rays, (3) visible light range, (4) infrared rays, and (5) long-wave, low-energy radiowaves. In general, about one half of the energy from the sun that reaches the earth's surface is in the form of infrared radiation, and the remaining half consists mostly of visible and ultraviolet light. The other forms of radiation such as x rays are screened out by the atmosphere.[1]

In the process of passing through the atmosphere, ultraviolet, visible, and infrared radiation are absorbed, scattered without loss of energy, and reflected in every direction, depending on the specific wavelength involved and the degree of atmospheric turbidity and cloudiness. In general the rate of scattering is inversely proportional to the wavelength; the shorter the wavelength, the greater the amount of scattering.[1,2]

Wavelengths shorter than 290 nm are shielded from reaching the earth by the formation of ozone (O_3). With chlorophyll in plants, the atmospheric oxygen is continually replaced by photosynthesis and converted to ozone by radiation of wavelengths shorter than 240 nm. Ozone absorbs ultraviolet radiation from about 200 to 320 nm and blocks radiation below 290 nm. In this manner, the ozone layer protects the biosphere from biocidal radiations shorter than 290 nm.

In terms of human adaptation to solar radiation, the narrow wavelength band between 290 and 310 nm is the most crucial, since it produces vitamin D and is responsible for killing microorganisms in the atmosphere. The functional influences of solar radiation on humans are several, both direct and indirect. Among these the most important include (1) the provision of light and heat, (2) synthesis of biochemical components such as vitamin D, and (3) influence of hormonal and neuronal changes of pigmentation. In general, these influences take place through the skin and its components.

SKIN STRUCTURE AND COLOR
Skin structure

Human skin consists of the dermis and epidermis, which are connected by a basement membrane and an intricate system of cells and blood vessels that enable the skin to function as one of the important factors in human thermoregulation and as protection against the deleterious effects of solar radiation. As shown in Fig. 7-1 the epidermis' outer surface has a stratum corneum (horny layer). This layer is extremely tough, chemically resistant, and almost impenetrable; its average thickness is about 15 μm. It consists of many flat cells that have lost most of their cytoplasm and nuclei but contain many filaments of keratin in a matrix formation. These cells are held together by an extremely strong cement substance of unknown composition. The thickness of the stratum corneum layer is remarkably consistent. This layer is produced by a cell line called *keratinocytes*, which because of their appearance are known as the *prickle cells*. These prickle cells migrate outward during cell duplication and division. As they approach the stratum corneum, or horny layer, they ac-

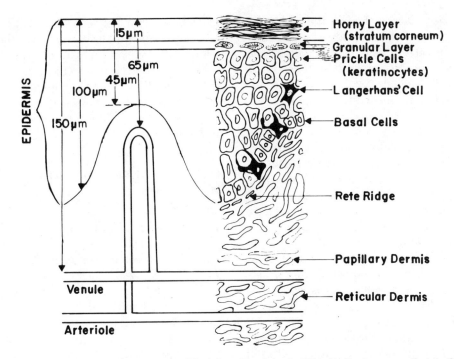

Fig. 7-1. Diagram of human skin. (Modified from Daniels, F. 1974. Radiant energy. Part A. Solar radiation. In N. B. Slonim, ed. Environmental physiology. The C. V. Mosby Co., Saint Louis.)

cumulate granules, becoming the granular layer located directly below the stratum corneum.

Below the prickle cells are located the basal cells and the Langerhans' cells; interspersed among these are the melanocytes, or melanoblasts. The melanocytes synthesize the pigment melanin in a process that begins with oxidation of the amino acid tyrosine, which is then acted on by the enzyme tyrosinase. Melanin is deposited along with protein in specific subcellular organelles called *melanosomes*. These melanosomes are then transferred to keratinocytes of the skin and hair through the dendritic processes.[3] It has been estimated that each melanocyte "services" about thirty-six keratinocytes. In other words, there is func-

tional as well as structural integration of a melanocyte with its associated keratinocytes.

Skin color and its measurement

The mature melanosome or melanin granule is dispersed into smaller melanin particles as the cells move outward. These cells range in color from brown to black. The melanin granules are about 1 μm in size and scatter themselves to form a cap over the nucleus of the keratinocyte, thus protecting the nuclear deoxyribonucleic acid (DNA) of the epithelium. As shown in recent studies, individual and population differences in skin color appear related to differences in both the amount of melanin synthesis and in the number of melanocytes.[2,4-6] Among blacks or dark-skinned populations, such as the Australian aborigines and Solomon Island natives, melanocyte cells are greater and melanin granules are larger and more dispersed than those found in whites or orientals.[2,4-6]

In addition to melanin, oxyhemoglobin, reduced hemoglobin, and carotene contribute to skin color. The most useful method of measuring these influences is by measurement of skin reflectance with either a photoelectric reflectometer or a reflectance spectrophotometer. Both these instruments work on the same principle of reflectance and have similar parts. Therefore, with appropriate statistical adjustments, their values are comparable.[7] The main unit includes a galvanometer, a constant voltage transformer, and controls; the search unit consists of a lamp and a photocell. Light from the lamp passes through exchangeable glass filters of known wavelength to the surface being measured. The light that is diffusely reflected from this surface acts on the photocell. Thus the amount of light reflected from a skin surface, as compared with reflectance by standard white magnesium surface (giving 100% reflectance), is measured by the photocell and recorded on the galvanometer.[7-12]

The first important characteristic of spectral reflectance of the human skin is that reflectance is directly proportional to wavelength; the lower the reflectance, the shorter the wavelength. Melanin has no specific absorption bands but general areas of absorption ranging from infrared to ultraviolet. According to Daniels[2] and as confirmed by recent studies, reflectometry picks up the absorption bands of oxyhemoglobin at 542 and 526 μm. Reduced hemoglobin has an absorption maximum of about 556 μm, hemoglobin has an absorption of about 420 μm, and carotene has an absorption of 482 μm. Further investigations have shown that readings at shorter wavelengths, such as that given by the red filter (620 to 685 μm) or an interference filter with a transmittance maximum between 620 and 720 μm, are most suitable for measuring the contribution of melanin to skin color. Although it is also subject to the effects of melanin, the absorption from oxyhemoglobin can be sampled with either a green transmittance filter or an interference filter in the maximum transmittance range of 542 to 566 μm.[7-12]

INFLUENCE OF RADIATION ON HUMAN SKIN
Sunburn

When solar radiation is intense, 290 to 320 nm, and the skin is not tanned, an individual develops sunburn. The general sequence of events includes a latent period of several hours, followed by blood vessel dilation manifested in erythema, which reaches its maximum between 8 and 24 hours after exposure. As a result of sunburn, there is general discomfort, a reduction in the pain threshold, and severe blistering. From sunburn the skin may also develop secondary infection or a suppression of sweating. Susceptible individuals, such as those with low melanization, may develop desquamation and peeling of the sunburned area with continued exposure; this in turn reduces the possibility of maintaining adequate melanization. Therefore, repeated sunburn may lead to degenerative changes in both the dermis and epidermis, and skin cancer is one of the possible consequences.[2]

Melanization

On exposure to ultraviolet radiation the skin becomes melanized or tanned by two distinct processes: (1) immediate tanning and (2) delayed tanning.[13] *Immediate tanning* is produced by both ultraviolet (320 to 380 nm) and visible light (400 to 700 nm). Within 5 to 10 minutes after exposure to midday summer sun the skin becomes hyperpigmented. When withdrawn from exposure to light for about 4 hours, the tanned area fades almost to nonexposure levels. The rate of depigmentation appears related to length of exposure to ultraviolet light; after prolonged exposure (90 to 120 minutes) residual hyperpigmentation may be visible for as long as 24 to 36 hours. The rapid rate of immediate tanning is brought about by (1) rapid darkening of preformed melanin, (2) rapid transfer of preformed melanosomes (melanin) from the basal location to the upper malpighian layer and stratum corneum, and (3) rapid distribution of melanosomes in melanocytes. The rapid darkening of preformed melanin occurs either because of photo-oxidation of melanosomes or because of the enzyme-mediated oxidation of melanin.

Delayed tanning is optimally stimulated by exposure to short ultraviolet radiation between 290 and 320 nm and to a lesser extent by exposure to longwave ultraviolet radiation and visible radiation. Because delayed tanning involves production of new melanosomes, it appears slowly over a period of 48 to 72 hours. Current theories[13] postulate that delayed melanization occurs from (1) an increased number of functional melanocytes resulting from a proliferation of melanocytes and possible activation of dormant or resting melanocytes, (2) hypertrophy of melanocytes and increased ramification of their dendrites, (3) increased melanosomal synthesis, (4) increased rate of melanization in melanosomes, (5) transfer of melanosomes from melanocytes to keratinocytes because of increased turnover in keratinocytes, and (6) activation of tyrosinase because of the direct effect of radiation on the tyrosinase-inhibiting sulfhydril compounds present in the epidermis.[14]

Fig. 7-2 illustrates the development of skin tanning in relation to length of exposure to summer sunlight in Idaho. These data show that with constant 40-minute exposures a rapid melanization (darkening) of the skin occurs, which is stabilized by the end of the second week (broken lines). However,

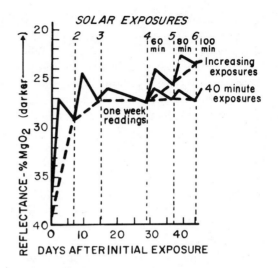

Fig. 7-2. Development of tanning in relation to length of exposure to summer light. After weeks of exposure, amount of melanization increases in proportion to length of time of daily exposure to solar radiation. (Modified from Daniels, F. 1974. Radiant energy. Part A. Solar radiation. In N. B. Slonim, ed. Environmental physiology. The C. V. Mosby Co., Saint Louis.)

these data also show that the greater the length of daily exposure to sunlight (straight lines), the greater the degree of melanization. In other words, the amount of melanization is proportional to amount of daily exposure to solar radiation.

Vitamin D synthesis

The same wavelengths of solar radiation that may cause sunburn, cataracts, and skin cancer, 290 to 320 nm, also assist in the synthesis of vitamin D. For humans there are two sources of vitamin D: cholecalciferol (vitamin D_3) and chemically related ergocalciferol (vitamin D_2). Ergocalciferol is the synthetic form of vitamin D made by irradiation of ergosterol from plants and fungi, whereas the natural form, cholecalciferol, is found in small amounts in most seafoods. As shown in Table 4, the dietary sources of vitamin D are limited to seafood and, to a lesser extent, dairy foods. To meet childhood requirements for vitamin D of 5 to 10 mg daily, one would have to consume between 11 and 23 g of swordfish, sardines, or mackerel or 100 g of herring. For littoral people these dietary sources might be easily accessible, but for the majority of populations they are not. Most people derive vitamin D directly from solar radiation.

Biochemical and photochemical studies have demonstrated that sunlight falling on human skin causes the photolytic conversion of 7-dehydrocholesterol into cholecalciferol (vitamin D_3) in the epidermis and dermis.[15,16] According to these investigations, if all the available 7-dehydrocholesterol in 8 cm² of human skin were converted to vitamin D, this would provide the daily requirement for vitamin D. It is evident, then, that the limiting factor in cutaneous vitamin D production is the amount of absorbed solar radiation.

As previously indicated, the intensity of solar radiation reaching the earth depends on the latitude, season, and time of day of exposure. Thus the closer one is to the equator and the higher the altitude, the greater the intensity. As shown in Fig. 7-3, despite the availability and consumption of vitamin D–fortified dairy products in Michigan, variations in plasma vitamin D levels paralleled variations in solar radiation between summer and winter. In contrast, in Puerto Rico where there are minimal seasonal differences in solar intensity, there are no seasonal variations in vitamin D levels.[17] In the same manner, in London variations in blood 25-OH vitamin D are associated with seasonal differences in solar intensity.[18,19] Reflecting these seasonal differences in vitamin D synthesis is the fact that in Swedish adults intestinal calcium absorption is more efficient

Table 4. Dietary sources of vitamin D*

Food	Vitamin D per portion
Swordfish	45 µg/100 g
Sardines, canned	29-39 µg/100 g
Salmon, raw	4-14 µg/100 g
Salmon, canned	6-12 µg/100 g
Mackerel, raw	28 µg/100 g
Herring, raw	8 µg/100 g
Herring, canned	8 µg/100 g
Halibut	1 µg/100 g
Shrimp	4 µg/100 g
Oysters	0.1 µg/3-4 medium-sized
Liver	
Beef	0.2 µg/100 g
Calf	0.0-0.3 µg/100 g
Chicken	1.2-1.7 µg/100 g
Eggs	0.6 µg/average yolk
Cow's milk	<0.2 µg/8 oz
Cream	0.4 µg/1 oz coffee cream
Butter	0.1 µg/2 pats
Cheese	0.3-.04 µg/100 g

*From Neer, R. M. 1975. The evolutionary significance of vitamin D, skin pigmentation, and ultraviolet light. Am. J. Phys. Anthropol. **43:**409-416.

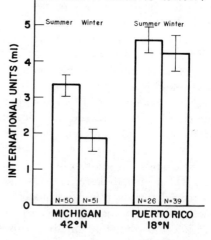

Fig. 7-3. Comparison of seasonal variation in plasma antirachitic activity between Michigan and Puerto Rico. In Michigan with low solar radiation in winter there are significant differences in plasma antirachitic activity; in Puerto Rico with uniform solar radiation throughout the year there are no seasonal variations in plasma antirachitic activity. (Modified from Smith, R. W., J. Rizek, and B. Frame. 1964. Am. J. Clin. Nutr. **14:**98-108.)

in the summer, declining progressively during the winter.[20] Another example illustrating the seasonal differences in vitamin D synthesis and its influence on calcium metabolism before the generalized use of vitamin D–fortified milk was the greater incidence of childhood rickets in the northern United States in the winter than in the summer.[21] The incidence of rickets in New Haven, Connecticut, at a latitude of 1 N, was greater than in Puerto Rico at a latitude of 18 N. Similarly, in Scotland the incidence of infantile hypocalcemia and defective teeth is much higher among children who developed in utero during the winter.[22,23]

As illustrated in Fig. 7-4, vitamin D synthesized in the skin or absorbed from the diet enters the liver where it is hydrolyzed. This process produces 25-hydroxycalciferol (25-HCC). From the liver 25-HCC is transported to the kidney where the compound undergoes further hydroxylation. In the kid-

ney the 25-HCC is converted to 1,25 dihydroxycalciferol (1,25 DHCC) under hypocalcemic conditions, or under normal conditions it is converted to 24,25 dihydroxycholecalciferol.[2,15,24] Thereafter, vitamin D, in either form, enters the circulation and is subsequently bound to the nuclei of intestinal epithelial cells. It is assumed that in these cells vitamin D acts as a messenger, instructing the DNA to transcribe information to RNA, which in turn transcribes a message to form the enzyme needed for calcium (Ca^{++}) transport from gut lumen into the circulation. In this manner, vitamin D presumably regulates calcium absorption through biochemical events, enabling the formation and maintenance of an internal calcified skeleton.

Although the direct mechanisms whereby vitamin D influences bone mineralization are not well known, there are several functions attributable to vitamin D that have a

METABOLISM (ACTIVATION) OF VITAMIN D

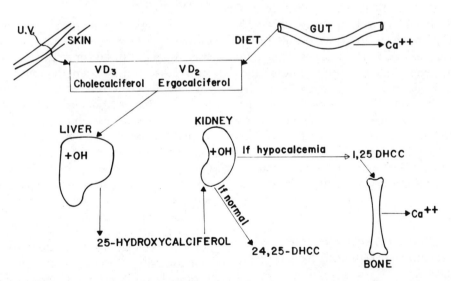

Fig. 7-4. Diagram of vitamin D synthesis. Through the action of ultraviolet radiation vitamin D is synthesized in skin or absorbed from diet, after which it is hydrolized in liver, transported to kidney, and from there enters the circulation to be used during calcium metabolism. (Modified from Neer, R. M. 1975. Am. J. Phys. Anthropol. **43**:409-416.)

direct effect on proper bone mineralization. First, it is well known that vitamin D stimulates intestinal calcium and phosphorus absorption. Second, vitamin D stimulates the mobilization of calcium and phosphate from the bone through resorption. By contributing calcium and phosphate to the blood pool, vitamin D helps maintain a plasma concentration of these minerals sufficient for proper bone calcification. Hormonal factors also interact with vitamin D in bone resorption as well as in mineralization. The influence of the parathyroid hormone in mobilizing calcium is decreased when there is a vitamin D deficiency.[16] Third, it has been suggested that vitamin D stimulates renal tubular transport of calcium and phosphorus.[16,25]

It is now evident that the observed abnormalities in calcium metabolism are directly related to the availability of vitamin D, which in turn depends on the availability of solar radiation. Clinical studies clearly indicate that childhood rickets is readily cured with 0.05 to 0.1 mg (2000 to 4000 I.U.) of vitamin D daily for 6 to 12 weeks, prolonged exposure to winter sunlight, or 5 minutes exposure to artificial ultraviolet radiation equivalent to strong summer sunlight at 36° latitude.[26] However, bone disorders associated with a vitamin D deficiency may occur in humans even though dietary intake of vitamin D and its precursors is normal, and there has been sufficient exposure to sunlight or ultraviolet radiation. Such bone disorders are usually related to metabolic factors that inhibit activation of vitamin D.[21,26]

EVOLUTIONARY SIGNIFICANCE OF POPULATIONAL DIFFERENCES IN SKIN COLOR

In general, populational differences in skin color are associated with two climatic and environmental factors. First, on each continent skin color is inversely related to latitude and temperature; the closer the population to the equator and the higher the temperature, the darker the skin color (Fig. 7-5). Second, the intensity of solar radiation is directly related to latitude and altitude; the closer the location to the equator and the higher the altitude, the greater the radiation intensity. Along with these climatic associations, skin color differences are also related to differences in incidence of skin cancer and malignant melanoma; the lighter the skin and the lower the latitude, the higher the incidence of skin cancer and malignant melanoma. With a view to the long-term consequences of these associations, biologists have postulated different theories to explain populational differences in skin color. Among these the most important are those concerned with skin cancer and melanoma incidence, vitamin D synthesis, and thermoregulation.

Skin cancer and malignant melanoma: adaptive significance of dark skin

According to United States mortality data, the death rate from skin cancer in whites is approximately three times greater than that for blacks. It has been demonstrated that this difference is related to the amount of melanin pigmentation by the fact that frequency of skin cancer is greater among albino Bantus than among nonalbino Bantus.[28] Furthermore, among whites the incidence of skin cancer is higher in the southern than in the northern United States.[28,29] Similarly, red-haired, blue-eyed, freckled individuals have a greater probability of developing carcinoma of the skin if engaged in outdoor occupations than do dark-skinned individuals.[30]

In early studies the influence of solar radiation on malignant melanoma was not well-defined. However, the importance of solar radiation as an etiological factor in the incidence of malignant melanoma in white

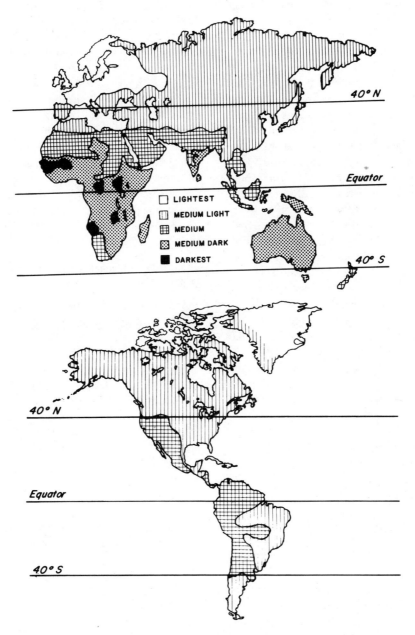

Fig. 7-5. Distribution of human skin color according to latitude. (Modified from C. L. Brace, and A. Montague. 1965. Man's evolution. The Macmillan Co., New York.)

populations has since been recognized.[32] Furthermore, like skin cancer, the incidence of malignant melanoma is greater among those with outdoor occupations and lighter pigmentation than with darker skin color.[32] These investigations clearly demonstrate the association of skin cancer and malignant melanoma with solar radiation and degree of pigmentation. It has been suggested that these differences result from genetic differences that evolved through the influence of natural selection. Others have questioned the evolutionary significance of skin cancer differences in view of the fact that mortality from skin cancer usually occurs after completion of the reproductive period. However, recent literature indicates that mortality from skin cancer and malignant melanoma together, although occurring at lower frequencies, does occur prior to completion of the reproductive period.

As shown in epidemiological data, in Australian whites living in a region of high solar radiation, approximately 669 deaths per 100,000 between the ages of 10 and 49 years were recorded to be caused by malignant melanoma, and about 8 deaths per 100,000 in the same age range were caused by other skin cancers.[31-33] In the United States and Australia the survival rate for individuals suffering from melanoma under the age of 50 years is approximately 50% because of improved medical care and is approximately 90% for skin cancer.[31-33] One would expect that among populations without access to adequate medical care, such as those of early man, the actual mortality rate from melanoma would equal about 1003 deaths per 100,000 and about 14.8 deaths per 100,000 for other skin cancers. The total combined mortality for these two diseases without modern medical care would equal 1017.8 per 100,000, or approximately 1/10,000. In view of the lower incidence of malignant melanoma and skin cancer

in dark-skinned populations, the selection against light skin color would equal about 0.0001, based on a mortality of 1:10,000. Given the nearly 3 million years of human evolution, it is conceivable that this level of selection could have had a strong influence on the evolution of dark skin color. Through computer simulation, it has been estimated that with optimizing selection and a 6% maximum difference in fitness, the evolution of the range of human skin color differences would have taken about 800 generations with no dominance and about 1500 generations with 80% dominance.[34] This would suggest that changes in skin color could have taken place within a range of 24,000 to 45,000 years.

Vitamin D synthesis: adaptive significance of light skin

As previously discussed, solar radiation is the most important source of vitamin D for humans. Its deficiency and the absence of artificial dietary supplement cause rickets in children, which by reducing the size of the female pelvic structure may even impair reproductive success in adulthood. Excessive vitamin D intake may result in hypervitaminosis D. In some individuals as little as 500,000 IU (1.25 mg) per day can be toxic, and an excess of 100,000 IU (2.5 mg) daily usually results in hypercalcemia.[25] Chronic hypercalcemia causes calcification of soft tissues such as the skin, heart, pancreas, stomach, lungs, thyroid, and especially the kidneys. In young children or adults in which the disease has advanced to renal fibrosis and hypertension the prognosis for chronic hypervitaminosis is grave and often fatal.[21]

According to spectrophotographic studies the rate at which ultraviolet radiation penetrates the epidermis is inversely related to the amount of melanin[35]; the darker the skin, the lower the absorption rate and, consequently, the lower the vitamin D synthesis.[21] Accordingly, various investigators have postulated that white skin evolved in order to maintain sufficient vitamin D synthesis in populations exposed to very little sunlight and that variations in human skin pigmentation among the world's populations arose from, and are maintained by, the necessity for regulating the synthesis of vitamin D within certain physiological limits.[21,36] Thus, the north-south distribution of human skin color is related to the amount and intensity of solar radiation.

A basic premise of this hypothesis is that the amount of melanin present in any particular population serves as a regulatory mechanism by which depigmentation facilitates synthesis of vitamin D and increased melanization prevents hypervitaminosis D. Therefore, in the northern latitudes there is selection for white skin that allows maximum photoactivation of 7-dehydrocholesterol into vitamin D at low-intensity ultraviolet radiation. On the other hand, in southern latitudes there is selection for dark skin, which prevents up to 95% absorption of the incident ultraviolet radiation from reaching the deeper layers of the skin where vitamin D synthesis takes place.

This hypothesis is supported by two major discoveries. First, blacks are more susceptible to rickets than whites in northern latitudes.[21] It is known that childhood rickets may result in reduced pelvic size (Fig. 7-6) and therefore can eventually affect reproduction. Before the widespread use of dietary vitamin D supplements that started in the 1930s, the incidence of deformed pelvis among black women studied in the 1950s was significantly greater (15%) than that of white women (2%)[37] (Fig. 7-6). The size reduction in the pelvic inlet and the absence of cesarean operations in any population would impair reproductive efficiency. Second, the human skin has a high capacity for synthesizing vitamin D. According to

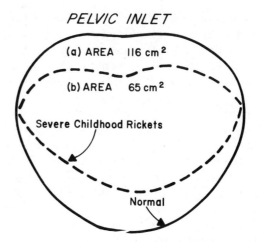

Fig. 7-6. Outline of normal pelvis and pelvis deformed by childhood rickets. Deformed pelvis impairs reproductive efficiency. (Modified from Eastman, N. J. 1956. Obstetrics, 11th ed. Appleton-Century-Crofts, New York.)

Beckemeir,[21] 1 cm² of human white skin synthesizes over a 3-hour exposure period to solar radiation up to 18 IU of vitamin D. Therefore Loomis[21] estimates that an individual exposing 1.5 m² surface area of skin for 6 hours at the equator would produce in excess of 800,000 IU of vitamin D without sufficient melanin in the stratum corneum to filter the intense solar radiation, an amount well within toxic quantities.

Thermoregulation: adaptive significance of dark- and light-colored skin

Two main hypotheses have been postulated to explain the origins of populational differences in skin color in terms of thermoregulation. The first hypothesis postulates that brunette and other intermediate-colored skins would be most adaptive under hot-dry conditions.[38] This hypothesis is based on two facts. (1) Dark skin, when exposed to solar radiation, absorbs more energy (heat); therefore it increases the gradient between skin and ambient temperature, enhancing the rate of heat radiation to portions of the environment cooler than the skin temperature and receiving less heat from the environment above that of skin temperature. On the other hand, very light skin does not easily tan and, when it is exposed to solar radiation, sunburn can result, and prolonged exposure might lead to skin cancer. (2) The distribution of skin color among world populations indicates that those persons inhabiting savanna and desert regions such as the Bushmen, Arabs, Hottentots, and Australian aborigines, do exhibit an intermediate skin color. The second hypothesis postulates that cold injury or frostbite may be an important factor in the evolution of white skin.[39] This hypothesis is based on evidence that during the two world wars, as well as the Korean War, the incidence of frostbite was greater among black soldiers than among whites. Furthermore, studies on tissue tolerance to severe cold indicate that pigmented skins of guinea pigs exposed to freezing temperatures suffered greater tissue damage than nonpigmented skins of the same species.[39] The proponents of adaptive significance of white skin postulate that as humans moved away from the equator toward the colder temperatures of the northern regions, and in the absence of well-developed technologies, white skin was favored by natural selection.

Infectious disease: dark skin as a by-product of adaptation to tropical disease

All the previous hypotheses have considered the pigmentary system as directly involved in responding to solar radiation. The disease hypothesis maintains that pigmentation is an indirect consequence of human adaptation to tropical disease.[40] This hypothesis is based on the following facts: (1) the organism's principal line of defense against disease is the reticuloendothelial system (RES), which covers the phagocytic action and production of gamma globulin antibodies; (2) there is an inverse relationship between the activity of RES and adrenocortical activity—the lower the adrenocortical activity, the higher the RES activity; and (3) a deficiency in the enzyme 11B-hydroxylase leads to cortical deficiency. The crux of this hypothesis is that the pituitary gland, in order to reactivate adrenal function, increases production of the adrenocorticotropic hormone (ACTH); parallel with ACTH production, it also secretes the melanocyte-stimulating hormone (MSH). Therefore this hypothesis delegates pigmentation to a secondary phenomenon resulting from an adaptation to tropical disease. Furthermore, it maintains that a single enzyme deficiency in the adrenal cortex may be the primary basis for human variations in skin color. In support of this hypothesis, Wasserman[40] indicates that pigmented populations such as American blacks, Indians, and Malayans, as shown by anatomical and physiological studies, do have decreased adrenocortical activity. Although these characteristics are accurate, a major flaw in this hypothesis is the assumption that infectious diseases were major selective factors during human evolution. Current anthropological and epidemiological data indicate that infectious disease became prevalent and had significant selective force only after the introduction of agriculture and the consequent increase in population size, which in evolutionary perspective occurred in too short a time to account for skin color variations.

CONCLUSION

Solar radiation is the major source of energy for the terrestrial biosphere. It affects all levels of life from a single photon acting on one electron in a molecule through all levels of molecular organization—organelles, cells, organs, individuals, and populations. In this chapter we have been concerned mostly with middle length and long-wave ultraviolet radiation. Depending on degree of acclimatization, the effects of solar radiation on the health and well-being of the organism can be both positive and negative.

When exposed to ultraviolet and visible solar radiation, the unacclimatized organism responds with reddening of the skin or erythema, followed by initial tanning from the darkening of peripheral melanin molecules. With continued exposure the melanocytes of the epidermis increase their synthesis of melanin and granules; the granules are then extruded toward the stratum corneum after which they are taken up into the keratinocytes. Along with this secondary hyperpigmentation, the thickness of the superficial stratum corneum or horny layer of the epidermis increases. The two processes represent a protective response in that they help retard the passage of ultraviolet light into the deeper layers of the skin. Without these two processes, excessive exposure to solar radiation in the unacclimatized organism might result in sunburn and related cellular injuries and possibly result in skin cancer.

Solar radiation plays an important role in the synthesis of vitamin D. As shown by studies indicating marked seasonal differences in plasma, vitamin D levels in regions characterized by seasonal differences in solar radiation, and use of fortified vitamin D foods, the majority of vitamin D is synthesized through solar radiation stimulus. Because vitamin D plays an important role in the metabolism of calcium, variations in solar radiation intensity are reflected in marked seasonal differences in the incidence of rickets. Therefore individual and populational differences in melanin-producing capacity have profound influences on the well-being and survival of the organism.

As shown by photochemical and photometric studies, populational differences in skin color appear related to different rates of melanin synthesis and the size of the melanin granules as well as to the number of melanocytes. Various hypotheses have been postulated to explain the origin of populational differences in skin color. These proposals suggest that cutaneous melanin pigmentation is, or has been, associated with (1) resistance to sunburn, solar degeneration, and skin cancer; (2) thermoregulation by enhancing absorption of solar energy or sensitivity to frostbite; and (3) regulation of vitamin D biosynthesis by regulating penetration of ultraviolet light into the skin. In addition, earlier hypotheses have postulated that melanin may have been adaptive as camouflage for early man in evading predators and for hunting.[41] These theories have directly linked cutaneous melanin with human fitness, thus emphasizing that skin pigmentation has been a major target for natural selection. Analysis of vital statistics from Australia indicates that the death from skin cancer and malignant melanoma, which are directly associated with intensity of solar radiation and inversely related to pigmentation, occurs at a rate of 1:10,000 for individuals under the age of 50 years. Given the nearly 3 million years of human evolution, it is conceivable that selection by skin cancer and malignant melanoma may indeed have been an important factor in the development of populational differences in skin color.

Other theories, although recognizing the role of melanin pigmentation, have identified variations in human skin color as by-products of other events of natural selection. This would include associating skin color with selection for eye color. Because decreasing pigmentation of the fundus of the eye results in an increased sensitivity to longer wavelengths of light (greater than 50 m), it has been postulated that this characteristic might have arisen in the cave dwelling period of European prehistory as an adaptive response to lower levels of light

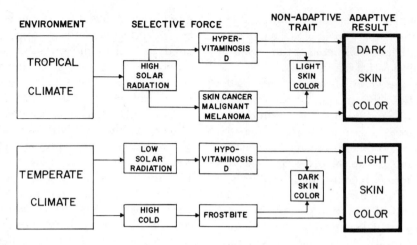

Fig. 7-7. Schematization of selective forces in tropical and temperate climates that affect human variation in skin color. Population differences in skin color are viewed as result of evolutionary compromise to selective forces present in world climates.

intensity.[42] However, experimental studies indicate that variations in retinal and iris pigmentation under varying conditions of light stress are not related to visual acuity.[43,44] Another theory states that selection for resistance to tropical disease by hypertrophy of the reticuloendothelial system is accompanied by a passive enhancement of cutaneous pigmentation. Still another theory postulates that dark skin color evolved as mimic response to the tropical forest.[40,41]

It is evident that populational differences in human skin color developed in response to more than one environmental factor, since no single selective force can account for the distribution of existing skin color variations. Therefore, as summarized in Fig. 7-7, populational differences in skin color probably evolved as a by-product of the competing selective forces of skin cancer, malignant melanoma, vitamin D synthesis, and cold injury.

REFERENCES

1. Thekaekara, M. P., and A. J. Drummond. 1971. Standard values for the solar constant and its spectral components. Nature Phys. Sci. **229**:6-9.
2. Daniels, F., Jr. 1974. Radiant energy. Part A. Solar radiation. In N. B. Slonim, ed. Environmental physiology. The C. V. Mosby Co., St. Louis.
3. Fitzpatrick, T. B., W. C. Quevedo, Jr., G. Szabo, and M. Seiji. 1971. The melanocyte system. In T. B. Fitzpatrick, ed. Dermatology in general medicine. McGraw-Hill, Inc., New York:
4. Garcia, R. I., R. E. Mitchell, J. Bloom, and G. Szabo. 1977. Number of epidermal melanocytes, hair follicles, and sweat ducts in the skin of Solomon Islanders. Am. J. Phys. Anthropol. **47**:427-434.
5. Mitchell, R. E. 1968. The skin of the Australian aborigine: a light and electromicroscopical study. Australas. J. Dermatol. **9**:314-328.
6. Szabo, G., A. B. Gerald, M. A. Pathak, and T. B. Fitzpatrick. 1972. The ultrastructure of racial color differences in man. In V. Riley, ed. Pigmentation: its genesis and biologic control. Appleton-Century-Crofts, New York.
7. Garrad, C., G. A. Harrison, and J. J. T. Owen. 1967. Comparative spectrophotometry of skin color with EEL and Photovolt instruments. Am. J. Phys. Anthropol. **27**:389-396.
8. Lasker, G. W. 1954. Seasonal changes in skin color. Am. J. Phys. Anthropol. **12**:553-558.

9. Weiner, J. S., G. A. Harrison, R. Singer, R. Harris, and W. Japp. 1964. Skin color in Southern Africa. Hum. Biol. **36**:294-307.

10. Harrison, G. A., J. T. T. Owen, F. J. DaRocha, and F. M. Salzano. 1967. Skin color in Southern Brazilian populations. Hum. Biol. **39**:21-31.

11. Hulse, F. S. 1967. Selection for skin color among Japanese. Am. J. Phys. Anthropol. **27**:143-156.

12. Conway, D., and P. T. Baker. 1972. Skin reflectance of Quechua Indians: the effects of genetic admixture, sex and age. Am. J. Phys. Anthropol. **36**:267-282.

13. Quevedo, W. C., Jr., T. B. Fitzpatrick, M. A. Pathak, and K. Jimbow. 1975. Role of light in human skin color variation. Am. J. Phys. Anthropol. **43**:393-408.

14. Pathak, M. A., Y. Hori, G. Szabo, and T. B. Fitzpatrick. 1971. The photobiology of melanin pigmentation in human skin. In T. Kawamura, T. B. Fitzpatrick, and M. Seiji, eds. Biology of normal and abnormal melanocytes. University of Tokyo Press, Tokyo.

15. DeLuca, H. F., J. W. Blunt, and H. Rikkers. 1971. The vitamins, 2nd ed. W. H. Sebrell, and R. S. Harris, eds. vol. 3. Academic Press, New York.

16. Omdahl, J. L., and H. F. DeLuca. 1973. Regulation of vitamin D metabolism and function. Physiol. Rev. **53**:327-372.

17. Smith, R. W., J. Rizek, and B. Frame. 1964. Determinants of serum antirachitic actvity. Special reference to involutional osteoporosis. Am. J. Clin. Nutr. **14**:98-108.

18. Stamp, T. C. B., and J. M. Round. 1974. Seasonal changes in human plasma levels of 25-hydroxy-vitamin D. Nature **247**:563-585.

19. Haddad, J. G., and K. J. Chyu. 1971. Competitive protein binding radioassay for 25-hydroxycholecalciferol. J. Clin. Endocrinol. Metab. **33**:992-995.

20. Malm, O. J. 1958. Calcium requirement and adaptation in adult men. Scand. J. Clin. Lab. Invest. (suppl.) **10**:36.

21. Loomis, W. F. 1967. Skin-pigment regulation of vitamin-D biosynthesis in man. Science **157**:501-506.

22. Roberts, S. A., M. D. Cohen, and J. O. Forfar. 1973. Antenatal factors associated with neonatal hypocalcemic convulsions. Lancet **2**:809-811.

23. Purvis, R. J., W. J. Barrie, G. S. MacKay, E. M. Wilkinson, F. Cockburn, N. R. Belton, and J. O. Forfar. 1973. Enamel hypoplasia of the teeth associated with neonatal tetany: a manifestation of maternal vitamin-D deficiency. Lancet **2**:811-814.

24. Neer, R. M. 1975. The evolutionary significance of vitamin D, skin pigment, and ultraviolet light. Am. J. Phys. Anthropol. **43**:409-416.

25. Yendt, E. R., H. F. DeLuca, D. A. Garcia, and M. Gohanim. 1970. Clinical aspects of vitamin D. In H. F. DeLuca, and J. W. Suttie, eds. The fat-soluble vitamins. University of Wisconsin Press, Madison, Wis.

26. Loomis, W. F. 1970. Rickets. Sci. Am. **223**:76-91.

27. Oettle, A. G. 1966. Epidemiology of melanoma in South Africa. In G. Della Porta, and O. Muhlbock, eds. The structure and control of the tulanocyte. Springer-Verlag New York, Inc., Heidelberg, N.Y.

28. Blum, H. F. 1959. Carcinogenesis by ultraviolet light: an essay in quantitative biology. Princeton University Press, Princeton, N.J.

29. Burdank, F. 1971. Patterns in cancer mortality in the United States: 1950-1967. NCI Monograph 33. U.S. Department of Health, Education, and Welfare, Washington, D.C.

30. Hall, A. F. 1950. Relationships of sunlight, complexion and heredity to skin carcinogenesis. Arch. Dermatol. Syph. **61**:589-610.

31. Lee, J. A. H. 1972. Sunlight and the etiology of malignant melanoma. In W. H. McCarthy, ed. Melanoma and skin cancer. Government Printer, Sydney, N.S.W. Australia.

32. Gellin, G. A., A. W. Kopf, and L. Garfinkel. 1969. Malignant melanoma: a controlled study of possibly associated factors. Arch. Dermatol. **99**:43-48.

33. Beardmore, G. L. 1972. The epidemiology of malignant melanoma in Australia. In W. H. McCarthy, ed. Melanoma and skin cancer. Government Printer, Sydney, N.S.W. Australia.

34. Livingstone, F. 1969. Polygenic models for the evolution of human skin color differences. Hum. Biol. **41**:480-493.

35. Thomson, M. L. 1955. Relative efficiency of pigment and horny layer thickness in protecting the skin of Europeans and Africans against solar ultraviolet radiation. J. Physiol. (Lond.) **127**:236-246.

36. Murray, F. G. 1934. Pigmentation, sunlight and nutritional disease. Am. Anthropol. **36**:438-445.

37. Eastman, N. J. 1956. Obstetrics, 11th ed. Appleton-Century-Crofts, New York.

38. Baker, P. T. 1958. The biological adaptation of man to hot deserts. Am. Naturalist **92**:337-357.

39. Post, P. W., F. Daniels, Jr., and R. T. Binford, Jr. 1975. Cold injury and the evolution of "white" skin. Hum. Biol. **47**:65-80.

40. Wasserman, H. P. Human pigmentation and environmental adaptation. Arch. Environ. Health **11**:691-694.

41. Cowles, R. B. 1959. Some ecological factors bearing on the origin and evolution of pigment in the human skin. Am. Naturalist **93:**283-293.

42. Daniels, F., Jr., P. W. Post, and B. E. Johnson. 1972. Theories of the role of pigment in the evolution of human races. In V. Riley, ed. Pigmentation: its genesis and biologic control. Appleton-Century-Crofts, New York.

43. Hoffman, J. M. 1975. Retinal pigmentation, visual acuity and brightness levels. Am. J. Phys. Anthropol. **43:**417-424.

44. Short, G. B. 1975. Iris pigmentation and photopic visual acuity: a preliminary study. Am. J. Phys. Anthropol. **43:**425-434.

8 | Biological effects and responses to high-altitude hypoxia

Environmental factors
    Nature of hypoxic stress
    Methods of studying hypoxic stress
    High-altitude areas of the world

Initial effects of and responses to high-altitude hypoxia
    Pulmonary function
    Circulation and heart functions
    Blood
    Retinal circulation
    Light sensitivity and visual acuity
    Memory and learning
    Hearing
    Motor function
    Taste
    Anorexia and weight loss
    Adrenal activity
    Thyroid function
    Testosterone secretion
    Sexual function

Individual factors and tolerance to high altitude
    Age
    Physical fitness
    Sex

Conclusion

ENVIRONMENTAL FACTORS

During their conquest of the Incas of Peru, the Spaniards were the first to notice the effects of high-altitude environments on the normal functioning of lowland natives.[1] In 1590 the chronicler Jose de Acosta in his *Historia Natural y Moral de las Indias* gave the first clear description of mountain sickness experienced by sea level man sojourning at a high altitude.[1] Three centuries later, Jourdanet[2] and Bert[3] began their scientific observations of the effects of high altitudes and low barometric pressures. Since then, study of the mechanisms whereby man adapts to the pervasive effects of high-altitude hypoxia has concerned the biological as well as the social scientists.

A high-altitude environment presents several stresses to man. The most important include (1) hypoxia, (2) high solar radiation, (3) cold, (4) humidity, (5) high winds, (6) limited nutritional base, and (7) rough terrain. From the physiological point of view hypoxia is the most important, since the other stresses are present in an equal or to a greater degree in other geographical zones. High-altitude hypoxia is a pervasive and ever-present stress that is not easily modified by cultural or behavioral responses. Furthermore, all organ systems and physiological functions are affected by hypoxia. For these reasons, the study of human adaptation to high-altitude hypoxia provides an excellent opportunity to learn about the flexibility and nature of the homeostatic processes that enable an organism to function and survive under extreme environmental stress.

Nature of hypoxic stress

Biological adaptation to high-altitude hypoxia depends mainly on the partial pressure of oxygen in the atmosphere, which decreases proportionately to an increase in altitude. Oxygen reaches the organic cells through the respiratory, cardiovascular, and hematological systems. All of these processes act synergically and enable gas molecules to pass through the tissues in adequate quantities. When tissues receive a deficient supply of oxygen, a physiological situation called *hypoxia* ("less oxygen" than required) develops. Hypoxia can be produced by any condition, physiological or pathological, that interferes with oxygen supply to the tissues. An interruption in oxygen supply can be produced by an alteration in gas acquisition at the cardiopulmonary level, such as occurs in anemic hypoxia. Hypoxia can also be produced by atmospheric conditions, for example, contamination of the air with carbon monoxide or other gases that displace the oxygen, or by normal depletion of oxygen in the atmosphere as occurs at high altitudes.

The atmosphere contains 20.95% oxygen, and this quantity is constant up to an altitude of 110,000 m. However, because air is compressible, it contains a greater number of gaseous molecules at low altitudes than at high altitudes; the barometric pressure, which depends on the molecular concentration of air, thus also decreases with an increase in altitude. This is the fundamental problem of high-altitude hypoxia: the oxygen in the air at high altitudes is less concentrated and, consequently, is at a lower pressure than it is at low altitudes.

Air consists of about 78.08% nitrogen, 0.03% carbon dioxide, 20.95% oxygen, as well as 0.01% trace elements. These gases together at sea level exert a pressure of 760 mm of mercury (Hg). This pressure is known as the *barometric pressure*. The pressure of each gas corresponds to its proportional amount. Therefore the pressure exerted by nitrogen is 78% of 760 = 593 mm Hg and that by oxygen is 20.95% of 760 = 159 mm Hg. These values are called the partial pressures of each gas. Hence, the partial pressure of oxygen, or P_{O_2}, at sea level is 159 mm

Hg, and the partial pressure of nitrogen, or P_{N_2}, at sea level is 593 mm Hg. At 3500 m (11,840 feet) the barometric pressure is reduced to 493 mm Hg, and the partial pressure of oxygen is 103 mm Hg; that is, at an altitude of 3500 m oxygen has about 35% less pressure than at sea level. At 4500 m (14,650 feet) the partial pressure of oxygen (P_{O_2} = 91 mm Hg) is decreased by as much as 40% with respect to sea level pressure (Fig. 8-1). Because of this decreased partial pressure of oxygen in ambient air, the partial pressure of oxygen in air reaching the trachea and alveoli is also reduced; this, in turn, reduces the amount of oxygen available to the tissues.

The drop in partial pressure of oxygen (P_{O_2}) at high altitude causes a reduction in oxygen saturation of arterial blood because the proportion of oxyhemoglobin (Hb_{O_2}) formation in the blood depends on the partial pressure of oxygen in the alveoli. When this pressure is high, as occurs at sea level, a greater proportion of hemoglobin is saturated with oxygen (greater formation of oxyhemoglobin, hence greater arterial oxygen saturation). On the other hand, when the partial pressure of oxygen is low, as occurs at high altitude, a lower proportion of hemoglobin is combined with oxygen (less formation of oxyhemoglobin and, hence, less arterial oxygen saturation). Thus, as shown in Table 5, if the partial pressure of oxygen in ambient air is 159 mm Hg and in the alveoli it is 104 mm Hg, as it is at sea level, the hemoglobin in arterial blood is 97% saturated with oxygen. On the other hand, if the partial pressure of oxygen in ambient air is 110

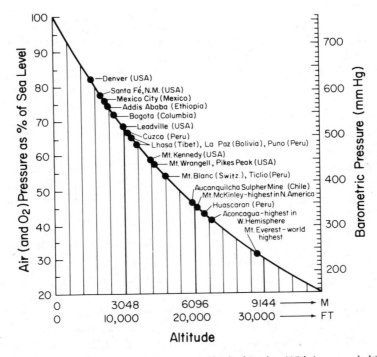

Fig. 8-1. Barometric pressure and oxygen pressure at high altitudes. With increased altitude there is percentage decrease in air and oxygen pressure. (Modified from Frisancho, A. R. 1975. Science **187**:313-319.)

Table 5. Effects of altitude and barometric pressure on partial pressure of oxygen in the air, inspired (tracheal) air, and alveoli and arterial oxygen saturation*

Altitude		Barometric pressure (mm Hg)	Partial pressure of oxygen (P$_{O_2}$)†			Arterial oxygen saturation (%)
meters	feet		Air (mm Hg)	Tracheal air (mm Hg)	Alveoli (mm Hg)	
0	0	760	159	149	104	97
3048	10,000	523	110	100	67	90
6096	20,000	349	73	63	40	70
9144	30,000	226	47	37	21	20
12,192	40,000	141	29	19	8	5
15,240	50,000	87	18	8	1	1

*Based on data from Folk, E. G. 1974. Textbook of environmental physiology. Lea & Febiger, Philadelphia.
†The partial pressure of oxygen (P$_{O_2}$) in the trachea is reduced because as inspired air enters the airways, it is warmed to almost body temperature (37° C) and saturated with water vapor, which exerts a vapor pressure of 47 mm Hg, regardless of barometric pressure. Therefore the P$_{O_2}$ of tracheal air at sea level = (760 − 47) × 0.2095 = 149 mm Hg, and 3048 m = (523 − 47) × 0.2095 = 100 mm Hg.

mm Hg and in the alveoli is 67 mm Hg, as it is at an altitude of 3048 m (10,000 feet), the hemoglobin in arterial blood is only 90% saturated with oxygen. This means that at an altitude of 3000 m there is a 10% decrease in oxygen for each unit of blood that leaves the lungs. Between 4000 and 5000 m this decrease might be as high as 30%.

Methods of studying hypoxic stress

The effects of high-altitude hypoxia are considered either acute or chronic. *Acute hypoxia* results from reduced oxygen availability that lasts for a few minutes, hours, or perhaps several weeks. *Chronic hypoxia* is a continuation of this condition for months, years, or a lifetime. The distinction between acute and chronic hypoxia results partly from the different mechanisms with which the organism responds to reduced oxygen availability.

The most common methods of studying the effects of and adaptation to high-altitude hypoxia include field or laboratory studies in a natural high-altitude environment and in low-pressure (decompression) chambers. A third method, sometimes used on labo-

ratory animals, is exposure to gas mixtures low in oxygen concentration but at sea level barometric pressures. In general, results derived from high-altitude environments are similar to those derived from altitude chambers.

During rest the physiological effects of hypoxia become evident at altitudes above 3000 m (about 10,000 feet), but during physical activity its effects are manifested above 2000 m (6600 feet). In this chapter the initial effects of high-altitude hypoxia, as well as factors affecting tolerance to high altitude, will be discussed. This will set the stage for a discussion in the next chapter of the process of acclimatization.

High-altitude areas of the world

As shown in Fig. 8-2 areas located above 3000 m include *(1)* the Rocky Mountains of the United States and Canada, *(2)* the Sierra Madre of Mexico, *(3)* the Andes of South America, *(4)* the Pyrenees between France and Spain, *(5)* the mountain ranges of Eastern Turkey, Persia, Afghanistan, and Pakistan, *(6)* the Himalayas, *(7)* the Tibetan Plateau and southern China, *(8)* the Atlas

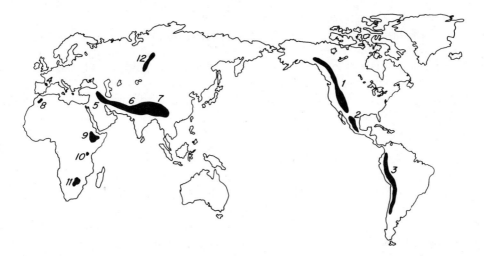

Fig. 8-2. Areas of the world exceeding 3000 m. *(1)* Rocky Mountains; *(2)* Sierra Madre; *(3)* Andes; *(4)* Pyrenees; *(5)* mountain ranges of Eastern Turkey, Persia, Afghanistan, and Pakistan; *(6)* Himalayas; *(7)* Tibetan Plateau and southern China; *(8)* Atlas Mountains; *(9)* high plains of Ethiopia; *(10)* Kilimanjaro; *(11)* the Basutoland; and *(12)* Tien Shan Mountains. (Modified from Heath, D., and D. R. Williams. 1977. Man at high altitude. The patho-physiology of acclimatization and adaptation. Churchill Livingstone, Edinburgh; and Pawson, I. G., and J. Corneille. 1978. The high-altitude areas of the world and their cultures. In P. T. Baker, ed. The biology of high altitude peoples. Cambridge University Press, New York.)

Mountains of Morocco, *(9)* the high plains of Ethiopia, *(10)* Kilimanjaro of East Africa, *(11)* Basutoland of South Africa, and *(12)* the Tien Shan Mountains of Russia. These areas are inhabited by more than 25 million people.

INITIAL EFFECTS OF AND RESPONSES TO HIGH-ALTITUDE HYPOXIA
Pulmonary function

Ventilation. On exposure to an altitude above 2500 m (8250 feet), the depth of pulmonary ventilation increases in linear association with an increase in altitude; the minute respiratory volume at 5000 m (16,500 feet) increases by about 45% to 69% above values attained at sea level.[4-9] Since the respiratory rate changes very little at high altitude, the increase in minute respiratory volume (minute respiratory volume = tidal volume × the respiratory rate) is caused by an increase in tidal volume, which is the volume of air inspired and expired with each normal breath. At sea level resting tidal volume equals about 500 ml, and the respiratory rate is 14.5 breaths per minute. Therefore minute respiratory volume equals 7.25 L. On exposure to 4000 m tidal volume averages about 700 ml, and resting respiratory rate increases to 15 breaths per minute, which results in a total minute respiratory volume of 10.5 L. However, during exercise the increase in both tidal volume and respiratory rate account for the increase in respiratory volume at high altitude.

According to current studies, increased pulmonary ventilation results from stimulation of carotid bodies and other peripheral chemoreceptors by hypoxemia. This increased pulmonary ventilation has adaptive significance—it increases the partial pressure of oxygen in the alveoli and improves the oxygenation of blood flowing through the pulmonary capillaries.

Respiratory alkalosis. As a result of increased ventilation, removal of carbon dioxide is also increased. During the first weeks of exposure to a high altitude the blood becomes alkaline (pH > 7.4), which must be compensated for during acclimatization (Chapter 9).

Lung volume. Several reports indicate that vital capacity and residual lung volume during the first month of exposure to high altitude decrease.[10-14] After about 1 month of exposure to high altitude these volumes become comparable to those at sea level.

Circulation and heart functions

With increasing hypoxia the resting heart rate increases from an average of 70 beats/min at sea level to as many as 105 beats/min at 4500 m. The mechanisms for increased heart rate are not well defined. Some investigators suggest that increased heart rate is related to stimulation of the carotid and aortic chemoreceptors; others attribute it to the influence of arterial hypocapnia and vagal afferent impulses from pulmonary stretch receptors. Concomitant with the increased pulse rate, systolic blood pressure either remains unchanged or decreases.[15]

It must be noted, however, that during exercise the heart rate does not increase to the high rates attained at sea level (170 to 210 beats/min). Most studies report a reduction in maximal exercise heart rate as great as 40 to 50 beats/min to a rate of 130 to 150 beats/min. Hence the cardiac output (quantity of blood pumped by the left ventricle of the heart into the aorta per minute) is reduced at high altitude. Furthermore, electrocardiographic studies indicate that among sea level natives the strength of the myocardium at high altitude is decreased.[16,17] In some cases, enlargement of the right ventricle has been reported.

Blood

Hemoglobin. When a sea level subject is exposed to high altitude and hypoxia develops, production of red blood cells exceeds destruction; the mean red cell count changes from about 5 million to 7 million/cu mm at 5000 m. Along with the increased red blood cell count, hemoglobin concentration also increases. The highest increase in hemoglobin takes place from 7 to 14 days after exposure, and during this time erythropoietic activity is about three times that observed at sea level. This process may continue for as long as 6 months, but the hemoglobin level stabilizes at about 18 g/100 ml,[18,19] and among high-altitude natives residing at 4000 m hemoglobin levels range from 16 to 20 g/100 ml.[20,21]

Blood volume. The pronounced polycythemia with exposure to high altitude results in an increased red cell volume. As shown in Fig. 8-3, the red cell volume, after a residence at 4540 m for 1 to 3 weeks, increases from 40 ml/kg at sea level to 50 ml/kg at high altitude. However, plasma volume decreases from an average of 48 ml/kg at sea level to 40 ml/kg at high altitude.[22] Therefore, in spite of red cell volume increases, total blood volume increases minimally. Consequently, the hematocrit increases from an average of 43% at sea level to about 60% after 2 weeks' exposure to high altitude; for this reason the viscosity of blood at high altitude is greater than at sea level. This increased viscosity results in greater strain on the heart; at a high altitude the heart must compensate for increased blood viscosity by doing more work. This explains the increased heart rate observed during initial exposure to high altitude.

Erythropoietic activity. The increased red blood cell production at high altitude is caused by an increase in erythropoietic activity. Within 2 hours of exposure to high altitude (4540 m) the average iron turnover rate increases on the average from 0.37 to 0.54 mg/day/kg body weight.[23] Furthermore, the iron turnover rate increases to a maximum of 0.91 mg/day/kg in 1 to 2 weeks; during this period erythropoietic activity is about three times that at sea level. The degree of erythropoietic stimulation has been found to be proportional to severity of the hypoxia; it is high during initial hours of exposure to high altitude and falls in a few days to a value intermediate between the initial peak response and that at sea level.[23]

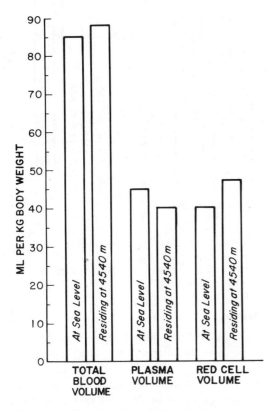

Fig. 8-3. Comparison of total blood volume, plasma volume, and red cell volume among sea level subjects and after residence for 1 to 3 weeks at high altitude. Exposure to high altitude results in increased red cell volume without increase in plasma volume. (Based on data from Merino, C. F. 1950. Blood 5:1-8.)

This secondary decrease in erythropoietic activity is related to the fact that after the first day several acclimatization processes operate and thus decrease the hypoxic stimuli. Furthermore, erythropoietic activity is not linearly related to altitude exposure because above 6000 m the rate of erythrocytic and hemoglobin formation is decreased.[24]

Retinal circulation

After only 2 hours of exposure to 5330 m the retinal arteries and veins increase in diameter about one fifth.[25] Fig. 8-4 shows that compared to sea level controls diameters increase 130% after 5 days, and after 5 to 7 weeks of exposure the increase still amounts to 100%. That the increased retinal blood flow is caused by hypoxia and not by alkalosis is inferred from the fact that hypoxia without hypocapnia results in increased dilation of retinal vessels and increased retinal blood flow, whereas hypocapnia without hypoxia results in reduced retinal blood flow.[62]

Light sensitivity and visual acuity

High-altitude hypoxia decreases light sensitivity. The higher the altitude, the more is sensitivity to light decreased; above 4500 m (14,850 feet) an intensity about 2.5 times greater than at sea level is required for a light to be seen.[26] With hypoxia, the response to light stimulus is not only slow, but also less consistent than at sea level.[26] These impairments appear caused by the effect of hypoxia on the visual system rather than by any psychological response of the subject. These decreases reach their maximum after about 1 hour of exposure, and in most cases visual performance is recovered by the forty-eighth hour of exposure.

Memory and learning

It has been reported that performance of unfamiliar tasks or difficult calculations is

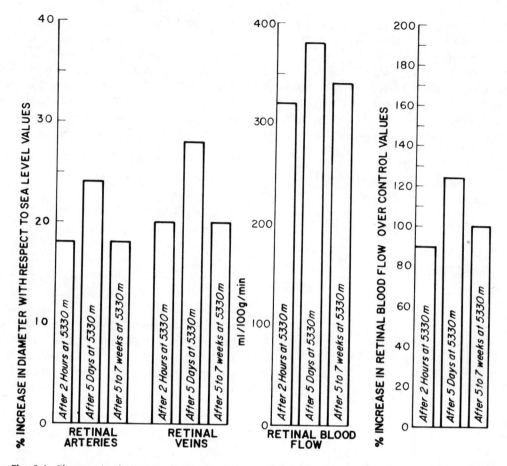

Fig. 8-4. Changes in diameter of retinal arteries and retinal veins, and retinal blood flow after 2 hours', 5 days', and 5 to 7 weeks' exposure to high altitude. Exposure to high altitude, especially during first 5 days, results in drastic dilation of retinal arteries and veins and concomitant increase in retinal blood flow. (Modified from Frayser, R., C. H. Houston, G. W. Gray, A. C. Bryan, and I. D. Rennie. 1971. Arch. Intern. Med. **127:**708-711.)

often considerably impaired during initial exposure to high altitude. As tested by paired-word association or pattern and position recall, immediate and recall memory has been observed to be diminished with an increase in altitude, especially at altitudes over 3660 m.[26] However, other studies indicate that the ability to learn a new procedure is affected more severely than the performance of a previously learned procedure.[27]

Hearing

Of the various sensory modalities, hearing is the least sensitive to hypoxia. Indeed, in progressive hypoxia the sense of hearing is the last to disappear, and only above an altitude of 6000 m (19,800 feet) have decreases in hearing acuity been reported.[28]

Motor function

Several investigators have reported signs of muscular weakness and incoordination on exposure to altitudes above 4500 m. At present, however, it is not known whether these deficiencies represent diminished functional capacity of the muscle itself or absence of muscle stimulation.[15]

A clear and well-defined effect of hypoxia is impairment of neuromuscular control. Neuromuscular control impairment increases with increasing altitude; at 6000 m handwriting may become undecipherable.[15] The physiological mechanisms responsible for this impairment are not known. It has been suggested that the increase in reflex muscle irritability observed above an altitude of 4000 m may result from the increased neuromuscular excitability associated with hyperventilation-induced alkalosis.[15]

Taste

Exposure to high altitude also influences food preference. In general at high altitudes preference for sugar increases, and the desire for fat decreases. For unknown reasons sugar tastes less sweet at high altitude, and about two times the normal amount is taken in drinks.[29] A high carbohydrate diet, along with increased sugar intake, results in reduced severity and duration of symptoms of the acute effects of high altitude, such as mountain sickness.[29] Reflecting the need for more sugar at high altitude, blood glucose levels are lower than at sea level; but when adequate carbohydrate intakes are maintained, the glucose levels are normal.[30] Altitude also seems to affect a person's ability to taste differences among four different compounds. It has been demonstrated that gustatory sensitivity to sweet (tested by sucrose), salt (sodium chloride), sour (citric acid or tartaric acid), and bitter (caffeine or quinine) were diminished during exposure to an altitude of 3450 m.[31,32] However, others indicate that rapid exposure to an altitude of 7620 m has no effect on taste perception.[33]

Anorexia and weight loss

High-altitude exposure, especially at elevations greater than 3500 m, results in anorexia and, as a consequence of reduced food consumption, weight loss. These responses are most pronounced during the first few days of exposure.[29]

In the Mount Everest expeditions the average daily food intake, between 5182 m (17,000 feet) and 6401 m (21,000 feet), was 2000 calories, and above 6401 m it averaged only 1500 calories. One of the major consequences of high-altitude anorexia is an imbalance between energy intake and energy output. The resulting energy deficits are affected by tissue catabolism, such as that of body fat and body protein.[29] Because of energy imbalance and body tissue catabolism body weight is reduced. In men the weight loss at Everest (6401 m) for a period of 4 weeks averaged 1 lb/week (0.45 kg) and 2.8 lb/week (1.26 kg) among poorly acclimated men.[29] At 4300 m the average weight loss for men for the first 7 days ranged from 3.49% to 5% of prealtitude weight.[34,35] In women, however, the average weight losses were less pronounced, and the loss over 7 days at 4300 m averaged only 1.76% prealtitude exposure weight.[36] Reduced body weight is not only caused by low caloric intake but also by loss of body water.[37,38] Body fluid loss increases at high altitudes because of increased urine output and increased water loss from the lungs associated with increased respiration,[37,38] together with the low humidity present at high altitude. Above 6706 m, despite a decrease in urine output, dehydration becomes progressive because of a blunting of the thirst sensation and the consequent decreased fluid intake.[29]

Adrenal activity

Adrenal cortex. Reflecting the general stress of the organism, exposure to high altitude results in increased adrenal activity. As shown by measurements of 17-hydroxycorticosteroids (17-OCHS) of the urine and blood plasma during the first week of exposure to altitudes above 2000 m, adrenocortical activity increases rapidly in the first week, and during the second week it returns to sea level values.[15,29,39]

Adrenal medulla. On exposure to altitudes above 3000 m adrenal medulla activity is increased as shown by the increased excretion of noradrenaline and catecholamine.[15,29,40] After about the second week, adrenal medulla activity returns to sea level values.

Aldosterone. With controlled dietary sodium and potassium intake, exposure to altitudes above 3500 m results in the reduction of aldosterone secretion.[15,41,42] The factors responsible for this reduction are not yet well defined. It has been postulated that the mechanism for suppressing aldosterone secretion may involve the right atrium of the heart. According to this hypothesis increased blood volume that occurs with acclimatization to high altitude stimulates the stretch receptors of the right atrium, which in turn depresses aldosterone secretion.[42] In support of this hypothesis is the fact that experimental animals exposed to high altitude show reduced width of the adrenal gland's zona glomerulosa, which is the source of aldosterone.[43]

Renin. As shown by experiments with animals and humans, exposure to high altitude results in an initial increase in plasma renin.[44,45]

Thyroid function

Experiments with animals indicate that exposure to high altitude for more than 3 days results in reduced thyroid function.[46-49] Iodine retention and thyroid concentrating power are also decreased. The mechanism for this reduced thyroid function has not

been clearly identified. It has been postulated that the mechanism is related to deficient secretion of the thyroid-stimulating hormone by the pituitary[46]; others suggest that altitude reduces the thyroxine requirements and hence results in a concomitant reduction in hormone synthesis.[49,50]

Testosterone secretion

Studies of sea level subjects transported to 4250 m indicate that during the first 3 days of exposure the 24-hour urinary testosterone secretion was reduced by more than 50% when compared to sea level values.[51-52] By the end of the first week of exposure to high altitude, testosterone secretion returned to normal. Since it is known that exposure of sea level subjects to high altitude results in decreased plasma luteinizing hormone (LH), Heath and Williams[15] suggest that decreased testosterone secretion at high altitude is caused by low levels of LH.

Sexual function

Spermatogenesis. Experiments with animals and humans indicate that exposure to high altitude results in decreased spermatozoid production and increased abnormal forms.[52,53] Studies of sea level subjects at sea level and during 8 and 13 days' exposure to an altitude of 4330 m indicate that (Fig. 8-5) by the eighth day of exposure to high altitude the sperm count declined from a mean of 216.2 million/ml to 150.2 million/ml and to 98.2 million/ml by the thirteenth day. Along with this decrease there was also an increase in abnormal forms from 0% at sea level to 39.3% by the eighth day and a decrease in the motile forms from 70% at sea level to 50% by the eighth day at high altitude. Subsequent studies[52,53] on the semen of sea level subjects transported from sea level to 4270 m for 4 weeks indicated that the sperm count (expressed as total number of sperm) from the first day to the twenty-eighth day of exposure dropped gradually from a control level of $7.42 \times 10.^8$ This gradual decline continued even 15 days after the descent to sea level. Furthermore, the motile cells decreased from control values of 85.8% to 53.4% at the end of the experimental period. The frequency of abnormal forms increased from a control level of 15.5% to 31.6%. Thus, it appears that high-altitude hypoxia has profound effects on spermatogenesis.

Histological changes in the testes. The effects of hypoxia on spermatogenesis appear related to alterations in the tissues of the testes. Experiments on rats[54] indicate that after the third day of exposure to a simulated altitude of 7580 m the germinal epithelium suffered considerable damage, which progressed through the end of the experiment.

Tissue alterations appear to continue for longer periods; even after 6 months exposure to an altitude of 4510 m the germinal epithelium of cats showed various degrees of destruction.[55] Similarly, guinea pigs after 2 weeks exposure to an altitude of 4330 m exhibited profound alterations in the epithelium of the seminiferous tubules with a marked decrease of all cellular types.[51]

Estrus cycle. As shown in studies with rats

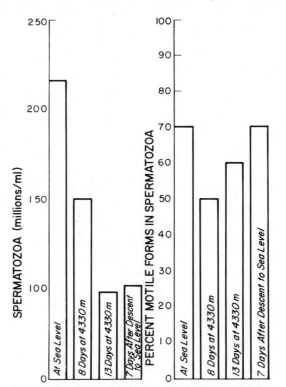

Fig. 8-5. Changes in spermatozoa count and motile forms after 8 days and 13 days of residence at high altitude and subsequent descent to sea level. Exposure to high altitude is associated with decreased spermatozoid count and reduced motility of spermatozoa, which return to normal with descent to sea level. (Modified from Donayre, J. 1966. Population growth and fertility at high altitude. In Life at high altitudes. Pub. 140. Pan American Health Organization, Washington, D.C.)

high-altitude hypoxia along with cold decreased the incidence of estrus. Rats exposed to cold in addition to hypoxia exhibited fewer instances of estrus than those rats exposed to hypoxia alone.[56] In other words, cold superimposes an anestrous effect on that produced by hypoxia, but these changes are reversible after return to sea level and temperate conditions.

Menstruation. Studies on females residing at high altitude indicated an increased incidence of menstrual disturbances such as amenorrhea, dysmenorrhea,[53] and increased menstrual flow.[53] However, the extent to which these variations in menstrual cycle are the result of hypoxia is not well defined because the majority of the subjects questioned were taking contraceptive pills.

INDIVIDUAL FACTORS AND TOLERANCE TO HIGH ALTITUDE
Age

From studies on animals and humans it is known that tolerance to acute high-altitude hypoxia is affected by age. It has been found that on exposure to 10,360 m in a decompression chamber for 6 hours the survival

of young rats (birth to 110 days) and old rats (older than 2 years) was poorer than those of adult rats (110 to 330 days).[57] Studies on humans showed that the decrease in light and auditory sensitivity associated with human aging is enhanced when sea level subjects are exposed to a simulated altitude of 4880 m.[26] Similarly, the resistance of healthy subjects (pilots) to acute oxygen deficiency in a decompression chamber simulating 7500 m increases between the ages of 18 and 40 years, and after 40 years of age tolerance decreases slowly.[58] Acclimatization studies indicate that among six 58- to 71-year-old subjects, five (83%) subjects exhibited a decrease in hemoglobin concentration during the first few days at high altitude[59]; this was in contrast to their responses 27 years earlier when all showed an increased hemoglobin concentration beginning with arrival at high altitude. This response appears to result from the fact that the mobilization of plasma water into interstitial or extracellular spaces and the associated increased hemoconcentration that occurs in young subjects exposed to high altitude does not occur in older subjects

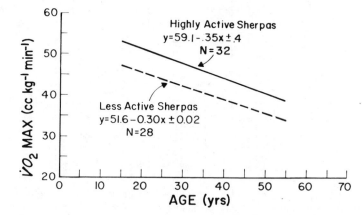

Fig. 8-6. Comparison of maximum oxygen uptake between highly active and less active Sherpas living at 3440 m in Nepal. At high altitude, as at sea level, active individuals of all ages maintain higher aerobic capacity than less active counterparts. (From Weiz, C. A. 1973. The effects of aging and habitual activity on exercise performance among a high altitude Himalayan population. Ph.D. Thesis. Pennsylvania State University, University Park, Pa.)

under similar conditions. Furthermore, it has been found that plasma aldosterone levels and probably secretion rates are reduced among older, but not among younger, subjects when exposed to high altitude.[60]

Physical fitness

Some of the major adaptive effects of physical training include increased vascularization, increased size of the striated and cardiac muscles, and increased maximum aerobic capacity. Although the influence of training has not been documented, one would expect that degree of physical fitness would affect degree of tolerance and rate of acclimatization to cold stress. Individuals with high fitness would be able to tolerate the stress of hypoxia better. As shown in Fig. 8-6, at all ages among the Nepalese Sherpas from Namche Bazar (3440 m) the most active natives such as porters, herders, and farmers attain a greater aerobic capacity than their less active counterparts (storekeepers, traders, and artisans) residing at the same altitude.[61]

Sex

Experimental studies indicate that female rats have a better survival rate than male rats when exposed to a simulated altitude of 10,360 m for 6 hours.[57] Circumstantial evidence from humans also indicates that the incidence and severity of acute mountain sickness and high-altitude pulmonary edema is greater in males than in females.[15,29]

CONCLUSION

The most important environmental stress at high altitude is the low oxygen availability that results from the decrease in barometric pressure. Therefore, in this chapter the physiological effects and responses that the organism makes to the stress of hypoxia associated with high altitude have been emphasized.

The physiological effects of hypoxia are multifaceted and complex. In response to low oxygen availability the organism increases its rate of pulmonary ventilation, as well as increasing the oxygen-carrying capacity of the blood. These adjustments are not completely adequate, as shown by the fact that sea level natives exposed to high altitude do experience disturbances of the sensory nervous system, adrenal activity, and reproductive function and reduced work capacity. Along with physiological disturbances, high-altitude hypoxia also affects appetite, producing anorexia which in turn results in weight loss. The weight loss is also caused by dehydration or loss of body water, which occurs because of inhibition of fluid intake and excessive fluid loss through the increased altitude-induced ventilation and low humidity of the high altitudes. Eventually the sea level organism is able to function at high altitude. This is achieved through the long-term process of acclimatization discussed in the next chapter.

Tolerance to high-altitude hypoxic stress is influenced by age, physical fitness, and sex. Thus very young and very old subjects are more impaired than adults, less active individuals experience a greater decline in aerobic capacity than more active individuals, and tolerance to hypoxic stress appears greater in females than in males.

REFERENCES

1. Kellogg, R. H. 1968. Altitude acclimatization, a historical introduction emphasizing the regulation of breathing. Physiologist **11**:37-57.

2. Jourdanet, D. 1861. Les altitudes de l'Amérique tropicale comparées au niveau des mers au point de vue de la constitution médicale. Baillière, Paris.

3. Bert, P. 1878. La pression barométrique: recherches de physiologie expérimentale. Masson, Paris.

4. Rahn, H., and A. B. Otis. 1949. Continuous analysis of alveolar gas composition during work, hypercapnea, hypercarbia, and anoxia. J. Appl. Physiol. 1:717-724.

5. Grover, R. F., J. T. Reeves, E. B. Grover, and J. E. Leathers. 1967. Muscular exercise in young men native to 3,100 m altitude. J. Appl. Physiol. 22:555-564.

6. Reeves, J. T., R. F. Grover, and J. E. Cohn. 1967. Regulation of ventilation during exercise at 10,200 ft. in athletes born at low altitude. J. Appl. Physiol. 22:546-554.

7. Sørensen, S. C., and J. W. Severinghaus. 1968. Respiratory sensitivity to acute hypoxia in man born at sea level living at high altitude. J. Appl. Physiol. 25:211-216.

8. Sørensen, S. C., and J. W. Severinghaus. 1968. Irreversible respiratory insensitivity to acute hypoxia in man born at high altitude. J. Appl. Physiol. 25:217-220.

9. Sørensen, S. C., and J. W. Severinghaus. 1968. Respiratory insensitivity to acute hypoxia persisting after correction of tetralogy of Fallot. J. Appl. Physiol. 25:221-223.

10. Rahn, H., and D. Hammond. 1952. The vital capacity at reduced barometric pressure. J. Appl. Physiol. 4:715-719.

11. Tenney, S. M., H. Rahn, R. C. Straud, and J. C. Mithoefer. 1952. Adaptation to high altitude: changes in lung volumes during the first seven days at Mount Evans, Colorado. J. Appl. Physiol. 5:607-613.

12. Ulvedal, F., T. E. Morgan, Jr., R. G. Cutler, and B. E. Welch. 1963. Ventilatory capacity during prolonged exposure to simulated altitude without hypoxia. J. Appl. Physiol. 18:904-908.

13. Shields, J. L., J. P. Hannon, C. W. Harris, and W. S. Platner. 1968. Effects of altitude acclimatization on pulmonary function in women. J. Appl. Physiol. 25:606-609.

14. Consolazio, C. F., H. L. Johnson, L. O. Mataush, R. A. Nelson, and G. J. Isaac. 1967. Respiratory function in normal young adults at 3475 and 4300 meters. Rep. 300. U.S. Army Medical Research and Nutrition Laboratory, Fitzsimons General Hospital, Denver, Colo.

15. Heath, D., and D. R. Williams. 1977. Man at high altitude. The pathophysiology of acclimatization and adaptation. Churchill Livingstone, Edinburgh.

16. Jackson, F., and H. Davies. 1960. The electro-cardiogram of the mountaineer at high altitude. Br. Heart J. 22:671-685.

17. Peñaloza, D., and M. Echevarria. 1957. Electrocardiographic observations on ten subjects at sea level and during one year of residence at high altitudes. Am. Heart J. 54:811-822.

18. Abbrecht, P. H., and J. K. Littell. 1972. Plasma erythropoietin in men and mice during acclimatization to different altitudes. J. Appl. Physiol. 32:54-58.

19. Reynafarje, C., J. Ramos, J. Faura, and D. Villavicencio. 1964. Humoral control of erythropoietic activity in man during and after altitude exposure. Proc. Soc. Exp. Biol. Med. 116:649-653.

20. Garruto, R. M. 1976. Hematology. In P. T. Baker and M. A. Little, eds. Man in the Andes: a multidisciplinary study of high altitude Quechua natives. Dowden, Hutchinson & Ross, Inc., Stroudsburg, Pa.

21. Frisancho, A. R., T. Velasquez, and J. Sanchez. 1975. Possible adaptive significance of small body size in the attainment of aerobic capacity among high altitude Quechua natives. In E. Watts, F. E. Johnston, and G. W. Lasker, eds. Biosocial interrelations in population adaptations. Mouton Publishers, Chicago.

22. Merino, C. F. 1950. Studies on blood formation and destruction in the polycythemia of high altitude. Blood 5:1-8.

23. Reynafarje, C. 1964. Hematologic changes during rest and physical activity in man at high altitude. In W. H. Weihe, ed. The physiological effects of high altitude. Pergamon Press Ltd., Oxford.

24. Hurtado, A., C. F. Merino, and D. Delgado. 1945. Influence of anoxemia on the hemopoietic activity. Arch. Intern. Med. 75:284-323.

25. Frayser, R., C. S. Houston, G. W. Gray, A. C. Bryan, and I. D. Rennie. 1971. The response of the retinal circulation to altitude. Arch. Intern. Med. 127:708-711.

26. McFarland, R. A. 1972. Psychophysiological implications of life at altitude and including the role of oxygen in the process of aging. M. K. Yousef, S. M. Horvath and R. W. Bullard, eds. In Physiological adaptations: desert and mountain. Academic Press, Inc., New York.

27. Cahoon, R. L. 1972. Simple decision making at high altitude. Ergonomics 15:157-163.

28. Curry, E. T., and F. Boys. 1956. Effects of oxygen on hearing sensitivity of simulated altitudes. Eye Ear Nose Throat Mon. 35:239-245.

29. Ward, M. 1975. Mountain medicine. A clinical study of cold and high altitude. Van Nostrand Reinhold Co. New York.

30. Consolazio, C. F., L. O. Matoush, H. L. Johnson, H. J. Krzywicki, T. A. Daws, and G. J. Isaac. 1969. Effects of high-carbohydrate diets on performance and clinical symptomatology after rapid ascent to high altitude. Fed. Proc. 28:937-943.

31. Grandjean, E. 1955. The effect of altitude on various nervous functions. Proc. R. Soc. (Lond.) 143:12-13.

32. Maga, J. A., and K. Lorenz. 1972. Effect of altitude on taste thresholds. Percept. Mot. Skills 34:667-670.

33. Finkelstein, B., and R. G. Pippett. 1958. Effect of altitude upon primary taste perception. J. Aviat. Med. 29:386-391.

34. Surks, M. I., K. S. K. Chinn, and L. O. Matoush. 1966. Alterations in body composition in man after acute exposure to high altitude. J. Appl. Physiol. 21:1741-1746.

35. Krzywicki, H. J., C. F. Consolazio, L. O. Matoush, H. L. Johnson, and R. A. Barnhart. 1969. Body composition changes during exposure to altitude. Fed. Proc. 28:1190-1194.

36. Hannon, J. P., J. L. Shields, and C. W. Harris. 1969. Anthropometric changes associated with high altitude acclimatization of women. Am. J. Phys. Anthropol. 31:77-83.

37. Hannon, J. P., G. J. Klain, D. M. Sudman, and F. J. Sullivan. 1976. Nutritional aspects of high altitude exposure. Am. J. Clin. Nutr. 29:604-613.

38. Krzywicki, H. J., C. F. Consolazio, H. L. Johnson, W. C. Nielsen, and R. A. Barnhart. 1971. Water metabolism in humans during acute high-altitude exposure (4,300 m). J. Appl. Physiol. 30:806-809.

39. Halhuber, M. J., and F. Gabl. 1964. 17-OHCS excretion and blood eosinophils at an altitude of 2000 M. In W. H. Weihe, ed. The physiological effects of high altitude. Pergamon Press Ltd., Oxford.

40. Pace, N., R. L. Groswold, and B. W. Grunbaum. 1964. Increase in urinary norepinephrine excretion during 14 days sojourn at 3800 meters elevation. Fed. Proc. 23:521-525.

41. Ayres, P. J., R. C. Hunter, E. S. Williams, and J. Rundo. 1961. Aldosterone excretion and potassium retention in subjects living at high altitude. Nature 191:78-80.

42. Williams, E. S. 1966. Electrolyte regulation during the adaptation of humans to life at high altitudes. Proc. R. Soc. Lond. (Biol.) 165:266-280.

43. Hartroft, P. M., M. B. Bischoff, and T. J. Bucci. 1969. Effects of chronic exposure to high altitude on the juxtaglomerular complex and adrenal cortex of dogs, rabbits and rats. Fed. Proc. 28:1234-1237.

44. Gould, A. B., and S. A. Goodman. 1970. Testos-terone metabolism in men exposed to high altitude. Acta Endocrinol. (Panama) 2:55-58.

45. Frayser, R., I. D. Rennie, G. W. Gray, and C. S. Houston. 1975. Hormonal and electrolyte response to exposure to 17,500 ft. J. Appl. Physiol. 38:636-642.

46. Surks, M. J. 1966. Effects of hypoxia and high altitude on thyroid iodine metabolism in the rat. Endocrinology 78:307-315.

47. Tryon, C. A., W. R. Kodric, and H. M. Cunningham. 1968. Measurement of relative thyroid activity on free-ranging rodents along an altitudinal transect. Nature 218:278-280.

48. Martin, L. G., G. E. Westenberger, and R. W. Bullard. 1971. Thyroidal changes in the rat during acclimatization to simulated high altitude. Am. J. Physiol. 221:1057-1063.

49. Galton, V. A. 1972. Some effects of altitude on thyroid function. Endocrinology 91:1393-1394.

50. Kotchen, T. A., E. H. Mougey, R. P. Hogan, A. E. Boyd III, L. L. Pennington, and J. W. Mason. 1973. Thyroid responses to simulated altitude. J. Appl. Physiol. 34:165-168.

51. Guerra-Garcia, R. 1971. Testosterone metabolism in men exposed to high altitude. Acta Endocrinol. (Panama) 2:55-62.

52. Donayre, J. R., R. Guerra-Garcia, F. Moncloa, and L. A. Sobrevilla. 1968. Endocrinological studies at high altitude. IV. Changes in the semen of men. J. Reprod. Fertil. 16:55-58.

53. Donayre, J. 1966. Population growth and fertility at high altitude. In Life at high altitudes. Pub. 140. Pan American Health Organization, Washington, D.C.

54. Altland, P. D. 1949. Effects of discontinuous exposure to 25,000 feet simulated altitude on growth and reproduction of the albino rat. J. Exp. Zool. 110:1-18.

55. Monge, M., and C. Mori-Charez. 1942. Fisiologia de la reproduccion en la altura. An. Fac. Med. Lima (Peru) 25:34-42.

56. Donayre, J. 1969. The oestrus cyle of rats at high altitude. J. Reprod. Fertil. 18:29-32.

57. Altland, P. D., and B. Highman. 1964. Effects of age and exercise on altitude tolerance in rats. In W. H. Weihe, ed. The physiological effects of high altitude. Pergamon Press Ltd., Oxford.

58. Klein, K. E. 1964. Discussion of paper by Altland and Highman (1964). In W. H. Weihe, ed. The physiological effects of high altitude. The Macmillan Co., New York.

59. Dill, D. B., J. W. Terman, and F. G. Hall. 1963. Hemoglobin at high altitude as related to age. Clin. Chem. 9:710-716.

60. Jung, R. C., D. B. Dill, R. Horton, and S. M. Horvath. 1971. Effects of age on plasma aldosterone levels and hemoconcentration at altitude. J. Appl. Physiol. **31**:593-997.
61. Weitz, C. A. 1973. The effects of aging and habitual activity on exercise performance among a high altitude Himalayan population. Ph.D. Thesis. Pennsylvania State University, University Park, Pa.
62. Hickam, J. B., and R. Frazer. 1966. Studies of the retinal circulation in man. Circulation. **33**:302-308.

9 | Functional adaptation to high altitude

After the initial effects of and responses to high altitude, usually characterized by the onset and disappearance of the symptoms of acute mountain sickness, gradual adaptive responses develop, some of which require months or many years for complete development. The various systemic and cell responses, which together permit the organism to function normally with low oxygen availability, develop at different rates. Some increase progressively for many months; others reach an early peak and then subside; and others require exposure during the organism's period of growth and development. It must be noted that many of the observed adjustments begin in the first few hours at high altitude, even though the results are manifested days or months later. For this reason, in this chapter the emphasis is not on tracing the chronological manifestation of a given response but on evaluating the relative interaction of various systemic and cell changes in the adaptive process. For this purpose, the physiological information derived from sea level natives exposed to high alti-

tudes for varying periods and from high-altitude natives will be compared. Furthermore, the discussion will also show that changes occurring during growth and development are of major importance in explaining the functional adaptation attained by the high-altitude native.

ACCLIMATIZATION

The various adaptive mechanisms triggered by exposure to high altitude are directed toward increasing the availability of oxygen and the pressure of oxygen at the tissue level. This is accomplished through modifications in (1) pulmonary ventilation, (2) lung volume and pulmonary diffusing capacity, (3) transport of oxygen in the blood, (4) diffusion of oxygen from blood to tissues, and (5) utilization of oxygen at the tissue level. (See Fig. 9-14.)

Pulmonary ventilation

On exposure to high-altitude hypoxia, sea level natives show, both at rest and during exercise, a progressive increase in pulmo-

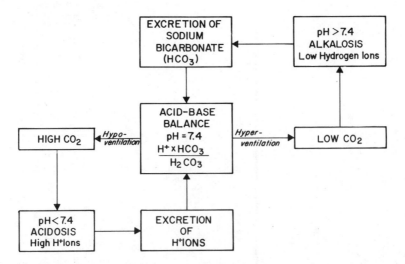

Fig. 9-1. Schematization of acid-base balance maintenance with acclimatization to high-altitude hypoxia. During acclimatization to high altitude excretion of sodium bicarbonate is increased to counteract alkalosis and maintain acid-base balance.

nary ventilation that may reach as much as 100% of sea level values.[1-3] Such hyperventilation is both adaptive and nonadaptive. It is adaptive because it increases the partial pressure of oxygen at the alveolar and arterial levels and consequently increases the diffusion gradient between blood and tissues. It is nonadaptive because it decreases the partial pressure of carbon dioxide at the alveolar level (Pa_{CO_2}) and, if this is not compensated for, it may change the pH of the blood from a normal (pH = 7.4) to an alkaline state (pH > 7.4), resulting in alkalosis. Since the pH is a function of hydrogen concentration as schematized in Fig. 9-1, the organism during acclimatization to high altitude increases the rate of bicarbonate excretion, which shifts the pH of the blood and cerebrospinal fluid back to normal.[4-6] In this manner the original homeokinetic relationship between the pH of the cerebrospinal fluid and the blood is restored to a sea level condition. It is this equilibrium that enables the lowland native acclimatized to high altitude to sustain an increased ventilation without the risk of alkalosis or hypocapnia.

As shown by recent analyses of both lowland and high-altitude natives,[5] the increase in pulmonary ventilation during exercise is directly proportional to the increase in altitude. However, at a given altitude, as shown in Fig. 9-2, pulmonary ventilation during exercise of the sea level native (sojourning on a short-term or long-term basis at high altitudes) is invariably higher than that of the high-altitude native.[6-17]

The sea level native's acclimatization to high altitude is associated unquestionably with an increase in pulmonary ventilation. In the highland native, however, acclimatization to high altitude is accompanied by a lesser increase in pulmonary ventilation. Since the increase in pulmonary ventilation permits the newcomer to maintain an increase in P_{O_2} at the alveolar level and an increase in arterial oxygen saturation,[5] it would

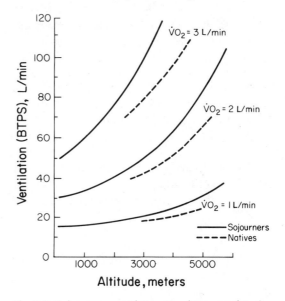

Fig. 9-2. Pulmonary ventilation in relation to altitude in lowlander sojourners to high altitude and highland natives measured at rest and at two levels of exercise. With exercise ($\dot{V}O_2$ = oxygen consumption of 2 and 3 L/min) ventilation increases much more at altitude than at sea level; this increase is much greater in sojourners than in highland natives. (From Lenfant, C., and K. Sullivan. 1971. Reprinted by permission from The New England Journal of Medicine **284:**1298-1309.)

appear that a hyperventilatory response is critical to the newcomer's acclimatization. However, after acclimatization occurs, the increase in pulmonary ventilation plateaus, probably reflecting the operation of other adaptive mechanisms. Studies on ventilatory sensitivity indicate that high-altitude natives have a hypoxic chemoreceptor insensitivity.[18-23] This insensitivity can be acquired by sea level natives if they are exposed to high altitudes throughout growth and development.[24,25] However, other studies indicate that it can also be acquired by adults through prolonged residence at high altitudes.[26,27]

Lung volume

On initial exposure to high-altitude hypoxia the vital capacities and residual lung volumes of sea level natives are reduced, but after 1 month at high altitudes, such subjects attain values which are comparable to those they had at sea level.[28-32] In contrast, as shown in Fig. 9-3, highland natives have larger lung volumes and residual volumes than sea level natives when adjustments are made for differences in body size.[6,7,34]

Investigations in Ethiopia demonstrated that highlanders living above 3000 m have a significantly greater forced vital capacity than their lower altitude counterparts (Fig. 9-4). Furthermore, evaluation of the respiratory function of migrant groups demonstrated that the enlarged forced vital capacity of the highland Ethiopian can be acquired by lowland natives who migrate to high altitudes.[33]

Current evidence suggests that the enlarged lung volume of the high-altitude native results from adaptations acquired during the developmental period.[25,34-38] As shown in Fig. 9-5, the sea level natives who were

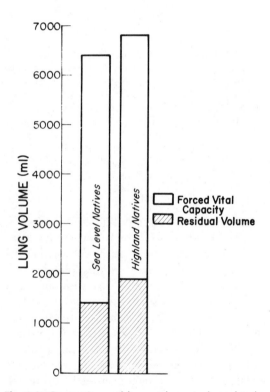

Fig. 9-3. Comparison of lung volumes of sea level and high-altitude natives. Lung volume, especially residual lung volume, is increased among highland natives. (From Hurtado, A. 1964. Animals in high altitudes: resident man. In D. B. Dill, E. F. Adolph, and C. G. Wilber, eds. Handbook of physiology. vol 4. Adaptation to the environment. American Physiological Society, Washington, D.C.)

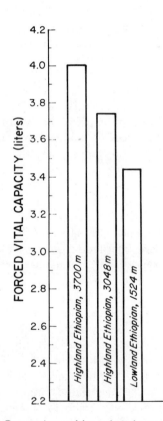

Fig. 9-4. Comparison of forced vital capacity of lowland and highland Ethiopean natives. The higher the altitude, the greater the lung volume. (Based on data from Harrison, G. A., C. F. Kuchemann, M. A. S. Moore, A. J. Boyce, T. Baju, A. E. Mourant, M. J. Godber, B. G. Glasgow, A. C. Kopec, D. Tills, and E. J. Clegg. 1969. Philos. Trans. R. Soc. Lond. **256:**147-182.)

acclimatized to high altitudes during growth, when adjustments were made for variations in body size, attained the same forced vital capacity as the high-altitude natives. In contrast sea level natives (Peruvian and white United States subjects) acclimatized as adults had significantly lower vital capacities than high-altitude natives.

The hypothesis that the enlarged lung volume of high-altitude natives results from developmental adaptation is supported by experimental studies on animals. Various

studies[39-43] have demonstrated that young rats, after prolonged exposure to high-altitude hypoxia (3450 m), exhibited an accelerated proliferation of alveolar units and accelerated growth in alveolar surface area and lung volume. In contrast adult rats, after prolonged exposure to high-altitude hypoxia, did not show changes in quantity of alveoli and lung volume.[41,42] Fig. 9-6 shows that rats acclimatized to a high altitude from birth to the age of 131 days develop a greater lung volume than sea level controls. In contrast

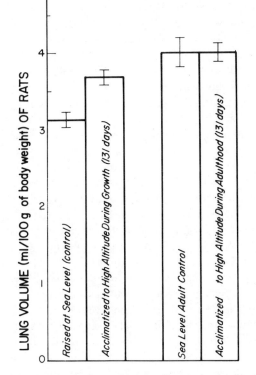

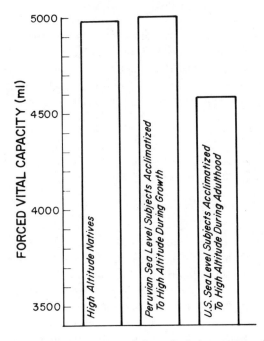

Fig. 9-5. Comparison of forced vital capacity of high-altitude natives, Peruvian sea level subjects acclimatized to high altitude during growth, and United States sea level subjects acclimatized to high altitude during adulthood. Acclimatization to high altitude during growth results in lung volumes similar to those of high-altitude native. (Based on data from Frisancho, A. R., T. Velasquez, and J. Sanchez. 1973. Hum. Biol. **45:**583-594.)

Fig. 9-6. Comparison of lung volume of rats raised at sea level and acclimatized to high altitude during growth and during adulthood. Like humans, acclimatization to high altitude during growth results in enlargement of lung volumes. (Based on data from Burri, P. H., and E. R. Weibel. 1971. Morphometric evaluation of changes in lung structure due to high altitudes. In R. Porter and J. Knight, eds. High altitude physiology. Cardiac and respiratory aspects. Churchill Livingstone, Edinburgh.)

adult rats, who were the mothers of the young rats studied, were acclimatized to a high altitude for the same number of days and had lung volumes similar to the sea level controls. These findings suggest that in experimental animals and humans the attainment of an enlarged lung volume at high altitude is probably mediated by developmental factors.

Pulmonary diffusion capacity

As shown by several studies, acclimatization to high altitudes does not change the oxygen pulmonary diffusing capacity of sea level subjects.[44-46] On the other hand, all studies indicate that the pulmonary diffusing capacity of the highland native is systematically greater than that attained by lowland natives at sea level.[46-50] This difference is probably caused by at least three factors. First, since pulmonary diffusing capacity is related in part to alveolar area, the enhanced pulmonary diffusing capacity of the highland native is probably caused by a greater alveolar area and increased capillary volume. Second, increased oxygen pulmonary diffusing capacity of the highland native may also be related to his high pulmonary pressure. It has been suggested that the high pulmonary pressure that occurs at high altitude is associated with a more uniform perfusion of the lung that may distend patent capillaries and perhaps perfuse capillaries unopened at sea level of sea level natives becoming acclimatized to a high altitude.[51] Third, another probable contributing factor is increased pulmonary ventilation which, along with the increased alveolar and capillary volumes, improves the ratio of ventilation to perfusion.

Transport of oxygen in the blood

The major function of hemoglobin in red blood cells is to transport oxygen from the lungs to the tissues. In response to delivery of insufficient oxygen, the bone marrow is stimulated by an erythropoietic factor to increase production of red blood cells.[52-54] For this reason, at altitudes above 3500 m both sea level and high-altitude natives have normal red blood cell counts ranging from 5 to 8 million/cu mm compared to the 4.5 million at sea level. Along with an increase in red blood cells, the hemoglobin is augmented; for sea level natives living above 3500 m the average concentrations range from 16 to 20 g/100 ml compared to the 14.8 g/100 ml for sea level natives.[53-58] In this way the oxygen-carrying capacity of the blood at high altitude is increased. It must be noted, however, that among high-altitude natives there are marked differences in hemoglobin concentration depending on the region of residence. For example, in Peru the mean hemoglobin concentration for natives of the central highlands residing at 4000 m is about 20 g/100 ml,[67,55] whereas for natives of the southern highlands residing at the same altitude the hemoglobin concentration does not exceed 18 g/100 ml.[57] These differences can be partially explained by the fact that in the central highlands high-altitude hypoxia is compounded by additional hypoxia from mining activities.

Diffusion of oxygen from blood to tissues

Capillaries. For oxygen to be used it must reach the cell mitochondria through a process of physical diffusion. The rate of such diffusion depends on the partial pressure of the oxygen. Because oxygen is consumed as it goes through successive layers, the partial pressure of oxygen declines with the increase in distance that the oxygen has to travel. Since the partial pressure of oxygen in the ambient air is already low at high altitudes, the organism must respond by shortening the distance the oxygen has to travel. This is accomplished by the opening up of existing capillaries and the formation of new capillaries. Through microscopic studies of experimental animals it has been found that the number of open muscle capillaries at high altitude are increased more than 40% when compared to sea level values.[59-62] A very important effect of an increased capillary bed is that it increases the blood perfusion; thus, oxygen is more readily diffused into tissue in spite of a lowered oxygen tension of the blood before it reaches the capillaries.[63]

Myoglobin. The rate of diffusion of oxygen from the capillaries to the cell mitochondria is also aided by increased amounts of tissue myoglobin.

Myoglobin is a protein found in high concentrations in muscles that carry out sustained or periodic work. It has a molecular weight of about 17,500 and consists of 152 amino acid residues and one iron-containing heme group. Studies on humans and animals at high altitudes indicate a high concentration of myoglobin in the sartorius muscle.[64-67] Proteins of low molecular weight such as myoglobin facilitate diffusion of oxygen from capillaries to the mitochondria by random movement interspersed with larger advances of translational and rotational movements.[68,69] It is quite reasonable to assume that at high altitude the increased concentration of myoglobin is an adaptive response to facilitate diffusion of oxygen from the capillaries to the cell mitochondria.

Oxygen-hemoglobin dissociation. The increased red cell count and hemoglobin concentration associated with exposure to high altitude results in increased oxygen-carrying capacity of the blood. However, in spite of an increased oxygen-carrying capacity at 3151 m, the arterial blood is only 87% saturated with oxygen compared to being 97% saturated at sea level. Therefore, at high altitude to provide an adequate supply of oxygen to the tissues the hemoglobin must increase the rate of oxygen delivery to the cell. It must be noted that one basis for oxygen transport from lung to tissues is that oxygen combines strongly with hemo-

globin when the partial pressure of oxygen is high, as in the pulmonary capillaries; when the partial pressure of oxygen is low, as in the tissue capillaries, oxygen is released freely. In other words, the hemoglobin affinity for oxygen is inversely related to the partial pressure of oxygen. Physiologists express this affinity in terms of the partial pressure of oxygen in plasma (P_{O_2}) associated with 50% oxygen saturation of blood at 37° C and a pH of 7.4, known as the *oxygen-hemoglobin dissociation curve*. Several studies have shown that at high altitude a decreased hemoglobin-oxygen affinity and a right shift of the oxygen dissociation curve is an adaptive response to hypoxia.[2,3,70-74] As shown in Table 6 and Fig. 9-7, at sea level 97% of the arterial blood is saturated with oxygen, and the venous blood is about 70% saturated with oxygen, resulting in a desaturation of 27% (97 − 70 = 27%). On the other hand, at 3151 m the arterial blood is 87% saturated with oxygen, and the venous blood is 62% saturated with oxygen. Thus, at high altitude hemoglobin, as shown by the low percent oxygen saturation of the venous blood, has a decreased affinity for oxygen, and the oxygen-dissociation curve is shifted to the right. As a result of the decreased hemoglobin-oxygen affinity at high altitude the proportion (87 − 62 = 25%) of available oxygen that is delivered to the tissues is similar to that delivered at sea level (97 − 70 = 27%).

The advantage of the decreased affinity for oxygen of hemoglobin depends on the altitude. Below an elevation of 3500 m a decrease in oxygen affinity is quite favorable, but at higher altitudes the advantage is very small.[5] At an altitude higher than 3500 m the partial pressure of oxygen in the alveoli decreases greatly, and the oxygen uptake of the blood in the lungs is impaired (Table 6). Therefore, at altitudes above 3500 m the beneficial effects of decreased oxygen affinity with hemoglobin in the tissues is counterbalanced by the decreased oxygen loading in

Table 6. Effects of altitude and barometric pressure on pressure of oxygen in the air, trachea, alveoli, and arterial and venous blood and oxygen saturation in the arterial and venous blood*

Altitude (m)	Barometric pressure (mm Hg)	Partial pressure of oxygen (P_{O_2})					Oxygen saturation	
		Air (mm Hg)	Trachea (mm Hg)	Alveoli (mm Hg)	Arterial blood (mm Hg)	Venous blood (mm Hg)	Arterial blood (%)	Venous blood (%)
0	760	159	149	96	90	42	97	70
3048	523	110	100	67	62	40	90	65
3151	515	108	98	65	60	36	87	62
3735	493	103	93	60	50	34	81	59
4340	458	96	86	50	46	33	75	55
4540	446	93	83	47	44	32	73	55
5791	364	79	69	45	40	26	60	50

*Based on data from Torrance, J. D., C. Lenfant, J. Cruz, and E. Marticorena. 1970-1971. **Respir. Physiol. 11:**1-15; Moore, L. G. 1973. Red blood cell adaptation to high altitude: mechanism of the 2,3 diphosphoglycerate response Ph.D. Thesis. University of Michigan, Ann Arbor, Mich.; Hurtado, A. 1964. Animals in high altitudes: resident man. In D. B. Dill, E. F. Adolph, and C. G. Wilber, eds. Handbook of Physiology. vol 4. Adaptation to the environment. American Physiological Society, Washington, D.C.; and Ward, M. 1975. Mountain medicine. A clinical study of cold and high altitude. Van Nostrand Reinhold Co., New York.

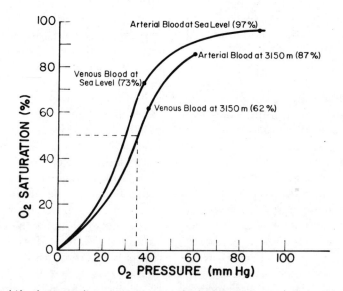

Fig. 9-7. Right shift of oxygen dissociation curve at high altitude compared to sea level. At high altitude the proportion of available oxygen delivered to tissues is equal to that at sea level. (Based on data from Moore, L. G. 1973. Red blood cell adaptation to high altitude: mechanism of the 2,3 diphosphoglycerate response. Ph.D. Thesis. University of Michigan, Ann Arbor, Mich.)

the lungs. For example, at 5791 m the arterial blood is only 70% saturated with oxygen, and the venous blood is 60% saturated with oxygen.

The decrease in hemoglobin affinity for oxygen appears to be related to an increase in intraerythrocytic 2,3-diphosphoglycerate (DPG), which in turn seems related to changes in blood pH.[2,3,71-75] Lenfant, Torrance, and Reynafarje[75] found that in subjects who were made acidotic with acetazolamide when exposed for 4 days to an altitude of 4400 m there were no changes in plasma pH, no increase in 2,3-DPG, and no shift in the oxygen dissociation curve.[75] In contrast, in the control subjects (who were not acidotic) on exposure to altitude the oxygen-hemoglobin dissociation curve shifted rapidly to the right when these subjects were exposed to high altitudes. This shift seemed to be caused by an increase in 2,3-DPG, which in turn was associated with an increase in plasma pH above sea level values.

Thus it appears that the erythrocytic organic phosphates affect the affinity of hemoglobin for oxygen. However, at present the biochemical mechanisms responsible for this change are not well defined. Furthermore, changes in the oxygen-hemoglobin dissociation curve appear more beneficial to the sea level newcomer than the highland native.[2] Studies using rodents and camelids (vicuña, alpaca, and llama) that are native to the highlands indicate a higher hemoglobin-oxygen affinity than those at sea level.[110,111] Similarly, experimental studies on rats indicate that a decreased hemoglobin-oxygen affinity is not adaptive in extreme high altitudes.[112]

Utilization of oxygen

The last step in the process of adaptation to hypoxia involves variations in the rate of oxygen utilization and generation of energy at the cellular level. Based on studies with guinea pigs, it is postulated that at high altitude the carbohydrate metabolism, during its glycolytic (anaerobic) breakdown, goes through the pentose-phosphate pathway rather than the Embden-Meyerhof pathway.[76-79] The advantage in using the pentose-phosphate pathway appears to be the fact that no additional adenosinetriphosphate (ATP) is required to generate glyceraldehyde-3-phosphate as is necessary in the Embden-Meyerhof pathway. According to Reynafarje[79] at high altitude, by relying on the pentose-phosphate pathway, the organism saves energy (ATP) or produces more chemical energy with the same oxygen consumption. This hypothesis is supported by the finding that the activity of oxidative enzymes in the sartorius muscles is greater at high altitudes than at sea level.[76] For example, in the homogenate of whole cells the reduced diphosphopyridine nucleotide (DPNH)-oxidase system and triphosphopyridine nucleotide (TPNH)-cytochrome-c reductase and transhydrogenase are significantly more active in the highland native than in the sea level native.[79] Thus among high-altitude natives the chemical and morphological characteristics related to energy utilization and production appear qualitatively and quantitatively different from those of lowland natives. It is not known whether such characteristics may be acquired by sea level natives residing for long periods at high altitudes.

Cardiovascular traits

Pulmonary circulation. Andean adults maintain an increased arterial pulmonary pressure.[80-83] As shown in Fig. 9-8, in both resting and exercise conditions the systolic and diastolic arterial pulmonary pressure of Peruvian highland natives living at 4330 m is nearly twice that of sea level natives tested at sea level. Histological studies have demonstrated that after the first months of postnatal development, children

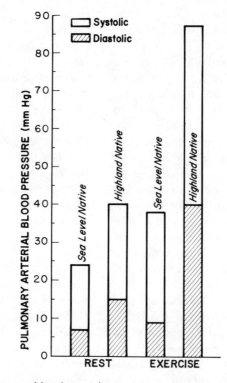

Fig. 9-8. Comparison of pulmonary blood arterial pressure among sea level and high-altitude natives. Both at rest and during exercise high-altitude natives exhibit higher pulmonary pressure than sea level natives. (Based on data from Peñaloza, D., F. Sime, N. Banchero, and R. Gamboa. 1962. Med. Thorac. **19**:449-460.)

born at high altitudes show a thickening of the muscular layer and muscularization of the pulmonary arteries and arterioles that resemble the development of the fetal pulmonary vascular tree.[84,85] These characteristics, along with the viscosity accompanying polycythemia, contribute to the development of greater pulmonary vascular resistance or pulmonary hypertension in the high-altitude resident and native.

Based on studies of steers the hypothesis has been put forward that pulmonary hypertension at high altitudes would favor a more effective perfusion of all the pulmonary areas and, therefore, increase the effective blood gas interfacial area of the alveoli.[51] In this manner perfusion of the entire lung coupled with an increased vascularization would enhance the diffusing capacity of the lung and should decrease the difference between arterial and alveolar blood. These changes would permit more effective arterial blood oxygenation.[51] However, this has not been proven in the acclimatized man, nor can one assume that there will be a consequent decrease in the arterial-alveolar gradient. Therefore the application of this hypothesis to human adaptation remains to be proven.

Heart. As a result of increased pulmonary resistance or hypertension, the workload of the right ventricle of the heart is increased at high altitude. As demonstrated by ana-

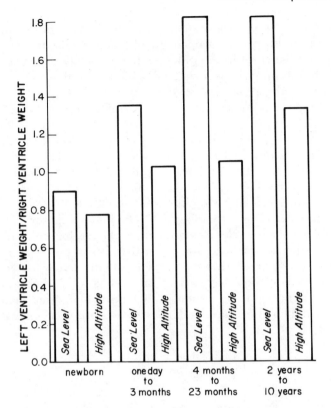

Fig. 9-9. Comparison of left ventricle weight; right ventricle weight ratio among sea level and high-altitude natives at birth, 1 day to 3 months, 4 to 23 months, and 2 to 10 years. Among high-altitude subjects the left ventricle weighs less than right ventricle, a characteristic that becomes apparent after the age of 3 months. (Modified from Arias-Stella, J., and S. Recavarren. 1962. Am. J. Pathol. **41:**55-59.)

tomical and electrocardiographic studies this increased workload leads to an enlargement or hypertrophy of the right ventricle.[80,81,87-90] Fig. 9-9 shows that after the age of 3 months the weight of the right ventricle is greater than that of the left ventricle (ratio is less than 1), and this characteristic is maintained through childhood to adulthood. On the other hand, at sea level from infancy to adulthood the left ventricle weighs more than the right ventricle (ratio greater than 1.0).

Another factor that may contribute to the enlargement of the right ventricle is the high incidence of patent ductus arteriosus. Of 5000 school children of both sexes born at high altitudes, 0.72% had a patent ductus

arteriosus compared to 0.04% of sea level children.[91,92] This increased incidence of patent ductus arteriosus is probably a consequence of fetal and newborn hypoxia. It should be noted that during the prenatal stage when the lungs are not yet expanded, blood pressure in the pulmonary arteries exceeds that in the aorta so that blood flows from the pulmonary artery to the aorta through the ductus arteriosus. After birth, with the interruption of umbilical circulation and expansion of the lungs, the blood pressure falls sharply in the pulmonary arteries and rises in the systemic circulation. As a result the flow of blood is from the aorta to pulmonary artery (rather than the prebirth flow from the pulmonary artery to the aorta). Thus, if the ductus arteriosus remains open it acts as a shunt from the aorta to the pulmonary artery where the pressure is lower, and hence the work of the right ventricle of the heart is increased. For these reasons it is quite possible that the incidence of patent ductus arteriosus may also be another source of the right ventricular hypertrophy of high-altitude populations. Lowland natives with patent ductus arteriosus commonly suffer from right ventricular hypertrophy and pulmonary stenosis. These findings demonstrate the influence of developmental factors in the acquisition of the cardiovascular characteristics of highland dwellers. This does not mean, however, that preponderance of the right ventricle cannot be acquired during adulthood because adult rats in a hypobaric chamber to 5500 m developed right ventricular enlargement over a period of only 5 weeks along with muscularization of the small pulmonary arterial vessels.[93]

Cardiac output and stroke volume. The stroke volume (SV) is defined as the volume of blood pumped from the heart with each beat. The cardiac output (Q) is the total volume of blood pumped by the heart each minute. It is the product of stroke volume and heart rate.

On initial exposure to high-altitude hypoxia the resting pulse rate of the sea level native, because of a generalized increase in sympathetic activity, increases rapidly from an average of 70 beats/min to as much as 105 beats/min. This increase is associated with an abrupt augmentation of the resting

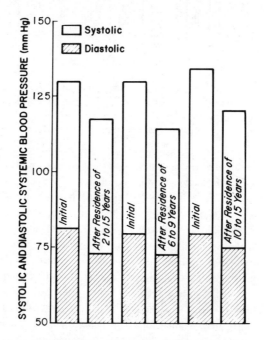

Fig. 9-10. Comparison of systemic blood pressure among sea level subjects acclimatized to high altitude. Prolonged residence at high altitude is associated with reduction in systolic and diastolic blood pressure. (Based on data from Marticorena, E., L. Ruiz, J. Severino, J. Galvez, and D. Peñaloza. 1969. Am. J. Cardiol. **23:**364-368.)

cardiac output.[94,95] With acclimatization the cardiac output and stroke volume decline; in about 1 week they are equal to or below those attained at sea level.[5,96-99] This decline in cardiac output and stroke volume seems associated with a decrease in heart rate, which usually remains above sea level values. The cardiac output of high altitude natives during rest and exercise was found to be equal to that attained at sea level.[83] Therefore oxygen requirements of the body at high altitude appear to be met by greater oxygen extraction rather than by greater blood flow.

Systemic blood pressure. Various studies indicate that the systemic blood pressure levels in adult high-altitude natives are lower than those observed at sea level.[100] Epidemiological studies report that among high-altitude natives the frequency of essential hypertension and ischemic heart disease are significantly lower than among their counterparts at sea level.[101] Furthermore, prolonged residence at high altitude results in lowering of systolic and diastolic pressures in sea level subjects.[102] As shown in Fig. 9-10 in adult sea level white males aged 25 to 66 years residing in Peru at an altitude of 3750 m, the systolic pressure after a residence of 2 to 15 years declines by as much as 14 mm Hg and diastolic pressure by as much as 7 mm Hg. The decrease in systemic blood pressure indicates that chronic hypoxia has a relaxing effect on smooth muscle—the effect on the arterial media is vasodilation.[103] Furthermore, because exposure to high-altitude hypoxia results in increased vascularization,[59-62] it is possible that the prevalence of low blood pressure at high altitude may be related to a reduction in peripheral vascular resistance to blood flow. In other words, lower blood pressure may also be considered a by-product of tissue adaptation to high-altitude hypoxia.

Work capacity and maximal oxygen intake

Oxygen consumption, or oxygen uptake, is a basic biological function that reflects the total metabolic work being done by the organism. With increased metabolic requirements during maximal exercise oxygen consumption may increase from an average resting value between 200 and 350 ml/min to as much as 5 L/min. The rate of oxygen consumption is a product of the cardiac output and the difference in oxygen content between the venous and arterial blood. The rate of oxygen consumption can also be expressed as a product of heart rate, stroke volume, and the difference in oxygen content between the venous and arterial blood. Therefore, the rate of oxygen consumption during exercise can be affected by changes in heart rate, stroke volume, and rate of oxygen extraction determined by the difference in oxygen content between the venous and arterial blood. Thus, during severe exercise the metabolic requirement for oxygen increases drastically, and all the processes involved in the transport, delivery, and utilization of oxygen are required to work at their maximum. For this reason the effects of high-altitude hypoxia are most evident during periods of hard work. Thus measurements of an individual's work capacity indicate the degree of success of the various adaptive responses he has made.

It is generally agreed that the maximum oxygen intake per unit of body weight (or aerobic capacity) during maximal work is a measure of the individual's work capacity because it reflects the capacity of the working muscles to use oxygen and the ability of the cardiovascular system to transport and deliver oxygen to the tissues. The rate of oxygen consumption increases linearly with the magnitude of work. As an exercising subject approaches the point of exhaustion or fatigue, his oxygen consumption will reach a maximum and remain at that level even with further increase in work. This peak value is referred to as the individual's *maximal oxygen intake*. Maximum oxygen intake may be obtained directly or indirectly. By the direct approach maximum oxygen intake, along with respiratory volume, is obtained while the subject is performing a maximal or exhaustive work task for short time periods (9 to 15 minutes), either on a stationary bicycle ergometer or a treadmill. By the indirect approach maximum oxygen intake is derived from measurements of oxygen intake and pulse rate (or respiratory frequency) while performing submaximal work for longer periods (20 to 45 minutes). The maximum oxygen intake is then applied to previously established regression equations. In general the indirect method is less accurate and gives lower values for maximum oxygen intake than those obtained by the direct method.

Newcomers to high altitudes. Studies among sea level newcomers to high altitude demonstrated a reduction in aerobic capacity of 13% to 22%.[10] As shown in Fig. 9-11, the maximum aerobic capacity of well-trained sea level subjects, when expressed as percent of the sea level values, declined by 11% for every 1000 m (3000 feet) ascended beyond 1500 m (5000 feet). In contrast, the aerobic capacity of high-altitude natives is comparable to that attained by lowland natives at sea level.[1,9-17,107-109] It must also be noted that the observed decreases in aerobic capacity at high altitude are influenced very little by physical conditioning. In fact the decrease in aerobic capacity at high altitude has been observed to be proportional to the extent of training; athletes show the greatest decrease, sedentary individuals the least, and active subjects an intermediate decrease.[10-12]

Developmental response. As demonstrated by studies of sea level migrants residing at high altitude, the attainment of a normal aerobic capacity at high altitude appears to be the result of adaptations acquired during the period of growth.[14,36] As shown in Fig. 9-12 sea level subjects, when acclimatized to high altitude during childhood and adolescence, attained an aerobic capacity (maximum oxygen intake) that was equal to that of the highland natives. In contrast sea level natives (Peruvian and white United States subjects), when acclimatized to high altitudes as adults, attained significantly lower aerobic capacities than the highland natives. Evaluations of the data indicated that in the sea level subjects who were acclimatized young the volume of air ventilated per unit of oxygen consumed (ventilation equivalent), maximum pulse rate, and the volume of

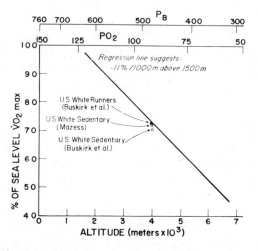

Fig. 9-11. Mean percentage reduction in maximal oxygen utilization (V̇O₂ max) from sea level values for groups abruptly exposed to a high altitude of 4000 m at Nuñoa, Peru. The aerobic capacity of sea level subjects on exposure to high altitude declines 11% for every 1000 m above 1500 m. (From Buskirk, E. R. 1976. Work performance of newcomers to the Peruvian highlands. In P. T. Baker and M. A. Little, eds. Man in the Andes: a multidisciplinary study of high-altitude Quechua natives. Dowden, Hutchinson, & Ross, Inc., Stroudsburg, Pa.)

oxygen consumption per pulse rate were comparable to those of the highland natives. On the other hand, the lowland subjects (Peruvian and United States) attained significantly higher ventilation ratios and lower heart rates than the highland natives.[14]

The extent to which developmental factors influence the attainment of aerobic capacity at high altitude is also illustrated in Fig. 9-13. These data show that among sea level natives acclimatized to high altitude in the developmental period, the attainment of aerobic capacity is directly related to age at migration and length of residency. In contrast when subjects were acclimatized to high altitude as adults, age at migration and length of residency did not influence the attainment of aerobic capacity. From these investigations it appears that the attainment of normal aerobic capacity at high altitude is

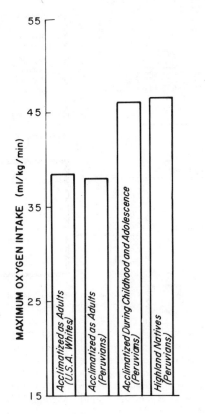

Fig. 9-12. Comparison of aerobic capacity among subjects acclimatized to high altitude during growth and adulthood and subjects native to high altitude. Acclimatization to high altitude during developmental period is associated with attainment of aerobic capacity similar to high-altitude native. (Based on data from Frisancho, A. R., C. Martinez, T. Velasquez, J. Sanchez, and H. Montoye. 1973. J. Appl. Physiol. **34:**176-180.)

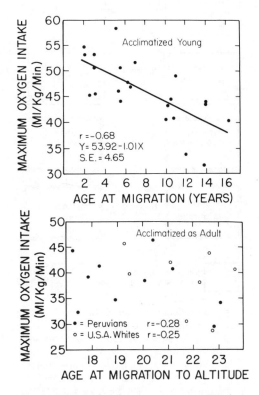

Fig. 9-13. Relationship between age at migration to high altitude and attainment of aerobic capacity among Peruvian and United States sea level natives. Among subjects acclimatized to high altitudes during developmental period, age at migration is significantly correlated with aerobic capacity; this is not the case if subjects are acclimatized as adults. (Modified from Frisancho, A. R., C. Martinez, T. Velasquez, J. Sanchez, and H. Montoye. 1973. J. Appl. Physiol. **34:**176-180.)

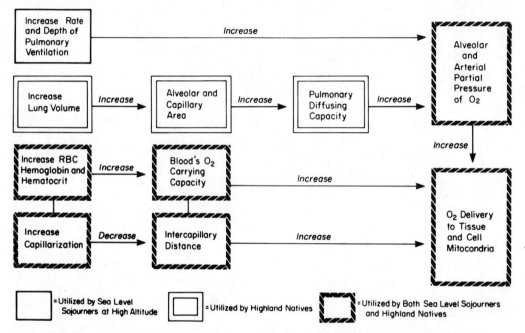

Fig. 9-14. Schematic representation of adaptive pathways elicited by high-altitude hypoxia. Adaptation to high-altitude hypoxia results in series of coordinated mechanisms oriented toward increasing oxygen supply at tissue level. Lowland and highland natives use different paths to acclimatize to high-altitude hypoxia. Whereas systems for increased oxygen-carrying capacity of the blood and augmented capillarization are operative in both lowland and the highland natives, increased pulmonary ventilation is used mostly by lowland native (RBC = red blood cell). (Modified from Frisancho, A. R. 1975. Science **187**:313-319.)

influenced by adaptations acquired during the developmental period.[14,36]

CONCLUSION

Acclimatization to high-altitude hypoxia is a complex phenomenon that develops through the modification and synchronized interdependence of the respiratory, circulatory, and cardiovascular systems to improve oxygen delivery and oxygen utilization. These various adaptive mechanisms that enable both the lowland and highland native to overcome the hypoxic stress of high altitudes are schematized in Fig. 9-14.

In both the sea level sojourner and the highland native adaptation to the low availability of oxygen results in the operation of a variety of coordinated mechanisms oriented toward increasing the oxygen supply and oxygen delivery to the tissue cells (Fig. 9-14). However, the lowland native and the highland native use different paths to acclimatize to high-altitude hypoxia. Whereas both the lowland and highland native use the increase in oxygen-carrying capacity of the blood, augmented capillarization, and enhanced enzymatic activity to acclimatize, it is mainly the lowland native who uses the increase in pulmonary ventilation. That acclimatization of the highland native does not depend on hyperventilation is perhaps caused in part by the highland native's enlarged lung volume that facilitates receiving an adequate oxygen supply at the alveolar level. The low dependence of hyperventilation in spite of arterial hypoxemia in the high-altitude native would suggest a difference in the reactivity of the peripheral chemoreceptors.

Recent investigations suggest that the acquisition of an enlarged lung volume and chest size[34,38] and attainment of normal aerobic capacity[14] at high altitude are in-fluenced by developmental factors. Studies of cardiac morphology[80-90] indicate that the enlarged right ventricle of the heart characteristic of the high-altitude native is acquired during the developmental period. Furthermore, studies on chemoreceptor sensitivity indicate that the hyposensitivity that characterizes the high-altitude native is acquired during growth and development.[24,25] From these studies emerges the conclusion that differences between highland and sea level natives in physiological performance and morphology of the organs of the oxygen transport system are caused in part by adaptations acquired during the developmental period.

During growth and development environmental factors are constantly conditioning and modifying the expression of inherited potentials. The environmental influences felt by the organism depend on the type of stress imposed and especially on the age at which the individual is subjected to the stress. Hence, the respective contributions of genetic and environmental factors vary with the developmental stage of the organism; in general, the earlier the age, the greater the environmental influence. For these reasons it would be surprising if developmental processes did not influence the functional performance and morphology of the high-altitude native. At present, however, the extent to which this conclusion is applicable to the other physiological traits that characterize the highland native is not known. For example, it is now generally accepted that the attainment of low systemic blood pressure at high altitude does not depend on developmental factors because it can be acquired by long-term residency at high altitude.[102] Similarly, it is not known how and by what mechanisms high-altitude hypoxia induces the development of highland native characteristics.

REFERENCES

1. Grover, R. F., J. T. Reeves, E. B. Grover, and J. S. Leathers. 1967. Muscular exercise in young men native to 3,100 m altitude. J. Appl. Physiol. **22**:555-564.
2. Torrance, J. D., C. Lenfant, J. Cruz, and E. Marticorena. 1970-1971. Oxygen transport mechanisms in residents at high altitude. Respir. Physiol. **11**:1-15.
3. Lenfant, C., J. D. Torrance, E. English, C. A. Finch, C. Reynafarje, J. Ramos, and J. Faura. 1968. Effect of altitude on oxygen binding by hemoglobin and on organic phosphate levels. J. Clin. Invest. **47**:2652-2656.
4. Severinghaus, J., and A. Carcelen. 1964. Cerebrospinal fluid in man native to high altitude. J. Appl. Physiol. **19**:319-323.
5. Lenfant, C., and K. Sullivan. 1971. Adaptation to high altitude. N. Engl. J. Med. **284**:1298-1309.
6. Hurtado, A. 1964. Animals in high altitudes: resident man. In D. B. Dill, E. F. Adolph, and C. G. Wilber, eds. Handbook of physiology. vol 4. Adaptation to the environment. American Physiological Society, Washington, D.C.
7. Hurtado, A., T. Velasquez, C. Reynafarje, R. Lozano, R. Chavez, H. Aste-Salazar, B. Reynafarje, C. Sanchez, and J. Muñoz. 1956. Mechanisms of natural acclimatization: studies on the native resident of Morococha, Peru, at an altitude of 14,000 feet. Rep. 56-1. U.S. Air Force School of Aviation Medicine, Randolph Field, Texas.
8. Lahiri, S., and J. S. Milledge. 1965. Sherpa physiology. Nature **207**:610-612.
9. Lahiri, S., J. S. Milledge, H. P. Chattopadhyay, A. K. Bhattacharyya, and A. K. Sinha. 1967. Respiration and heart rate of Sherpa highlanders during exercise. J. Appl. Physiol. **23**:545-554.
10. Buskirk, E. R. 1976. Work performance of newcomers to the Peruvian highlands. In P. T. Baker and M. A. Little, eds. Man in the Andes: a multidisciplinary study of high-altitude Quechua natives. Dowden, Hutchinson, & Ross, Inc., Stroudsburg, Pa.
11. Kollias, J., E. R. Buskirk, R. F. Akers, E. K. Prokop, P. T. Baker, and E. Piconreategui. 1968. Work capacity of long-time residents and newcomers to altitude. J. Appl. Physiol. **24**:792-799.
12. Mazess, R. B. 1969. Exercise performance of indian and white high altitude residents. Hum. Biol. **41**:494-518.
13. Mazess, R. B. 1969. Exercise performance at high altitude (4000 meters) in Peru. Fed. Proc. **28**: 1301-1306.
14. Frisancho, A. R., C. Martinez, T. Velásquez, J. Sanchez, and H. Montoye. 1973. Influence of developmental adaptation on aerobic capacity at high altitude. J. Appl. Physiol. **34**:176-180.
15. Velásquez, T. 1966. Acquired acclimatization to sea level. In Life at high altitudes. Pub. 140. Pan American Health Organization, Washington, D.C.
16. Velásquez, T. 1970. Aspects of physical activity in high altitude natives. Am. J. Phys. Anthropol. **32**:251-258.
17. Velásquez, T., and B. Reynafarje. 1966. Metabolic and physiological aspects of exercise at high altitude. Part 2. Response of natives to different levels of workload breathing air and various oxygen mixtures. Fed. Proc. **25**:1400-1402.
18. Chiodi, H. 1957. Respiratory adaptation to chronic high altitude hypoxia. J. Appl. Physiol. **10**:81-87.
19. Lefrançois, R., H. Gautier, and P. Pasquis. 1968. Ventilatory oxygen drive in acute and chronic hypoxia. Respir. Physiol. **4**:217-228.
20. Lahiri, S., F. F. Kao, T. Velásquez, C. Martinez, and W. Pezzia. 1969. Irreversible blunted respiratory sensitivity to hypoxia in high altitude natives. Respir. Physiol. **6**:360-374.
21. Lahiri, S., F. F. Kao, T. Velásquez, C. Martinez, and W. Pezzia. 1970. Respiration of man during exercise at high altitude: highlander vs lowlander. Respir. Physiol. **8**:361-375.
22. Velásquez, T., C. Martinez, W. Pezzia, and N. Gallardo. 1968. Ventilatory effects of oxygen in high altitude natives. Respir. Physiol. **5**:211-220.
23. Severinghaus, J. W., C. R. Bainton, and A. Carcelen. 1966. Respiratory insensitivity to hypoxia in chronically hypoxic man. Respir. Physiol. **1**:308-334.
24. Forster, H. V., J. A. Dempsey, M. L. Birnbaum, W. G. Reddan, J. Thoden, R. F. Grover, and J. Rankin. 1971. Effect of chronic exposure to hypoxia on ventilatory response to CO_2 and hypoxia. J. Appl. Physiol. **31**:586-592.
25. Lahiri, S., R. G. Delàney, J. S. Brody, M. Simpser, T. Velásquez, E. K. Motoyama, and C. Polgar. 1976. Relative role of environmental and genetic factors in respiratory adaptation to high altitude. Nature **261**:133-135.
26. Byrne-Quinn, E., I. E. Sodal, and J. V. Weil. 1972. Hypoxic and hypercapnic ventilatory drives in children native to high altitude. J. Appl. Physiol. **32**:44-46.
27. Weil, J. V., E. Byrne-Quinn, I. E. Sodal, G. F. Filley, and R. F. Grover. 1971. Acquired attenuation of chemoreceptor function in chronically hy-

poxic man at high altitude. J. Clin. Invest. **50:** 186-195.

28. Tenney, S. M., H. Rahn, R. C. Stroud, and J. C. Mithorfer. 1952. Adaptation to high altitude: changes in lung volumes during the first seven days at Mt. Evans, Colorado. J. Appl. Physiol. **5:**607-613.

29. Rahn, H., and D. Hammond. 1952. The vital capacity at reduced barometric pressure. J. Appl. Physiol. **4:**715-722.

30. Ulvedal, F., T. E. Morgan, Jr., R. G. Cutler, and B. E. Welch. 1963. Ventilatory capacity during prolonged exposure to simulated altitude without hypoxia. J. Appl. Physiol. **18:**904-908.

31. Consolazio, C. F., H. G. Johnson, L. O. Matoush, R. A. Nelson, and G. J. Isaac. 1967. Respiratory function in normal young adults at 3475 and 4300 meters. Rep. 300 U.S. Army Medical Research and Nutrition Laboratory, Fitzsimons General Hospital, Denver, Colo.

32. Shields, J. L., J. P. Hannon, C. W. Harris, and W. S. Platner. 1968. Effects of altitude acclimatization on pulmonary function in women. J. Appl. Physiol. **25:**606-609.

33. Harrison, G. A., C. F. Kuchemann, M. A. S. Moore, A. J. Boyce, T. Baju, A. E. Mourant, M. J. Godber, B. G. Glasgow, A. C. Kopec, D. Tills, and E. J. Clegg. 1969. The effects of altitudinal variation in Ethiopian populations. Philos. Trans. R. Soc. Lond. **256:**147-182.

34. Frisancho, A. R., T. Velásquez, and J. Sanchez. 1973. Influences of developmental adaptation on lung function at high altitude. Hum. Biol. **45:**583-594.

35. Frisancho, A. R. 1976. Growth and functional development at high altitude. In P. T. Baker and M. A. Little, eds. Man in the Andes: a multidisciplinary study of high-altitude Quechua natives. Dowden, Hutchinson and Ross, Inc., Stroudsburg, Pa.

36. Frisancho, A. R. 1975. Functional adaptation to high altitude hypoxia. Science **187:**313-319.

37. Frisancho, A. R. 1978. Human growth and development among high-altitude populations. In P. T. Baker, ed. The biology of high-altitude peoples. Cambridge University Press, New York.

38. Brody, J. S., S. Lahiri, M. Simpser, E. K. Motoyama, and T. Velásquez. 1977. Lung elasticity and airway dynamics in Peruvian natives to high altitude. J. Appl. Physiol. **42:**245-251.

39. Burri, P. H., and E. R. Weibel. 1971. Morphometric estimation of pulmonary diffusion capacity.

Part 2. Effect of PO_2 on the growing lung. Adaptation of the growing rat lung to hypoxia and hyperhypoxia. Respir. Physiol. **11:**247-264.

40. Bartlett, D. 1972. Postnatal development of the mammalian lung. In R. Goss, ed. Regulation of organ and tissue growth. Academic Press, Inc., New York.

41. Burri, P. H., and E. R. Weibel. 1971. Morphometric evaluation of changes in lung structure due to high altitudes. In R. Porter and J. Knight, eds. High altitude physiology. Cardiac and respiratory aspects. Churchill Livingstone, Edinburgh.

42. Cunningham, E. L., J. S. Brody, and B. P. Jain. 1974. Lung growth induced by hypoxia. J. Appl. Physiol. **37:**362-366.

43. Bartlett, D., Jr., and J. E. Remmers. 1971. Effects of high altitude exposure on the lungs of young rats. Respir. Physiol. **13:**116-125.

44. Kreuzer, F., and P. Van Lookeren Campagne. 1965. Resting pulmonary diffusing capacity for CO and O_2 at high altitude. J. Appl. Physiol. **20:**519-524.

45. Degraff, A. C., Jr., R. F. Grover, J. W. Hammond, Jr., J. M. Miller, and R. L. Johnson, Jr. 1965. Pulmonary diffusing capacity in persons native to high altitude. Clin. Res. **13:**74.

46. DeGraff, A. C., Jr., R. F. Grover, R. L. Johnson, J. W. Hammond, and J. M. Miller. 1970. Diffusing capacity of the lung in Caucasians native to 3,100 m. J. Appl. Physiol. **29:**71-76.

47. Velásquez, T. 1956. Maximal diffusing capacity of the lungs at high altitudes. Rep. 56-108. U.S. Air Force School of Aviation Medicine, Randolph, Texas.

48. Velásquez, T., and E. Florentini. 1966. Maxima capacidad de difucion del pulmon en nativos de la altura. Arch. Inst. Biol. Andina **1:**179-187.

49. Remmers, J. E., and J. C. Mithoefer. 1969. The carbon monoxide diffusing capacity in permanent residents at high altitudes. Respir. Physiol. **6:**233-244.

50. Guleria, J. S., J. N. Pande, P. K. Sethi, and S. B. Roy. 1971. Pulmonary diffusing capacity at high altitude. J. Appl. Physiol. **31:**536-543.

51. Grover, R. F., J. T. Reeves, D. H. Will, and S. G. Blount. 1963. Pulmonary vasoconstriction in steers at high altitudes. J. Appl. Physiol. **18:**567-570.

52. Abbrecht, P. H., and J. K. Littell. 1972. Plasma erythropoietin in men and mice during acclimatization to different altitudes. J. Appl. Physiol. **32:**54-58.

53. Reynafarje, C. 1957. The influence of high altitude on erythropoietic activity. Brookhaven Symp. Biol. **10**:132-146.

54. Reynafarje, C. 1959. Bone-marrow studies in the newborn infant at high altitudes. J. Pediatr. **54**: 152-167.

55. Merino, C. F. 1950. Blood formation and blood destruction in polycythemia of high altitude. Blood **5**:1-31.

56. Bharadwaj, N., A. P. Singh, and M. S. Malhotra. 1973. Body composition of the high altitude natives of Ladakh. A comparison with sea level residents. Hum. Biol. **45**:423-434.

57. Garruto, R. M. 1976. Hematology. In P. T. Baker and M. A. Little, eds. Man in the Andes: a multidisciplinary study of high-altitude Quechua natives. Dowden, Hutchinson & Ross, Inc., Stroudsburg, Pa.

58. Quilici, J. C., and H. Vergnes. 1978. The hematological characteristics of high-altitude peoples. In P. T. Baker, ed. The biology of high-altitude peoples. Cambridge University Press, New York.

59. Becker, E. L., R. G. Cooper, and G. D. Hathaway. 1955. Capillary vascularization in puppies born at simulated altitude of 20,000 feet. J. Appl. Physiol. **8**:166-168.

60. Valdivia, E., M. Watson, and C. M. Dass. 1960. Histologic alterations in muscles of guinea pigs during chronic hypoxia. Arch. Pathol. **69**:199-208.

61. Cassin, S., R. D. Gilbert, and E. M. Johnson. 1966. Capillary development during exposure to chronic hypoxia. SAM-TR-66-16. U.S. Air Force School of Aerospace Medicine, Brooks Air Force Base, Texas.

62. Tenney, S. M., and L. C. Ou. 1970. Physiological evidence for increased tissue capillarity in rats acclimatized to high altitude. Respir. Physiol. **8**: 137-150.

63. Rahn, H. 1966. Introduction to the study of man at high altitudes: conductance of O_2 from the environment to the tissues. In Life at high altitudes. Pub. 140. Pan American Health Organization, Washington, D.C.

64. Hurtado, A., A. Rotts, C. Merino, and J. Pons. 1937. Studies of myoglobin at high altitude. Am. J. Med. Sci. **194**:708-713.

65. Tappan, D. V., and B. Reynafarje. 1957. Tissue pigment manifestations of adaptation to high altitude. Am. J. Physiol. **190**:99-103.

66. Reynafarje, B. 1962. Myoglobin content and enzymatic activity of muscle and altitude adaptation. J. Appl. Physiol. **17**:301-305.

67. Anthony, A., E. Ackerman, and G. K. Strother. 1959. Effects of altitude acclimatization on rat myoglobin: changes in myoglobin of skeletal and cardiac muscle. Am. J. Physiol. **196**:512-516.

68. Wittenberg, J. B. 1965. Myoglobin-facilitated diffusions of oxygen. J. Gen. Physiol. **49** (1):57-74.

69. Scholander, P. F. 1960. Oxygen transport through hemoglobin solutions. Science **131**:585-590.

70. Aste-Salazar, H., and A. Hurtado. 1944. The affinity of hemoglobin for oxygen at sea level and at high altitudes. Am. J. Physiol. **142**:733-743.

71. Brewer, G. J., J. W. Eaton, J. V. Weil, and R. F. Grover. 1970. Studies of red cell glycolysis and interactions with carbon monoxide, smoking and altitude. In G. Brewer, ed. Red cell metabolism and function. Plenum Publishing Corp., New York.

72. Rorth, M., S. Nygaard, and H. Parving. 1972. Effects of exposure to simulated high altitude on human red cell phosphates and oxygen affinity of hemoglobin. Influences of exercise. Scand. J. Clin. Lab. Invest. **29**:329-333.

73. Moore, L. G. 1973. Red blood cell adaptation to high altitude: mechanism of the 2,3 diphosphoglycerate response. Ph.D. Thesis. University of Michigan, Ann Arbor, Mich.

74. Moore, L. G., G. Brewer, and F. Oelshlegel. 1972. Red cell metabolic changes in acute and chronic exposure to high altitude. In G. Brewer, ed. Hemoglobin and red cell structure and function. Plenum Publishing Corp., New York.

75. Lenfant, C., J. D. Torrance, and C. Reynafarje. 1971. Shift of the O_2-Hb dissociation curve at altitude: mechanisms and effect. J. Appl. Physiol. **30**:625-631.

76. Reynafarje, B. 1966. Physiological patterns: enzymatic changes. In Life at high altitudes. Pub. 140. Pan American Health Organization, Washington, D.C.

77. Reynafarje, B., L. Loyola, R. Cheesman, E. Marticorena, and S. Jimenez. 1969. Fructose metabolism in sea-level and high-altitude natives. Am. J. Physiol. **216**:1542-1547.

78. Reynafarje, B., and T. Velásquez. 1966. Metabolic and physiological aspects of exercise at high altitude. Part 1. Kinetics of blood lactate, oxygen consumption and oxygen debt during exercise and recovery breathing air. Fed. Proc. **25**:1397-1399.

79. Reynafarje, B. 1971. Mecanismos moleculares en la adaptacion a la hypoxia de las grandes alturas. Thesis Doctoral en Medicina. Universidad Nacional Mayor de San Marcos, Lima, Peru.

80. Peñaloza, D., F. Sime, N. Banchero, and R. Gamboa. 1962. Pulmonary hypertension in healthy men born and living at high altitude. Med. Thorac. **19**:449-460.

81. Sime, F., N. Banchero, D. Peñaloza, R. Gamboa, J. Cruz, and E. Marticorena. 1963. Pulmonary hypertension in children born and living at high altitudes. Am. J. Cardiol. **11**:143-149.

82. Peñaloza, D., F. Sime, N. Banchero, R. Gamboa, J. Cruz, and E. Marticorena. 1963. Pulmonary hypertension in healthy men born and living at high altitudes. Am. J. Cardiol. **11**:150-157.

83. Banchero, N., F. Sime, D. Peñaloza, J. Cruz, R. Gamboa, and E. Marticorena. 1966. Pulmonary pressure, cardiac output, and arterial oxygen saturation during exercise at high altitude and at sea level. Circulation **33**:249-262.

84. Saldana, M., and J. Arias-Stella. 1963. Studies on the structure of the pulmonary trunk. Part 2. The evolution of the elastic configuration of the pulmonary trunk in people native to high altitudes. Circulation **27**:1094-1100.

85. Arias-Stella, J., and S. Recavarren. 1962. Right ventricular hypertrophy in native children living at high altitude. Am. J. Pathol. **41**:55-59.

86. Keith, J. D., R. D. Rowe, and P. Vlad. 1958. Heart diseases in infancy and childhood. The Macmillan Co., New York.

87. Rotta, A., A. Canepa, A. Hurtado, T. Velásquez, and R. Chavez. 1956. Pulmonary circulation at sea level and at high altitudes. J. Appl. Physiol. **9**:328-332.

88. Peñaloza, D., R. Gamboa, J. Dyer, M. Echevarria, and E. Marticorena. 1960. The influence of high altitudes on the electrical activity of the heart. Part 1. Electrocardiographic and vectorcardiographic observations in the newborn, infants and children. Am. Heart J. **59**:111-128.

89. Peñaloza, D., R. Gamboa, J. Dyer, M. Echevarria, and E. Marticorena. 1961. The influence of high altitudes on the electrical activity of the heart. Electrocardiographic and vectorcardiographic observations in adolescence and adulthood. Am. Heart J. **61**:101-107.

90. Peñaloza, D., J. Arias-Stella, F. Sime, S. Recavarren, and E. Marticorena. 1964. The heart and pulmonary circulation in children at high altitude. Physiological anatomical and clinical observations. Pediatrics **34**:568-582.

91. Marticorena, E., D. Peñaloza, J. Severino, and K. Hellriegel. 1962. Incidencia de la persistencia del conducto arterioso en las grandes alturas. Memorias del IV Congreso Mundial de Cardiologia, Mexico, **I-A**:155-159.

92. Alzamora-Castro, V., G. Battilana, R. Abugatas, and S. Sialer. 1960. Patent ductus arteriosus and high altitude. Am. J. Cardiol. **5**:761-765.

93. Heath, D., C. Edwards, M. Winson, and P. Smith. 1973. Effects on the right ventricle, pulmonary vasculature, and carotid bodies of the rate of exposure to, and recovery from, simulated high altitude. Thorax **28**:24-28.

94. Stenberg, J., B. Ekblom, and R. Messin. 1966. Hemodynamic response to work at simulated altitude, 4,000 m. J. Appl. Physiol. **21**:1589-1594.

95. Vogel, J. A., J. E. Hansen, and C. W. Harris. 1967. Cardiovascular responses in man during exhaustive work at sea level and high altitudes. J. Appl. Physiol. **23**:531-539.

96. Klausen, K. 1966. Cardiac output in man in rest and work during and after acclimatization to 3,800 m. J. Appl. Physiol. **21**:609-616.

97. Saltin, B., and G. Grimby. 1968. Physiological analysis of middle-aged and old former athletes: comparison with still active athletes of the same ages. Circulation **38**:1104-1115.

98. Hartley, L. H., J. Alexander, M. Modelski, and R. F. Grover. 1967. Subnormal cardiac output at rest and during exercise in residents at 3,100 m. altitude. J. Appl. Physiol. **23**:839-848.

99. Hoon, R. S., V. Balasubramanian, O. P. Mathew, S. C. Tiwari, S. S. Sharma, and K. S. Chadha. 1977. Effect of high-altitude exposure for 10 days on stroke volume and cardiac output. J. Appl. Physiol. **42**:722-727.

100. Monge, M. C., and C. Monge. 1966. High-altitude diseases: mechanism and management. Charles C Thomas, Publisher, Springfield, Ill.

101. Ruiz, L. 1973. Epidemiologia de la hipertencion arterial y de la cardiopatia isquemica en las grandes alturas. Thesis Doctoral en Medicina. Universidad Peruana Cayetano Heredia, Lima, Peru.

102. Marticorena, E., L. Ruiz, J. Severino, J. Galvez, and D. Peñaloza. 1969. Systemic blood pressure in white men born at sea level: changes after long residence at high altitudes. Am. J. Cardiol. **23**:364-368.

103. Heath, D., and D. R. Williams. 1977. Man at high altitude. The pathophysiology of acclimatization and adaptation. Churchill Livingstone, Edinburgh.

104. Balke, B. 1960. Work capacity at altitude. In W. R. Johnson, ed. Science and medicine of exercise and sports. Harper & Row, Publishers, Inc., New York.

105. Dill, D. B., L. G. Myhre, D. K. Brown, K. Burrus, and G. Gehlsen. 1967. Work capacity in chronic exposures to altitude. J. Appl. Physiol. **23**:555-560.

106. Faulkner, J., J. Kollias, C. Favour, E. Burskirk and B. Balke. 1968. Maximum aerobic capacity and running performance at altitude. J. Appl. Physiol. **24**:685-691.

107. Elsner, R. W., A. Bolstad, and C. Forno. 1964. Maximum oxygen consumption of Peruvian Indians native to high altitude. In W. H. Weihe, ed. The physiological effects of high altitude. Pergamon Press Ltd., Oxford.

108. Baker, P. T. 1976. Work performance of highland natives. In P. T. Baker and M. A. Little, eds. Man in the Andes: a multidisciplinary study of high-altitude Quechua natives. Dowden, Hutchinson & Ross, Inc., Stroudsburg, Pa.

109. Way, A. B. 1976. Exercise capacity of high altitude Peruvian Quechua Indians migrant to low altitude. Hum. Biol. **48**:175-191.

110. Banchero, N., and R. F. Grover. 1972. Effects of different levels of simulated altitude on O_2 transport in llama and sheep. Am. J. Physiol. **222**:1239-1245.

111. Monge, C. M., and C. Monge. 1968. Adaptation to high altitude. In E. S. E. Hafez, ed. Adaptation of domestic animals. Lea & Febiger, Philadelphia.

112. Eaton, J. W., T. D. Skelton, and E. Berger. 1974. Survival at extreme altitude: protective effect of increased hemoglobin-oxygen affinity. Science **183**:743-744.

10 Prenatal and postnatal growth and development at high altitude

From conception an individual's growth and development depend on the interaction of genetic and internal and external environmental conditions. It is a basic principle that the environment provides external factors that make development possible and permit the expression of genetic potentials. Research with animals and humans has demonstrated that high-altitude hypoxia directly or indirectly affects growth and development. In this chapter the results of studies of prenatal and postnatal human growth conducted in the South American Andes, Ethiopian highlands, Himalayas, India, and Tien Shan Mountains of the Soviet Union will be summarized along with the results of experimental studies on animals. The objective is to derive an overview of the mechanisms whereby a high-altitude environment influences human growth and development.

PRENATAL GROWTH AND DEVELOPMENT

The fetus even at sea level develops in a hypoxic environment[1] and, therefore, at high altitude is subject to an even greater hypoxic stress than at sea level. For example, at sea level the intrauterine umbilical arterial oxygen tension is about 20 mm Hg, which corresponds to an atmospheric oxygen tension of 61 mm Hg found at an altitude of 7500 m.[2] For this reason, and as shown by experimental studies[3-5] and observations on humans residing at high altitudes,[6-13] the prenatal structures and especially the placenta are modified by a high-altitude environment. This modification results in (1) increased surface area available for diffusion of oxygen and transfer between maternal and fetal blood and (2) decreased resistance of the placental barrier to the transfer of oxygen.

Human studies indicate that the frequency of "irregular shape," rather than the usual round or oval placentas, at high altitude is three times greater than at sea level.[6-10]

Furthermore, the average weight of the placenta is between 10% and 15% greater than the average weight at sea level.[6-11] In contrast, the average birth weight at high altitude is between 10% and 15% below the average birth weight at sea level.[6-14] Therefore, as illustrated in Fig. 10-1, the placental weight/birth weight ratio at high altitude is greater (0.16 to 0.21) than at sea level (0.12 to 0.15). The placentas at high altitude are also thinner, and they contain greater amounts of cord hemoglobin than those at sea level.[6-10,15] In view of the fact that placental surface area is highly correlated with placental capillary area and with the capacity

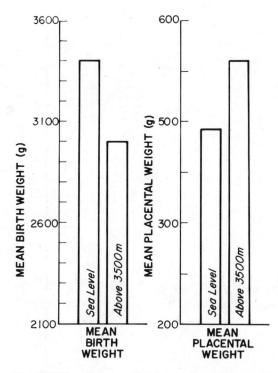

Fig. 10-1. Comparison of birth weight and placental weight of sea level and high-altitude natives. Residence at high altitude is associated with lower birth weight but increased weight of placenta. (Based on data from Kruger, H., and J. Arias-Stella. 1970. Am. J. Obstet. Gynecol. **106:**586-591.)

of the placenta to nourish and oxygenate the fetus,[16] the observed morphological characteristics of the placenta of high-altitude populations reflect a compromise between increasing the placental area and diminishing the placental barrier for oxygen transfer.[10] Through these modifications, despite a reduction of approximately one half in the oxygen pressure gradient between maternal and fetal bloods, the rate at which oxygen reaches the fetal blood per kilogram of tissue supplied approaches sea level values.[3]

The association between a reduced birth weight and high altitude has also been found in the populations of the mountain states of the United States. For example, in Leadville situated in Colorado at 3050 m the frequency of birth weights less than 2500 g ranges between 20% to 31% compared to an average of 10% for sea level populations.[17] Comparing these findings with those found in Peru at equivalent altitudes, it becomes evident that the frequency of birth weight depression in Peru is less severe than in the United States.[8] For example, the frequency of low birth weight infants at 3400 m in the city of Cusco is 10%, which is less than half the frequency reported for comparable altitudes in the United States. This difference is probably related to differences in sampling and maternal nutritional factors. On the other hand, this difference may also be related to variations in degree of acclimatization between United States' and Peruvian Andean populations. Populations who have lived longest at high altitude and therefore have the greatest degree of adaptation can have newborns with weights that approach the weight of sea level newborns. For example, evaluation of a large number of births occurring in the city of Puno situated at 3850 m in southern Peru[9] indicate that the frequency of low birth weight infants (less than 2500 g) among the low altitude native mestizo women is 23%, whereas among highland native women the percent of low birth weight approaches sea level values. Similarly, the mean birth weight for newborns of highland native women of the city of Puno was greater than those of the mestizo women who presumably are low-altitude natives.[18,19] Recent studies in La Paz, Bolivia,[20] also indicate that the mestizo women or descendants of Europeans have newborns with lower birth weights than newborns of native women. These findings together suggest that with prolonged residence sea level women can adapt to high altitude and thus have newborns with weights that approach sea level values. However, in all the studies reviewed the mean birth weights even for the highland native women are still lower than those attained at sea level, which suggest that the high-altitude effects are only partially overcome.

POSTNATAL GROWTH AND DEVELOPMENT
Height and weight

In the previous section we have seen that prenatal growth and development is delayed at high altitude. This pattern of slow growth and development continues during the postnatal period and is evident in experimental animals as well as in humans. In general experimental studies in animals exposed to hypoxic conditions, whether it be in altitude chambers with low oxygen mixtures or at high altitudes under favorable nutritional conditions, show that weight increases at a slower rate than at sea level.[21-28] This retarded growth has been attributed to anorexia (lack of appetite) that experimental animals suffer from[29] and to a deficiency in the intestinal absorption of nutrients.[30,31] However, these factors alone cannot explain the growth pattern in body size, body morphology, and the organ systems concerned with the transport of oxygen. Microscopic studies reveal that the retarded growth associated with high-altitude hypoxia is caused

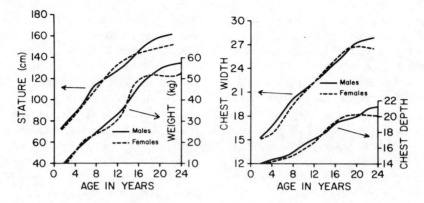

Fig. 10-2. Development of stature, weight, chest width, and chest depth of Nuñoa Quechua Indians. Pattern of growth in body size is characterized by late sexual dimorphism. (Modified from Frisancho, A. R., and P. T. Baker. 1970. Am. J. Phys. Anthropol. **32:**279-292.)

by a lesser number of cells, whereas the retarded growth associated with malnutrition is caused by a decreased amount of cytoplasm.[25] Other investigations indicate that high-altitude hypoxia interferes with cellular and protein multiplication of the brain.[26,27] From all these studies it is evident that high-altitude hypoxia plays an important role in delayed growth at high altitude.

Studies of Andean populations, such as those from the Peruvian, Chilean, and Bolivian highlands, indicate that postnatal growth is delayed compared to that of low-altitude populations with comparable nutritional and socioeconomic status.[18,32-37,42,43,72,76] Results of an extensive study based on semi-longitudinal and cross-sectional samples of the Quechua population of the District of Nuñoa situated at a mean altitude of 4250 m are presented in Figs. 10-2 to 10-4. From these data it is evident that growth in stature in both sexes is delayed, and until the age of 14 years there is no clear sex differentiation. In men growth in height continues until about the age of 22 years and in women until 20 years. The rapid growth associated with adolescence occurs after the age of 16 years in males and 14 years in females. In other

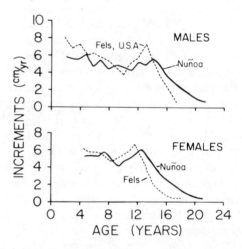

Fig. 10-3. Stature growth rate of Nuñoa Indians. Compared to United States Fels Standards, Nuñoa males and females have late and poorly defined spurt. (Modified from Frisancho, A. R., and P. T. Baker. 1970. Am. J. Phys. Anthropol. **32:**279-292.)

words, the growth of highland Quechuas is characterized by (1) late sexual dimorphism, (2) slow growth and prolonged periods of growth, and (3) late adolescent height spurt.

The pattern of slow growth in stature observed among Andean populations can also be found among populations from the Hima-

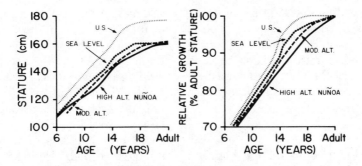

Fig. 10-4. Comparison of absolute and relative development in stature of Nuñoa Quechua boys and Peruvians from sea level and a moderate altitude of 2300 m. (Modified from Frisancho, A. R., and P. T. Baker. 1970. Am. J. Phys. Anthropol. **32:**279-292.)

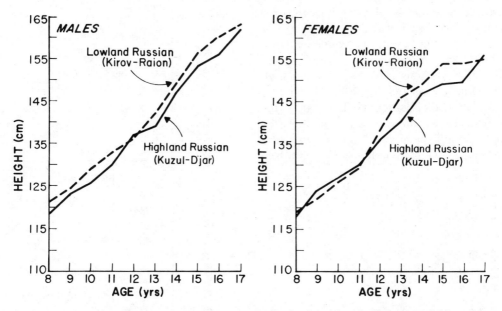

Fig. 10-5. Comparison of growth in stature among lowland and highland Russian children from Tien Shan Mountains. During adolescence highland children are shorter than their lowland counterparts. (Modified from Miklashevskaia, N. N., V. S. Solovyeva, and E. Z. Godina. 1972. Vopros Anthropologii **40:**71-91.)

layas and the Tien Shan Mountains.[38,39] As shown in Fig. 10-5, between the ages of 12 and 18 Russian highland children are shorter than their low-altitude counterparts.[39] However, it must be pointed out that not all populations that live at high altitudes necessarily have slow growth. It has been demonstrated

in studies of Africans that the populations of the mountains of Ethiopia, because they live in better nutritional and socioeconomic conditions, have a faster growth rate than their low-altitude counterparts.[40] These findings agree with investigations conducted with Peruvian Quechua populations situated in the district of Junin at 4300 m and those situated in the district of Lamas at 1000 m in the Peruvian eastern lowlands.[41] In these studies we found that growth in stature and weight, because of the better nutritional reserves of the highlanders, was faster than those at low altitudes.

Chest size

A distinguishing feature of the highland native is an enlarged thorax.[42] As shown by studies done in the central and southern highlands of Peru and Chile the increased chest size of the highland native is acquired through rapid and accelerated growth, especially after the end of childhood[33-37,42,43,76,77] (Fig. 10-6). Studies of an Ethiopian population[40,44] indicate that the trend toward greater chest size is also present among highland children and adults. Fig. 10-7 depicts the relationship, as derived from regression analysis, of age to chest circumfence (Log 10) of Ethiopian children[40] and shows that at a given age the highland boys and girls have a larger chest size than their low-altitude counterparts. Fig. 10-8 shows that the highland adult Ethiopians have a greater maximum chest circumference than their low-altitude counterparts. Furthermore, evaluations of the anthropometric measurements of migrant groups demonstrated that the enlarged chest size of the highland Ethiopian could be attained by lowland natives who migrated to high altitude.[44] A recent study by Malik and Singh[45] conducted among the Bod natives of the mountains of Ladakh situ-

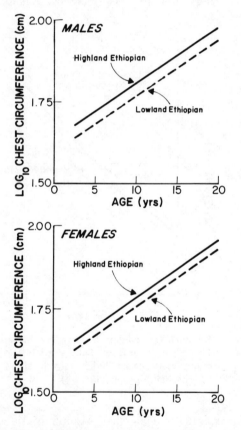

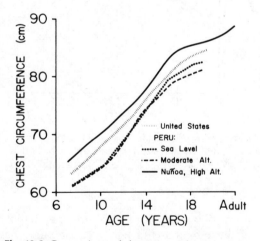

Fig. 10-6. Comparison of chest circumference among Peruvian children and adults from sea level, moderate altitude, and high altitude. Highland Quechuas from Nuñoa exhibit accelerated growth in chest size. (From Frisancho, A. R., and P. T. Baker. 1970. Am. J. Phys. Anthropol. **32:**279-292.)

Fig. 10-7. Relationship of age to chest circumference (Log 10) among highland and lowland Ethiopean children. At a given age highlanders show greater chest size for their stature than do lowlanders. (Based on data from Clegg, E. J., I. G. Pawson, E. H. Ashton, and R. M. Flinn. 1972. Philos. Trans. R. Soc. Lond. [Biol.] **264:**403-437.)

ated at 3514 m in India demonstrated that the growth in chest circumference of the highlanders is significantly faster than the low-altitude Indian norm.

In summary, since the adult Sherpas also exhibit an enlarged thorax,[74] it would appear that, with the exception of the Russians from the Tien Shan Mountains,[39] residence and/ or acclimatization to high altitude results in enlarged chest dimensions. That prolonged residence at high altitude can result in enlarged chest size is also inferred from the fact that United States adult women who resided at Pikes Peak for 2½ months exhibited an increase in maximum chest circumference despite a significant reduction in subcapsular skinfold thickness.[46]

Lung volume

Concomitant with increased chest size, the lung volume of high-altitude natives is greater than that for persons at low altitudes. As illustrated in Fig. 10-9, greater lung volume of highland natives is acquired through a rapid and accelerated growth.[33-36,42,47,75,77] In view of the fact that during childhood at sea level growth in lung volume is associated with an enhanced quantity of alveolar units and alveolar surface area,[48] the rapid growth in lung volume at high altitude is probably also associated with an enhanced quantity of alveolar units and alveolar surface area. Since there is a direct relationship between alveolar surface area and rate of oxygen diffusion from the lungs to the capillary bed,

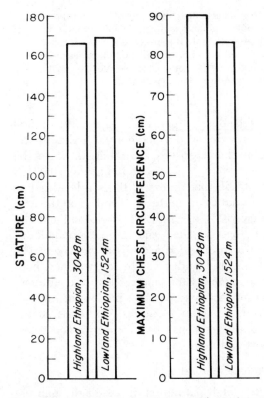

Fig. 10-8. Comparison of stature and maximum chest circumference among highland and lowland Ethiopians. Highland adults, despite their similar statures, have greater chest size than lowland counterparts. (Based on data from Harrison, G. A., G. F. Kuchemann, M. A. S. Moore, A. J. Boyce, T. Baju, A. E. Mourant, M. J. Godber, B. G. Glasgow, A. C. Kopec, D. Tills, and E. J. Clegg. 1969. Philos. Trans. R. Soc. Lond. [Biol.] **256B**:147-182.)

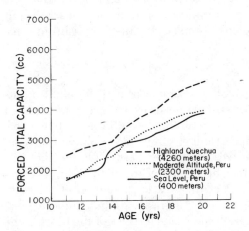

Fig. 10-9. Comparison of forced vital capacity among Peruvian boys from sea level, moderate altitude, and high altitude. Highland boys from Nuñoa exhibit accelerated development of lung volume. (Based on data from Frisancho, A. R., and P. T. Baker. 1970. Am. J. Phys. Anthropol. **32**:279-292.)

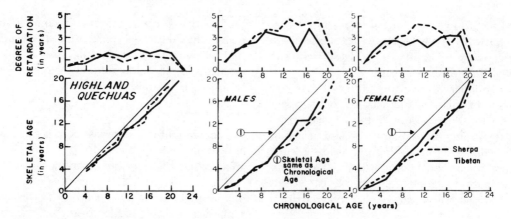

Fig. 10-10. Relationship between skeletal age and chronological age among highland Quechuas, highland Sherpas, and lowland Sherpas (Tibetan). In both highland samples skeletal maturation, especially during childhood, is delayed. During adolescence this difference decreases. (Based on data from Frisancho, A. R. 1969. Growth, physique, and pulmonary function at high altitude: a field study of a Peruvian Quechua population. Ph.D. Thesis. Pennsylvania State University, University Park, Pa., and Pawson, I. G. 1977. Am. J. Phys. Anthropol. **47**:473-482.)

the rapid growth in lung volume at high altitude surely reflects an adaptation to high-altitude hypoxia. As discussed in Chapter 9, evidence suggests that the low-altitude native through growth and development at high altitude can acquire an enlarged lung volume similar to the high-altitude native.[35,40,50,76]

Heart

Another characteristic of the highland native is that the heart is bigger and heavier than that of the low-altitude native. Anatomical and electrocardiographic studies conducted mostly in Peru indicate that the larger heart size of the highland native is a result of the lack of involution of the right ventricle.[51-53] These studies indicate that at birth the characteristics of the heart in the highlander and the sea level native are the same; in both environments the newborns show a similar preponderance of the right ventricle, but after the second month regression of the right ventricle that is natural in the sea level native does not occur in the

highlander.[51-53] That is, during the period of growth and development at high altitude, fetal characteristics are retained, so in the adult state the preponderance of the left ventricle that occurs in the sea level native does not occur in the highlander; on the contrary, it is the right ventricle and not the left that is bigger and more preponderant.

The preponderance of the right ventricle of the highlander has been explained both as a compensatory mechanism to counteract pulmonary hypertension present at high altitude (Chapter 9) and as part of a systemic adaptive response to increase oxygen transport and delivery.

Skeletal maturation

Skeletal maturation, assessed through estimates of skeletal age with reference to the Greulich and Pyle atlas,[54] of Andean, Himalayan, and Ethiopian high-altitude populations prior to the age of 16 years is quite retarded.[34-36,38,40] However, in both the Himalayan Sherpas and Peruvian Quechuas after the age of 16 years the retardation decreases drastically, so by about the age of 20 years in males and 18 years in females the high-altitude native approaches western standards (Fig. 10-10). Compared to United States norms, before the age of 16 years the high-land Sherpas and Quechuas exhibit an average delay in skeletal age of about 20%, but between the ages of 16 and 20 the difference amounts to only 10%. This indicates that age at which complete epiphyseal union occurs (reflected by the measurement of skeletal age during adolescence) at high altitude is retarded by 10%. This delay coincides with the increase in age of attainment of adult stature. As pointed out earlier, growth in height continues up to age 22 in males and 20 in females, which compared to United States norms equals a delay of about 10%. For this reason, the origins of the short adult stature of high-altitude populations is explained mostly by the marked growth delay that occurs during childhood, a retardation which is not recuperated by the lengthened period of growth.

Sexual maturation

Concomitant with retardation in adolescent skeletal maturation, sexual maturation among high-altitude Andean populations is delayed. Investigations of a large sample of Peruvian girls aged 11 to 17 years indicate that the age of menarche at high altitude averaged 13.58 years compared to 12.58 years at sea level[55] (Fig. 10-11). Furthermore, it has been found that in both males and females the age at which the secondary sexual characteristics develop is markedly delayed at high altitude.[55-57] Similarly, measurements of luteinizing hormones indicate that adult values in girls are attained 1 year later at high altitude than at sea level.[57] Thus it appears that adolescent maturation by any criteria is delayed among Andean high-altitude populations. On the other hand, among Ethiopian high-altitude populations second-

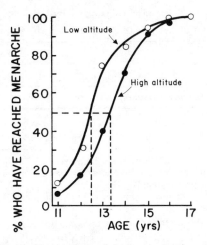

Fig. 10-11. Comparison of age at menarche among Peruvian mestizos from sea level and central highlands. The mean age at menarche is later for the highland girls than for those of sea level. (Modified from Donayre, J. 1966. Population growth and fertility at high altitude. In Life at high altitudes. Pub. 140. Pan American Health Organization, Washington, D.C.)

ary sexual maturation does not show any altitude-related differences.[40] Nevertheless, studies in the Himalayas report that the age at menarche among the highland Sherpas averaged 18.1 years, which is one of the latest ever recorded for a human population.[38] The extent to which these data correspond to actual sexual maturation remains to be seen.

DETERMINANTS OF GROWTH

Obviously the pattern of growth and development at high altitude reflects the interaction of genetic and environmental factors. For this reason, to determine the causes of the highland pattern of growth and development it is necessary to consider the role of each of these factors.

Genetic factors

One way of determining the role of genetic factors in human growth is to assess the par-

Table 7. Parent-offspring correlation in height among high-altitude Quechuas from the District of Nuñoa, situated at a mean altitude of 4250 m in southern Peru*

| | Father | | | | Mother | | | |
| | Son | | Daughter | | Son | | Daughter | |
Age group (years)	N	r	N	r	N	r	N	r
5-10.9	115	0.31†	98	0.29†	96	0.36†	86	0.32†
11-16.9	80	0.4†	60	0.42†	60	0.48†	50	0.52†

*Based on data from Frisancho, A. R. 1976. Growth and functional development at high altitude. In P. T. Baker and M. A. Little, eds. Man in the Andes: a multidisciplinary study of high altitude Quechua natives. Dowden, Hutchinson & Ross, Inc., Stroudsburg, Pa.
†Weighted mean r is derived from Z-transformed age-specific values of R; probability < 0.01.

ent-offspring correlation. In general a high correlation coefficient implies that the phenotypic expression is under a high genetic control, whereas a low correlation implies a low genetic control. As shown in Table 7 the parent-offspring correlations in the Quechua highlanders from Nuñoa range from 0.29 to 0.52.[35] These values are similar to those found among western populations with good nutritional status. Thus it appears that the genetic contributions to phenotypic variations in growth and stature among high-altitude Quechuas is comparable to that of sea level populations. With respect to this conclusion, it must be pointed out that comparative studies of Andean Aymara populations from Chile indicate that the most important factor explaining differences in anthropometric measurements is the altitude difference, whereas geographic and genetic differences contribute the least.[58] Another approach for determining the role of genetic factors on growth is to compare populations of similar genetic composition living at sea level and at high altitude. Studies of highland and lowland Peruvian populations of the same Quechua stock[19,43,47] suggest that most of the differences in growth are traceable to altitude differences and not to genetic differences.

In summary, at the present stage of knowledge it appears that differences in growth between highland and lowland populations are not caused by differences in genetic composition.

Nutrition

In general, at high altitude because of the joint effect of hypoxia and cold agriculture is limited, and the nutritional base is less than at low altitudes. Therefore one would expect undernutrition to contribute to delayed growth at high altitude.[73] A way of determining the role of nutritional reserves in human growth is to evaluate the amount of nutritional reserves a population has.[59] Through anthropometric measurements the caloric and protein reserves are easily determined, and in general a high amount of subcutaneous fat and body muscle implies high calorie and protein reserves. As shown in Fig. 10-12, the mean triceps skinfold thickness of the highland Nuñoa children[34-36] is between the fiftieth and fifteenth percentile of the United States Ten State Nutritional Survey.[59] These findings indicate that in this highland population the children have adequate calorie reserves. Both metabolic balance studies[60] and dietary surveys[61,62] demonstrate that the dietary intake of Nuñoa samples meet the United States recommended dietary allowances (Fig. 10-13). Furthermore, as shown in Figs. 10-14 and 10-15, in Nuñoa fatter children are not taller

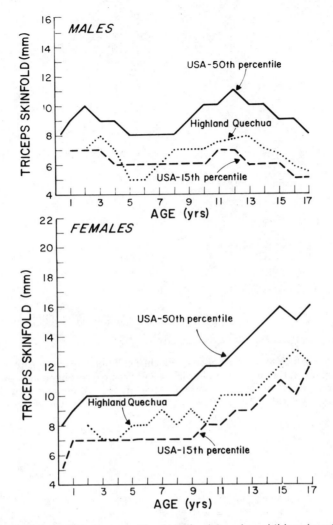

Fig. 10-12. Triceps skinfold in the fiftieth percentile of highland Quechua children from Nuñoa and fiftieth and fifteenth percentiles of United States children. The highland children's subcutaneous fat is within lower normal range of United States standards. (Based on data from Frisancho, A. R., and P. T. Baker. 1970. Am. J. Phys. Anthropol. **32:**279-292, and Frisancho, A. R. 1974. Am. J. Clin. Nutr. **27:**1052-1058.)

than their leaner counterparts,[34] suggesting that greater calorie reserve is not associated with increased dimensional growth. This finding is contrary to those of sea level populations in which increased fatness is associated with advanced maturity and growth.[63]

Thus it would appear that among those high-altitude Quechuas from Nuñoa nutri-

tional limitation alone does not appear to account for their pattern of growth. However, it is possible that a high-altitude environment may indirectly affect energy balance. First, as indicated in Chapter 5 the natives of Nuñoa, in spite of efficient technological adaptations to cold, are frequently exposed to severe cold stress because of

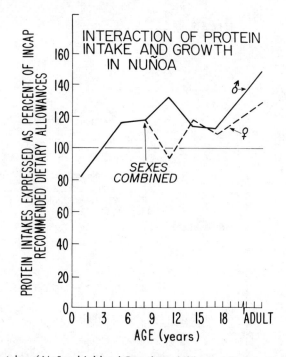

Fig. 10-13. Protein intake of Nuñoa highland Quechua children and adults expressed as percent of INCAP (Institute of Nutrition of Central America and Panama) recommended dietary allowances. (Calculated from individual values given by Gursky, M. 1969. A dietary survey of three Peruvian highland communities. M.A. Thesis. Pennsylvania State University, University Park, Pa.)

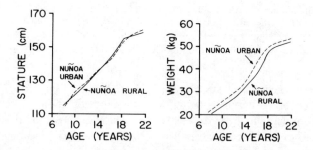

Fig. 10-14. Comparison of stature and weight among highland Quechua boys from urban and rural areas of district of Nuñoa. Although there are marked differences in weight, urban and rural boys exhibit similar statures. (Based on data from Frisancho, A. R., and P. T. Baker. 1970. Am. J. Phys. Anthropol. **32:**279-292.)

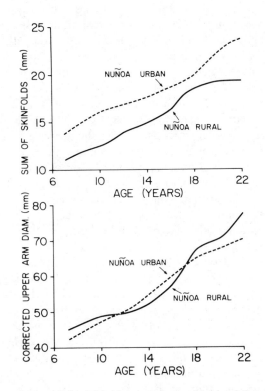

Fig. 10-15. Comparison of sum of skinfold thickness among highland Quechua boys from urban and rural areas of district of Nuñoa. (Based on data from Frisancho, A. R., and P. T. Baker. 1970. Am. J. Phys. Anthropol. **32:**279-292.)

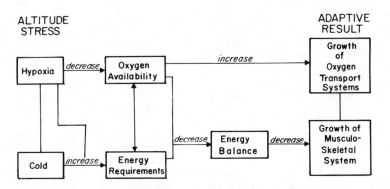

Fig. 10-16. Schematization of two-directional patterns of growth at high altitude. At high altitude because of combined effects of hypoxia and cold and increased energy requirements, growth of musculoskeletal system is delayed, whereas in response to low oxygen availability, growth of oxygen-transport system organs is accelerated.

the requirements of a subsistence economy. Laboratory studies indicate that high-altitude Quechuas have a higher basal metabolic rate (produce more heat) than sea level residents[64,65] and maintain body temperatures at higher levels when exposed to cold stress than sea level inhabitants.[66-68] Furthermore, when exposed to cold both children and adults are able to maintain hand and foot temperatures at comfortable levels, which is in marked contrast to sea level residents.[66-68] Such cold exposure is bound to increase the individual's food energy requirements. The balance metabolic studies conducted on high-altitude Quechuas from Nuñoa indicate that to maintain body weight without modifying body composition an active adult man residing at an altitude of 4000 m must increase his calorie intake by about 14.8% over the requirements of a man with the same physical characteristics who resides at sea level.[60] Second, investigations of glucose metabolism demonstrate that among high-altitude adult male and pregnant female natives the rate of blood glucose utilization and glucose tolerance is greater than at sea level.[69-71]

CONCLUSION

At high altitude the pattern of growth and development in body size and the organ systems concerned with oxygen transport differs from the low-altitude pattern. This high-altitude pattern follows two directions of response in which accelerated and slow patterns occur simultaneously. As schematized in Fig. 10-16, high-altitude hypoxia accelerates the growth of oxygen transport organ systems such as the placenta, lungs, heart, and thorax. On the other hand, joint effects of hypoxia and cold increase energy requirements; this in turn affects the energy balance and results in prenatal and postnatal growth retardation of the musculoskeletal system, which affects both birth weight and stature. Because of this two-directional response, human growth in high-altitude populations must be viewed as the result of interaction and adaptation of the organism to competing stresses of hypoxia, cold, and energy requirements that characterize the high-altitude environment.

REFERENCES

1. Barcroft, J. 1936. Fetal circulation and respiration. Physiol. Rev. **16**:103-1108.
2. Dawes, G. S. 1965. Oxygen supply and consumption in late fetal life, and the onset of breathing at birth. In W. O. Fenn and H. Rahn, eds. Handbook of physiology. Section 3. Respiration. vol. 2. American Physiological Society, Washington, D.C.
3. Barron, D. H., J. Metcalf, G. Mechia, A. Hilligers, H. Prystovsky, and W. Huckabee. 1964. Adaptations of pregnant ewes and their fetuses to high altitude. In W. H. Weihe, ed. The physiological effects of high altitude. Pergamon Press, Inc., New York.
4. Eastman, N. J. 1930. Foetal blood studies. Part 1. The oxygen relationships of umbilical cord blood at birth. Bull. Johns Hopkins Hosp. **47**:221-224.
5. Metcalfe, J., G. Meschia, A. Hellegers, H. Prystowski, W. Huckabee, and D. H. Barron. 1962. Observations on the placental exchange of the re-

spiratory gases in pregnant ewes at high altitude. Q. J. Exp. Physiol. **47**:74-92.
6. Rendon, H. 1964. Aspectos microscopico de la placenta a 2,300 mts. de altitud. Thesis de Bachillerato, Universidad Nacional de San Agustin, Facultad de Medicina, Arequipa, Peru.
7. Chabes, A., J. Perada, L. Hyams, N. Barrientos, J. Perez, L. Campos, A. Monroe, and A. Mayorga. 1968. Comparative morphometry of the human placenta at high altitude and at sea level. Part 1. The shape of the placenta. Obstet. Gynecol. **31**: 178-185.
8. McClung, J. 1969. Effects of high altitude on human birth. Harvard University Press, Cambridge, Mass.
9. Passano, S. 1969. Observaciones humanas de la placenta en Puno 3812 m. de altura. Ginecologia y Obstetricia **15**:45-57.
10. Frisancho, A. R. 1970. Developmental responses to

high altitude hypoxia. Am. J. Phys. Anthropol. **32:** 401-408.

11. Kruger, H., and J. Arias-Stella. 1970. The placenta and the newborn infant at high altitudes. Am. J. Obstet. Gynecol. **106:**586-591.

12. Kadar, N., and M. Saldana. 1971. La placenta en la altura. Part 1. Caracteristics macroscopicas y morfometria. In R. Guerra-Garcia, ed. Estudio sobre la gestacion y el recien nacido en la altura. Universidad Peruana Cayetano Heredia, Lima, Peru.

13. Saldaña, M., K. Kadar, and S. Recavaren. 1971. La placenta en la altura. Part 2. Estudio ultraestructural cuantitative de placentas de Cerro de Pasco (4330 m), Puno (3850 m) y Lima (150 m). In R. Guerra-Garcia, ed. Estudio sobre la gestacion y el recien nacido en la altura. Universidad Peruana Cayetano Heredia, Lima, Peru.

14. Sobrevilla, L. A. 1971. Analysis matematico de la relacion ponderal placenta: recien nacido en la altura. In R. Guerra-Garcia, ed. Estudio sobre la gestacion y el recien nacido en la altura. Universidad Peruana Cayetano Heredia, Lima, Peru.

15. Guerra-Garcia, R., R. Lozano, and M. Cateriano. 1971. Bioquimica de la sangre materna y del cordon umbilical en Cerro de Pasco (4200 m). In R. Guerra-Garcia, ed. Estudio sobre la gestacion y el recien nacido en la altura. Universidad Peruana Cayetano Heredia, Lima, Peru.

16. Aherne, W., and M. S. Dunnill. 1966. Morphometry of the human placenta. Br. Med. Bull. **22:**5-8.

17. Lichty, J. A., R. Y. Ting, P. D. Bruns, and E. Dyar. 1957. Studies of babies born at high altitude. Part 1. Relation of altitude to birth weight. Am. J. Dis. Child. **93:**666-669.

18. Haas, J. D. 1976. Infant growth and development. In P. T. Baker and M. A. Little, eds. Man in the Andes: a multidisciplinary study of high-altitude Quechua natives. Dowden, Hutchinson & Ross, Inc., Stroudsburg, Pa.

19. Haas, J. D., P. T. Baker, and E. E. Hunt, Jr. 1977. The effects of high altitude on body size and composition of the newborn infant in Southern Peru. Hum. Biol. **49:**611-628.

20. Haas, J. D., D. A. Small, and J. L. Beard. 1978. Prenatal growth at high altitude: ethnic variation related to differential maternal adaptability. Am. J. Phys. Anthropol. **48**(abstract):401.

21. Timiras, P. S., A. A. Krum, and N. Pace. 1957. Body and organ weights of rats during acclimatization to an altitude of 12,470 feet. Am. J. Physiol. **191:**598-604.

22. Timiras, P. S. 1964. Comparison of growth and development of the rat at high altitude and at sea level. In W. H. Weihe, ed. The physiological effects of high altitudes. Pergamon Press, Inc., New York.

23. Metcalfe, J., G. Meschia, A. Hellegers, H. Prystowsky, W. Huckabee, and D. H. Barron. 1962. Observations on the growth rates and organ weights of fetal sheep at altitude and sea level. Q. J. Exp. Physiol. **47:**305-313.

24. Delaquerriere-Richardson, L., E. S. Forbes, and E. Valdivia. 1965. Effect of simulated high altitude on the growth rate of albino guinea pigs. J. Appl. Physiol. **20:**1022-1025.

25. Naeye, R. L. 1966. Organ and cellular development in mice growing at simulated high altitude. Lab. Invest. **15:**700-705.

26. Cheek, D. J., A. Graystone, and R. A. Rowe. 1969. Hypoxia and malnutrition in newborn rats: effects on RNA, DNA, and protein tissues. Am. J. Physiol. **217:**642-645.

27. Petropoulos, E. A., K. B. Dabal, and P. S. Timiras. 1972. Biological effects of high altitude on myelinogenesis in brain of the developing rat. Am. J. Physiol. **223:**951-957.

28. Clegg, E. J. 1978. Fertility and early growth. In P. T. Baker, ed. The biology of high-altitude peoples. Cambridge University Press, New York.

29. Schnakenberg, D. D., L. F. Krabill, and P. C. Weiser. 1971. The anorexic effect of high altitude on weight gain, nitrogen retention and body composition of rats. J. Nutr. **101:**787-796.

30. Van Liere, E. J., W. V. Crabtree, D. W. Nothup, and J. C. Stickney. 1948. Effect of anoxic anoxia on propulsive activity of the small intestine. Proc. Soc. Exp. Biol. Med. **67:**331-332.

31. Chinn, K. S. K., and J. P. Hannon. 1969. Efficiency of food utilization at high altitude. Fed. Proc. **28:** 944-947.

32. Bouloux, C. J. 1968. Contribution a l'etude biologique des phenomens pubertaires en tres haute altitude (La Paz). Centre d'hematypologie du dentre national de la recherche scientifique. Centre Regional de Transfussion Sanguine et d'Hemalogie, Toulouse, France.

33. Frisancho, A. R. 1969. Human growth and pulmonary function of a high altitude Peruvian Quechua population. Hum. Biol. **41:**365-379.

34. Frisancho, A. R., and P. T. Baker. 1970. Altitude and growth: a study of the patterns of physical growth of a high altitude Peruvian Quechua population. Am. J. Phys. Anthropol. **32:**279-292.

35. Frisancho, A. R. 1976. Growth and functional development at high altitude. In P. T. Baker and M. A. Little, eds. Man in the Andes: a multidisciplinary study of high altitude Quechua natives.

Dowden, Hutchinson & Ross, Inc., Stroudsburg, Pa.

36. Frisancho, A. R. 1978. Human growth and development among high altitude populations. In P. T. Baker, ed. The biology of high-altitude peoples. Cambridge University Press, New York.

37. Hoff, C. 1974. Altitudinal variations in the physical growth and development of Peruvian Quechua. Homo 24:87-99.

38. Pawson, I. G. 1977. Growth characteristics of populations of Tibetan origin in Nepal. Am. J. Phys. Anthropol. 47:473-482.

39. Miklashevskaia, N. N., V. S. Solovyeva, and E. Z. Godina. 1972. Growth and development in high-altitude regions of Southern Kirghizia, U.S.S.R. Vopros Anthropologii 40:71-91.

40. Clegg, E. J., I. G. Pawson, E. H. Ashton, and R. M. Flinn. 1972. The growth of children at different altitudes in Ethiopia. Philos. Trans. R. Soc. Lond. (Biol.) 264:403-437.

41. Frisancho, A. R., G. A. Borkan, and J. E. Klayman. 1975. Patterns of growth of lowland and highland Peruvians of similar genetic composition. Hum. Biol. 47:233-243.

42. Hurtado, A. 1932. Respiratory adaptation in the Indian natives of the Peruvian Andes. Studies at high altitude. Am. J. Phys. Anthropol. 17:137-165.

43. Beall, C. M., P. T. Baker, T. S. Baker, and J. D. Haas. 1977. The effects of high altitude on adolescent growth in southern Peruvian Amerindians. Hum. Biol. 49:109-124.

44. Harrison, G. A., G. F. Kuchemann, M. A. S. Moore, A. J. Boyce, T. Baju, A. E. Mourant, M. J. Godber, B. G. Glasgow, A. C. Kopec, D. Tills, and E. J. Clegg. 1969. The effects of altitudinal variation in Ethiopian populations. Philos. Trans. R. Soc. Lond. (Biol.) 256B:147-182.

45. Malik, S. L., and I. P. Singh. 1978. Growth trends among male Bods of Ladakh—a high altitude population. Am. J. Phys. Anthropol. 48:171-176.

46. Hannon, J. P., J. L. Shields, and C. W. Harris. 1969. Anthropometric changes associated with high altitude acclimatization in females. Am. J. Phys. Anthropol. 31:77-84.

47. Boyce, A. J., J. S. J. Haight, D. B. Rimmer, and G. A. Harrison. 1974. Respiratory function in Peruvian Quechua Indians. Ann. Hum. Biol. 1:137-148.

48. Dunnill, M. S. 1962. Postnatal growth of the lung. Thorax 17:329-333.

49. Frisancho, A. R., T. Velásquez, and J. Sanchez. 1973. Influence of developmental adaptation on lung function at high altitude. Hum. Biol. 45:583-594.

50. Frisancho, A. R. 1977. Developmental adaptation to high altitude hypoxia. Int. J. Biometeorol. 21:135-146.

51. Arias-Stella, J., and S. Recavarren. 1962. Right ventricular hypertrophy in native children living at high altitude. Am. J. Pathol. 41:55-62.

52. Peñaloza, D., J. Arias-Stella, F. Sime, S. Recavarren, and E. Marticorena. 1964. The heart and pulmonary circulation in children at high altitude. Physiological anatomical and clinical observations. Pediatrics 34:568-582.

53. Peñaloza, D., R. Gamboa, E. Marticorena, M. Echevarria, J. Dyer, and E. Gutierrez. 1961. The influence of high altitudes on the electrical activity of the heart: electrocardiographic and vectocardiographic observations in adolescence and adulthood. Am. Heart J. 61:101-107.

54. Greulich, W. W., and S. I. Pyle. 1959. Radiographic atlas of skeletal development of the hand and wrist, 2nd ed. Stanford University Press, Stanford, California.

55. Donayre, J. 1966. Population growth and fertility at high altitude. In Life at high altitudes. Pub. 140. Pan American Health Organization, Washington, D.C.

56. Penaloza, J. B. 1971. Crecimiento y desarrollo sexual del adolescente Andino. Thesis Doctoral. Universidad Nacional de San Marcos, Lima, Peru.

57. Llerena, L. A. 1973. Determinacion de hormona luteinizante por radioinmunoensayo. Variaciones fisiologicas y por efecto de la altura. Doctoral Thesis. Universidad Peruana Cayetano Heredia, Instituto de Investigaciones de Altura, Lima, Peru.

58. Rothammer, F., and R. Spielman. 1972. Anthropometric variation in Aymara: genetic, geographic and topographic contributions. Am. J. Hum. Genet. 24:371-380.

59. Frisancho, A. R. 1974. Triceps skinfolds and upper arm muscle size norms for the assessment of nutritional status. Am. J. Clin. Nutr. 27:1052-1058.

60. Picon-Reategui, E. 1976. Nutrition. In P. T. Baker and M. A. Little, eds. Man in the Andes: a multidisciplinary study of high altitude Quechua natives. Dowden, Hutchinson & Ross, Inc., Stroudsburg, Pa.

61. Mazess, R. B., and P. T. Baker. 1964. Diet of Quechua Indians living at high altitude: Nuñoa, Peru. Am. J. Clin. Nutr. 15:341-351.

62. Gursky, M. 1969. A dietary survey of three Peruvian highland communities. M.A. Thesis. Pennsylvania State University, University Park, Pa.

63. Garn, S. M., and D. J. A. Haskell. 1960. Fat thickness and developmental status in childhood and adolescence. Am. J. Dis. Child. 99:746-751.

64. Picon-Reategui, E. 1961. Basal metabolic rate body composition at high altitude. J. Appl. Physiol. **16:**431-434.

65. Mazess, R. B., E. Picon-Reategui, R. B. Thomas, and M. A. Little. 1969. Oxygen intake and body temperature of basal and sleeping Andean natives at high altitude. Aerospace Med. **40:**6-9.

66. Baker, T. P., E. R. Buskirk, J. Kollias, and R. B. Mazess. 1967. Temperature regulation at high altitude: Quechua Indians and U.S. whites during total body cold exposure. Hum. Biol. **39:**155-169.

67. Little, M. A. 1976. Physiological responses to cold. In P. T. Baker and M. A. Little, eds. Man in the Andes: a multidisciplinary study of high altitude Quechua natives. Dowden, Hutchinson & Ross, Inc., Stroudsburg, Pa.

68. Little, M. A., and J. M. Hanna. 1978. The responses of high-altitude populations to cold and other stresses. In P. T. Baker, ed. The biology of high-altitude peoples. Cambridge University Press, New York.

69. Picon-Reategui, E. 1962. Studies on the metabolism of carbohydrates at sea level and at high altitudes. Metabolism **11:**1148-1154.

70. Picon-Reategui, E. 1963. Intravenous glucose tolerance test at sea level and at high altitudes. J. Clin. Endocrinol. **23:**1256-1261.

71. Calderon, L., A. Llerena, L. Munive, and F. Kruger. 1966. Intravenous glucose tolerance test in pregnancy in women living in chronic hypoxia. Diabetes **15:**130-132.

72. Stinson, S. 1978. Child growth, mortality and the adaptive value of children in rural Bolivia. Ph.D. Thesis. University of Michigan, Ann Arbor, Mich.

73. Malina, R. M. 1974. Growth of children at different altitudes in Central and South America. Am. J. Phys. Anthropol. **40:**144.

74. Sloan, A. W., and M. Masali. 1978. Anthropometry of Sherpa men. Ann. Hum. Biol. **5:**453-458.

75. Anderson, H. R., J. A. Anderson, H. M. King, and J. E. Cotes. 1978. Variations in the lung size of children in Papua, New Guinea: genetic and environmental factors. Ann. Hum. Biol. **5:**209-218.

76. Mueller, W. H., V. N. Schull, W. J. Schull, P. Soto, and F. Rothhammer. 1978. A multinational Andean genetic and health program: growth and development in an hypoxic environment. Ann. Hum. Biol. **5:**329-352.

77. Mueller, W. H., F. Yen, F. Rothhammer, and W. J. Schull. 1978. A multinational Andean genetic and health program. VI. Physiological measurements of lung function in a hypoxic environment. Hum. Biol. **5:**489-541.

11

Altitude pathophysiology, athletic performance, and cross-acclimatization

As we have seen in the preceding chapters, high-altitude hypoxia elicits direct and indirect responses, some of which are evidently adaptive in reducing the severe oxygen deficiency in the cells to permit the organism to function normally. However, the adaptive significance of other responses is less obvious, and some of them can cause from mild to severe malfunction, eventually becoming deleterious and even fatal to the organism. The most important of these conditions are acute mountain sickness, pulmonary edema, and Monge's disease, which will be discussed under the heading of pathophysiology.

It is evident that responses that might be adaptive under a given condition may also enhance adaptation to another stressful condition. Conversely, responses that are adaptive under one condition might have negative effects when the organism is exposed to another environmental stress. This multifaceted response is known as cross-acclimatization. Since an organism is exposed to multiple stresses, studies on cross-acclimatization provide important information about the organism's adaptive range of responses.[1] For this reason under the heading of cross-acclimatization, the effects of altitude on athletic performance at sea level and at moderate altitude, anoxic stress, hypothermia, and hyperoxia will be discussed.

PATHOPHYSIOLOGY AND HIGH ALTITUDE

Three clinical entities specific to a high-altitude environment have been identified. These include acute mountain sickness, pul-

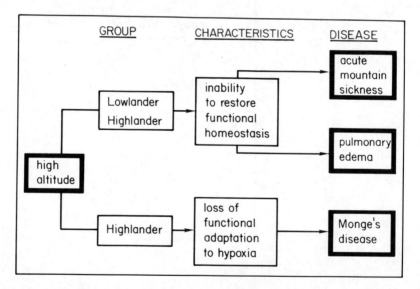

Fig. 11-1. Schematization of group incidence and general characteristics of diseases associated with high-altitude environment. Acute mountain sickness and pulmonary edema occur mostly among sea level natives or highlanders returning from sea level. Both diseases are characterized by an inability to restore functional homeostasis when exposed to stress of high altitude. In contrast Monge's disease occurs mostly among highlanders who for some reason lose their functional adaptation.

monary edema, and Monge's disease (Fig. 11-1). In this section the symptoms, cause, and treatment of these diseases will be briefly summarized. Extensive discussions of these topics are given in other works.[2-5]

Acute mountain sickness

Symptoms. Acute mountain sickness, or soroche, occurs during the first few days of exposure to high-altitude hypoxia. There is great individual variability in the altitude threshold at which it occurs. The usual symptoms include anorexia, nausea and vomiting, marked dyspnea, physical and mental fatigue, interrupted sleep, and headaches intensified by activity. There may also occur some digestive disorders, which result in weight loss and dehydration. In some cases the individual may feel an increased sensitivity to cold, dizziness, weakness, palpitation, transient leg, back, and chest pains, nasal congestion, and rhinorrhea. In very rare cases at altitudes above 4500 m a diminution of visual acuteness, painful menstruation, and bleeding of the gums may occur.[3]

In general the onset of acute mountain sickness may be sudden when ascent is very rapid, but more often it develops gradually over a period of hours, with maximal severity reached after 24 to 48 hours. The symptoms then decrease even more slowly and tend to disappear within 6 to 8 days.

There also appears to be a certain individual predisposition for the symptoms. Some persons may experience acute sickness as low as 1500 m (4920 feet), whereas occasionally subjects are unaffected at 4500 m (15,000 feet). At 5000 m[2] all nonacclimatized subjects are affected. At any altitude the onset of mountain sickness is increased by physical activity and alcohol consumption. The physiological limits of human tolerance appear to be reached at 8545 m (33,000 feet).

The symptoms of acute mountain sickness probably occur because of poor adjustment to the normal physiological reflex activities that are triggered by hypoxia. The onset and severity of the symptoms are governed by the body's inability to respond rapidly to internal homeostatic disruption. The severity of acute mountain sickness is less in females than in males.[4]

Cause. Although the cause of acute mountain sickness has been attributed specifically to hypoxia, the mechanisms that induce its symptoms are not well defined.[3,9] It has been postulated that the onset of acute mountain sickness is related to hypoxic effects on the brain, which is highly sensitive to changes in oxygen level. Exposure to high altitude results in a shift of water from the extracellular compartment into the cells, together with a slight increase in total body water.[4] The result is an intracellular edema that, in the case of the brain, may be responsible for some of the neurological symptoms of acute mountain sickness.[6] However, other studies have found little relationship between body dehydration and the incidence and severity of acute mountain sickness.[6] Recent investigations report that subjects who developed acute mountain sickness had multiple coagulation abnormalities[7] and suggested that problems of coagulation may be a contributing factor in the etiology of acute mountain sickness. Others attribute the onset of acute mountain sickness to hypocapnia and respiratory alkalosis resulting from hyperventilation.[8]

According to Singh et al,[3] on ascending to high altitude there is an initial hypersecretion of adrenal corticosteroids and vasopressin. Excessive secretion of vasopressin results in the initial retention of urine (oliguria), which coupled with the effects of hypoxia, brings about reduced peripheral blood flow and increased pulmonary blood volume and leads to pulmonary congestion. Both oliguria and the resulting increased sodium retention are associated with increased cerebral edema and elevated cerebrospinal fluid pressure. All these factors cause headache, retinal hemorrhages, and neurological disorders that characterize mountain sickness.[3]

Treatment. Because the cause of acute mountain sickness is not known, aside from oxygen administration, its treatment and prevention have been empiric. The symptoms and severity are usually diminished by avoiding sudden ascent, elevation, alcohol, and by restraint in eating, especially fats. Carbonic anhydrase inhibitors, such as acetazolamide (Dimox), have been used with some success.[10] It has been reported that the administration of this drug results in increased renal excretion of bicarbonate ions and thus speeds correction of respiratory alkalosis resulting from hyperventilation.[10,11] The benefit appears to increase when the drug is administered several days before exposure to high altitude.

Diuretics such as furosemide have been used to counteract the initial urine retention and to treat acute mountain sickness.[3] However, some studies cast doubt on the efficacy of furosemide[4-7,12] because subjects suffering from acute mountain sickness are usually already dehydrated from the efforts of climbing, low humidity, and vomiting. It has been found that high intakes of potassium along with low intakes of sodium decrease the symptoms of acute mountain sickness.[8] A high carbohydrate and low fat diet also reduces the symptoms of acute mountain sickness.[4,13] Experimental studies have found that a high carbohydrate diet increases ventilation and improves oxygenation during acute exposure to simulated high altitude[13] and increases endurance in heavy physical work at high altitude.[14] In any event an important way to decrease the symptoms of acute mountain sickness is to ascend to higher altitudes gradually and if possible spend many days at around 2000 or 3000 m before ascending to higher altitudes.

Pulmonary edema

Symptoms. Since the early 1930s it has been recognized that some high-altitude natives and mountain climbers, who after a visit to sea level return to the mountains, develop acute pulmonary edema that declines after descent to sea level.[15]

The main pathological features of pulmonary edema include widespread edema of the alveoli, extensive plugging of alveolar capillaries with sludged red blood cells, and uneven pulmonary vascular constriction, giving a patchy distribution of edema. At sea level pulmonary edema usually involves a disturbance in the Starling forces, such as increased pulmonary capillary pressure or increased pulmonary capillary permeability that normally permits leakage of plasma proteins and thus facilitates the transudation of fluid from pulmonary capillaries.

The risk of pulmonary edema appears greater among sea level subjects well acclimatized to high altitude who return to high altitude after a stay of 1 or 2 weeks at low altitudes.[16] When pulmonary edema occurs among highlanders, the condition is usually associated with pronounced right ventricular hypertrophy,[17-19] which is indicative of pulmonary hypertension. The main period of risk is between 12 and 72 hours after ascent. Males in the late teens and early twenties are known to be more at risk than females.[4,5,14] Rapid exposure to high altitude when associated with increased physical activity is also a precipitating situation for pulmonary edema. Most reported cases occur between 3500 and 4500 m.

Cause. It has been suggested that at high altitude the likely cause of pulmonary edema is an increased capillary pressure.[20] It has been suggested that the pathogenesis of pulmonary edema is related to the unequal pulmonary vasoconstriction induced by high-altitude hypoxia, which in turn results in reduced blood flow and sludging of platelets and erythrocytes in some areas and increased blood flow to nonvasoconstricted areas.[20] These two factors cause an increased filtration pressure in open capillaries and a patchy distribution of edema. According to others, the likely factor for the pathogenesis of pulmonary edema is increased plasma volume that occurs when highland subjects descend to sea level for a short period and thereafter return to high altitude.[16] These investigators point out that highland subjects on return to sea level during the first 2 weeks experience a decreased red cell volume, and this is accompanied by an excessive rise in plasma volume. Therefore, if a highlander returns from sea level to high altitude during this period, he may become more susceptible to the development of pulmonary edema than the newcomer who will have a lower plasma volume. In fact most subjects who developed pulmonary edema at high altitude were at sea level from 5 to 21 days, and only in few cases did pulmonary edema occur in newcomers.[16]

Treatment. Improvement is usually rapid with bed rest, oxygen administration, treatment with corticosteroids, and transport to lower altitudes. The most important preventive measure includes avoidance of excessive physical activity for a few days following ascent to high altitude for the first time or after returning to high altitude from sea level.[4,5,16,21]

Monge's disease

Characteristics. In 1928 Monge described a complex clinical syndrome as the sickness of the Andes, and it is currently termed *chronic mountain sickness,* or *Monge's disease,* in his honor. Monge's disease is a complex pathophysiological condition that occurs when individuals normally acclimatized to high altitude lose their ability to adapt to the altitude at which they have been living for long periods without symptoms. It is prevalent only among Andean populations, and no cases have been reported among Himalayan populations.[5] It occurs at altitudes exceeding 3000 m, and in most cases the disease seems to occur in young and middle-aged males.[2,4,5]

Clinical features. Patients with Monge's disease appear cynotic with nearly black lips and dark purple ear lobes and facial skin.[2,4,5] The conjunctival vessels of the eyes are extremely suffused, congested, and dark red-purple in color, reflecting excessive polycythemia and diminished arterial oxygen saturation.[4,5] Hemorrhages beneath the fingernails are also characteristic of subjects with Monge's disease.[5]

Patients with Monge's disease exhibit an exaggeration of the normal hematological and cardiovascular characteristics of the high-altitude native. In general hemoglobin exceeds 22 g/100 ml, the hematocrit level is greater than 70%, and the mean arterial pressure is about 50 mm Hg compared to 25 mm Hg of the high-altitude native.[2,4,5] Similarly, compared to healthy highland natives the right ventricle of the heart and overall size of the ventricles is excessively enlarged.[17] The arterial blood oxygen saturation is usually lower than that predicted for the altitude, and the arterial partial pressure of carbon dioxide is high, indicating poor ventilation.[2,22]

Cause. The clinical features of Monge's disease are usually associated with other clinical traits such as neuromuscular disorders affecting the thoracic cage, pulmonary tuberculosis, pneumoconiosis, kyphoscoliosis, and pulmonary emphysema.[2] These characteristics by themselves are capable, even at sea level, of producing chronic hypoxia.[5] For this reason, it has been concluded that Monge's disease is a collective term for a heterogenous group of conditions and does not indicate a distinct pathological entity.[5]

Treatment. An effective treatment for patients showing the signs and symptoms of Monge's disease is transport to lower altitudes. On removal of the patients to sea level the cyanosis, fatigue, right ventricular hypertrophy, hematocrit, and hemoglobin decrease rapidly; in 2 months normal values are restored.[18]

CROSS-ACCLIMATIZATION
Athletic performance

At sea level. Because the effects of altitude exposure produce cardiovascular changes similar to that of physical conditioning, several investigations have been conducted to determine the extent to which exposure to altitude improves work capacity at sea level. Earlier investigations reported that altitude training improved running performance and increased maximal aerobic capacity on return to sea level.[23-25] Recent investigations showed that well-trained athletes, on return to sea level after training at about 3000 m, have an improved work capacity.[26,27] On the other hand, other studies have found little or no effect,[28-31] and any differences in work performance have been attributed to a significant training effect during the course of the experiments.[30] In fact a recent study indicates that there is no major effect of hard endurance training at 2300 m over equivalent sea level training on aerobic power or on 2-mile run times at sea level in already well-trained middle-distance runners.[32]

Thus the hypothesis that training at high altitude has a potential effect on sea level performance appears inconclusive. This is not surprising when one considers that at high altitudes, especially above 4000 m, it is quite difficult for a sea level subject to maintain and tolerate intensive training equivalent to that of sea level. Therefore any altitude potentiating effects are counterbalanced by the lower intensity of physical conditioning. An answer to this important question could be obtained by studying sea level natives well acclimatized to high altitude, so intensive training could be maintained at both high altitude and sea level.

At moderate altitude. The 1968 Olympics held in Mexico City called attention to the possibility of altitude effects on athletic performance. The fact that the moderate altitude of 2380 m of Mexico City might affect athletic performance also raised the possibility that the effects of high altitude might not be the same for all events, and not all athletes would be equally affected. For some the altitude effects would be an advantage. This concern is exemplified by a letter in the *Times* signed by twenty-six British Olympic medalists in April, 1966.[5] They pointed out the possibility that natives or long-term residents at high altitude would have an advantage over those ascending from sea level. Exercise physiologists were called on to make predictions about the advantages and disadvantages of athletic performances in Mexico City. These predictions were based both on empirical information about altitude work physiology and statistics of athletic performance during the 1955 Pan American Games held in Mexico City and those held at sea level.[33,34] These investigators made the following predictions:

1. Improvements in time of running events of 100 to 400 m because of decreased wind resistance
2. Slower times for long-distance endurance events, which at 5000 and 10,000 m equaled 6% to 7%. In the marathon

at 42,000 m the times were 17% to 22% slower.

3. Time loss of 6% to 8% for sea level athletes performing at moderate altitude
4. Time gain of 2% to 4% in long-distance events for high-altitude natives performing at moderate altitude

Results from the 1968 Olympics in Mexico City confirmed these predictions. Thus 29% of the competitors in the short-distance events broke world records, and the average winning margin was 0.9% below the world record.[35,36] Furthermore, although both track and swimming events were performed in less time, the events lasting more than 1 minute showed an increase in time of 3% for those lasting 4 minutes and 8% for those lasting 1 hour.[36]

The prediction that high-altitude natives would be at an advantage in long-distance events has been confirmed by the results of the Olympics. The first five places in the 10,000 m race were taken by athletes who were either born or acclimatized for several years at around 1500 to 2500 m. First was Naftali Temu from Kenya (1500 m to 2000 m), second Mamowolde from Ethiopia (2000 to 2500 m), third Mohamed Gammoudi from Tunisia (1500 to 2000 m), fourth Juan Martinez from Mexico (2380 m), and fifth Nikolay Sviridov from Leminakan (1500 m) of the Soviet Union. However, the actual times were slower than those in previous Olympics. The first place was won with 29 minutes, 27.4 seconds, which is almost 2 minutes slower than Ron Clarke's world record, proving that moderate altitude does affect athletic performance even in those with previous acclimatization.

Anoxic stress and muscle relaxation

Several investigators have shown that the cardiac muscle of high-altitude acclimated rats, when exposed to anoxic stress and ex-perimental cardiac necroses, resists better and resumes function better than that of sea level controls.[37-42] Furthermore, the cardiac muscle of altitude-acclimated rats has been found more resistant than that of sea level controls to the necrogenic effect of isoproterenol as well as the necroses resulting from myocardial ischemia.[43,44]

Several hypotheses have been postulated to explain the underlying mechanisms for the increased resistance of an altitude-acclimated heart. First, it has been suggested that since the hearts of high altitude exposed animals have an increased capacity for anaerobic glycolysis,[39,40,45,46] acclimation to altitude may protect the heart by causing metabolic shifts, which interfere with the metabolic effects of anoxia and isoproterenol. Second, the greater resistance to anoxic stress of the cardiac muscle, derived from studies on acclimated rats, is related to an increased oxygen-carrying capacity that results from exposure to hypoxia.[41]

An important question is the extent to which these findings are applicable to cardiac diseases in humans. Medical observations indicate that high-altitude Peruvian natives exhibit a low frequency of atherosclerosis when compared to ethnically related low-altitude natives.[2] Furthermore, epidemiological studies indicate that the severity of atherosclerosis for inhabitants of Bogota (altitude 2600 m), Mexico (2380 m), and Guatemala (1750 m) is much greater than their counterparts situated at sea level.[47] Also among Peruvian high-altitude populations situated above 4000 m the manifestation of ischemic heart disease is much lower than among the United States or Jamaican populations.[48] For this reason a publication of the World Health Organization concludes its section on altitude effects by saying, "Available results justify the extension of such investigations to high altitude areas in other continents and to intermediate altitudes between 2000 and 3000 m. Experiments in hypertension and ischemic heart disease and investigations of the application of these phenomena in the prevention of such conditions are a logical further future development."[49] There is a need for more research in this important area.

Hypothermia

Experimental studies indicate that rats acclimated to an equivalent altitude of 4400 m for 4 weeks were able to maintain both rectal temperatures and oxygen uptake at higher levels than the control animals when swimming in water at 22° C.[50-52] The increased metabolic heat production and decreased rate of heat loss enabled the altitude-acclimated rats to swim a significantly longer time than the nonaltitude-acclimated controls.[50,51] It has been postulated that the observed differences are a result of physiological changes such as increased vascularity, and hemoglobin and myoglobin concentrations that occur with altitude acclimation.[50] Thus there appears to be a positive cross-acclimation between altitude and cold. However, other studies indicate that intermittent exposure to altitudes above 9000 m did not produce cross-acclimation between altitude and cold.[53]

Hyperoxia

In the same manner that low oxygen pressure impairs the organism's function, high oxygen pressure causes negative effects. Harmful effects of the high pressure of oxygen range from mild oxygen poisoning to direct lung tissue damage and convulsions similar to grand mal seizures; if prolonged, these effects may result in death.

As shown by experimental studies, acclimation to high-altitude hypoxia protects the lungs from the effects of high oxygen pressure. Rats acclimated to an altitude of 5272 m (17,400 feet) for 8 weeks showed a later occurrence of lung tissue damage and greater length of survival than nonacclimated controls.[54] Since inadequate blood oxygenation is the main cause of lung tissue injury and consequent death, it has been postulated that the differences between acclimated and nonacclimated rats are related to the increased capacity for oxygen delivery that occurs from altitude acclimation.[54] Thus, in this context there is a positive cross-acclimation between altitude and hyperoxia. Obviously, with increasing interest in using high oxygen pressure for therapeutic and medical purposes and in exploring the underwater world in which oxygen has high pressure, the potential for altitude acclimation protection warrants further research.

CONCLUSION

Three clinical entities specific to altitude have been identified: acute mountain sickness, pulmonary edema, and Monge's disease (Fig. 11-1). Acute mountain sickness has been clearly associated with hypoxic stress and is characterized by headache, malaise, dizziness, shortness of breath, sleep difficulties, and stomach upset. As schematized in Fig. 11-1 acute mountain sickness occurs in lowlanders as well as highlanders who are unable to restore functional homeostasis when exposed to hypoxia. Several factors precipitate the onset of acute mountain sickness, among which rapid ascent, dehydration, and excessive activity are the most important. Usually symptoms of acute mountain sickness disappear without treatment. In contrast, pulmonary edema is a severely debilitating disease and can be fatal if the patient is not treated rapidly. The disease is associated with excessive pulmonary hyper-

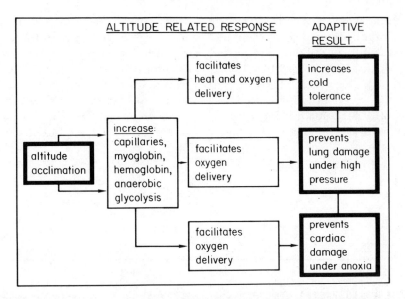

Fig. 11-2. Schematization of cross-acclimation between altitude hypoxia, hypothermia, hyperoxia, and anoxia. As a result of improved oxygen transport system elicited by high-altitude hypoxia oxygen delivery to cell is enhanced enabling the organism to tolerate cold, protecting lung tissue, and preventing cardiac muscle damage from high oxygen pressure or anoxia.

tension, impaired pulmonary oxygen exchange, and histological alterations of the pulmonary vessels. As a result the lowlander or highlander with pulmonary edema suffers a greater loss of functional homeostasis than with acute mountain sickness. Furthermore, there are multiple causes of the inability to restore functional homeostasis with pulmonary edema. For this reason treatment includes oxygen administration, corticosteroids, and transport to lower altitudes. Preventive measures include initial avoidance of excessive physical activity when ascending to altitude either for the first time or when returning from sea level. Monge's disease or chronic mountain sickness is a severely debilitating disease that occurs mostly among highland natives with prolonged residence at high altitude and is associated with a loss

of functional adaptation. It is characterized by an excessive hypoxemia and polycythemia, but the etiology is not well defined. Treatment includes transfer to a lower altitude.

Adaptation to high-altitude hypoxia, as learned from cross-acclimatization and cross-acclimation studies, affects the organism's response to other environmental stresses. Acclimation to high-altitude hypoxia appears to have positive cross-acclimation effects on the organism's response to anoxic stress, hyperoxia, and cold stress (Fig. 11-2). There is evidence suggesting that altitude acclimation may be related to the low incidence of hypertensive and other cardiac diseases in high-altitude populations. Athletic performance at sea level does not appear enhanced by acclimatization to high altitude. On the other hand, the advantages of acclimatization to moderate altitude are evident in the middle and long distance runs of the 1968 Olympics held in Mexico in which highland athletes excelled.

The beneficial effects of altitude acclimation on functional performance during cold stress appear related to increased capillarization and increased oxygen-carrying capacity, which together improve heat delivery and oxygen supply to the cell when the organism is exposed to cold stress. Similarly, the protective role of altitude acclimation on lung tissue and cardiac muscle during exposure to high oxygen pressure and anoxic stress appears to result from an improved oxygen transport system elicited by hypoxic stress.

REFERENCES

1. Folk, G. E., Jr. 1974. Textbook of environmental physiology. Lea & Febiger, Philadelphia.
2. Monge, M. C., and C. Monge. 1966. High-altitude diseases: mechanism and management. Charles C Thomas, Publisher, Springfield, Ill.
3. Singh, I., P. K. Khanna, M. C. Srivastava, M. Lal, S. B. Roy, and C. S. V. Subramanyan. 1969. Acute mountain sickness. N. Engl. J. Med. **280:**175-184.
4. Ward, M. 1975. Mountain medicine, a clinical study of cold and high altitude. Van Nostrand Reinhold Co. New York.
5. Heath, D., and R. R. Williams. 1977. Man at high altitude. The pathophysiology of acclimatization and adaptation. Churchill Livingstone, Edinburgh.
6. Aoki, V. S., and S. M. Robinson. 1971. Body hydration and the incidence and severity of acute mountain sickness. J. Appl. Physiol. **31:**363-367.
7. Maher, J. T., P. H. Levine, and A. Cymerman. 1976. Human coagulation abnormalities during exposure to hypobaric hypoxia. J. Appl. Physiol. **41:** 702-707.
8. Waterlow, J. C., and H. W. Bunje. 1966. Observations on mountain sickness in the Colombian Andes. Lancet **2:**655-661.
9. Hansen, J. E., and W. O. Evans. 1970. A hypothesis regarding the pathophysiology of acute mountain sickness. Arch. Environ. Health **21:**666-669.
10. Carson, R. P., W. D. Evans, J. L. Shields, and J. P. Hannon. 1969. Symptomatology, pathophysiology and treatment of acute mountain sickness. Fed. Proc. **28:**1085-1091.
11. Gray, G. W., A. C. Bryan, R. Frayser, C. S. Houston, and I. D. Rennie. 1970. Control of acute mountain sickness. Aerospace Med. **42:**81-84.
12. Wilson, R. 1973. Acute high-altitude illness in mountaineers and problems of rescue. Ann. Intern. Med. **78:**421-427.
13. Hansen, J. E., L. H. Hartley, and R. P. Hogan. 1972. Arterial oxygen increase by high carbohydrate diet at altitude. J. Appl. Physiol. **33:**441-445.
14. Consolazio, C. F., L. O. Matoush, H. L. Johnson, H. J. Krzywicki, T. A. Daws, and G. J. Isaac. 1969. Effects of high carbohydrate diets on performance and clinical symptomatology after rapid ascent to high altitude. Fed. Proc. **28:**937-943.
15. Hurtado, A. 1937. Aspectos físicos y patológicos de la vida en las alturas. Imprenta Rimac, Lima, Peru.
16. Hultgren, H. N., W. B. Sprikard, J. Hellriegel, and C. S. Houston. 1961. High altitude pulmonary edema. Medicine **40:**289-313.
17. Peñaloza, D., and F. Sime. 1971. Chronic cor pulmonale due to loss of altitude acclimatization (chronic mountain sickness). Am. J. Med. **50:**728-743.
18. Peñaloza, D., F. Sime, and L. Ruiz. 1971. Cor pulmonale in chronic mountain sickness: present concept of Monge's disease. In R. Porter and J. Knight, eds. High altitude physiology: cardiac and respiratory aspects. Ciba Foundation Symposium. Churchill Livingstone, Edinburgh.
19. Marticorena, E., F. A. Tapia, J. Dyer, J. Severino, N. Banchero, R. Gamboa, H. Kruger, and D. Peñaloza. 1964. Pulmonary edema by ascending to high altitudes. Dis. Chest **45:**275-279.
20. Fred, H. L., A. M. Schmidt, T. Bates, and H. H. Hecht. 1962. Acute pulmonary edema of altitude. Clinical and physiologic observations. Circulation **25:**929-937.
21. Menon, N. D. 1965. High-altitude pulmonary edema. N. Engl. J. Med. **273:**66-73.

22. Lozano, R., and M. C. Monge. 1965. Renal function in high-altitude natives and in natives with chronic mountain sickness. J. Appl. Physiol. **20:** 1026-1027.

23. Balke, B. 1964. Work capacity and its limiting factors at high altitude. In W. H. Weihe, ed. The physiological effects of high altitude. Pergamon Press, Inc., New York.

24. Balke, B., F. J. Nagle, and J. T. Daniels. 1965. Altitude and maximum performance in work and sports activity. J.A.M.A. **194:**646-649.

25. Faulkner, J. A., J. T. Daniels, and B. Balke. 1967. Effects of training at moderate altitude on physical performance capacity. J. Appl. Physiol. **23:**85-89.

26. Daniels, J. T., and N. Oldridge. 1970. The effects of alternate exposure to altitude and sea level on world-class middle-distance runners. Med. Sci. Sports **2:**107-112.

27. Dill, D. B., and W. C. Adams. 1971. Maximal oxygen uptake at sea level and at 3090 m altitude in high school champion runners. J. Appl. Physiol. **30:**854-859.

28. Reeves, J. T., R. F. Grover, and J. E. Cohn. 1967. Regulation of ventilation during exercise at 10,200 ft. in athletes born at low altitude. J. Appl. Physiol. **22:**546-554.

29. Saltin, B. 1967. Aerobic and anaerobic work capacity at an altitude of 2,250 meters. In R. F. Goddard, ed. The effects of altitude on physical performance. Athletic Institute, Chicago.

30. Faulkner, J. A., J. Kollias, C. B. Favour, E. R. Buskirk, and B. Balke. 1968. Maximum aerobic capacity and running performance at altitude. J. Appl. Physiol. **24:**685-691.

31. Buskirk, E. R., J. Kollias, R. F. Akers, E. K. Prokop, and E. P. Reategui. 1967. Maximal performance at altitude and on return from altitude in conditioned runners. J. Appl. Physiol. **23:**259-266.

32. Adams, W. C., E. M. Bernauer, D. B. Dill, and J. B. Bomar, Jr. 1975. Effects of equivalent sea level and altitude training on VO$_2$ max and running performance. J. Appl. Physiol. **39:**262-266.

33. Jokl, E., and P. Jokl. 1968. The effect of altitude on athletic performance. Exercise and altitude. University Park Press, Baltimore.

34. Faulkner, J. A. 1967. Training for maximum performance at altitude. In R. F. Goddard, ed. The effects of altitude and athletic performance. Athletic Institute, Chicago.

35. Faulkner, J. A. 1971. Maximum exercise at medium altitude. In R. J. Shephard, ed. Frontier of fitness. Charles C Thomas, Publisher, Springfield, Ill.

36. Craig, A. B. 1969. Olympic 1968: a post mortem. Med. Sci. Sports **1:**177-183.

37. Martin, L. G., G. E. Wertenberger, J. R. Hippensteele, and R. W. Bullard. 1972. Thyroidal influence on myocardial changes induced by simulated high altitude. Am. J. Physiol. **222:**1599-1603.

38. Burlington, R. F., and J. T. Maher. 1968. Effect of anoxia on mechanical performance of isolated atria from ground squirrels and rats acclimatized to altitude. Nature **219:**1370-1371.

39. McGrath, J. J., and R. W. Bullard. 1968. Altered myocardial performance in response to anoxia after high-altitude exposure. J. Appl. Physiol. **25:**761-764.

40. McGrath, J. J., J. Procházka, V. Pelouch, and B. Ostadal. 1973. Biological responses of rats to intermittent high-altitude effects of age. J. Appl. Physiol. **34:**289-293.

41. Souhrada, J., B. Mrzena, O. Poupa, and R. W. Bullard. 1971. Functional changes of cardiac muscle in adaptation to two types of chronic hypoxia. J. Appl. Physiol. **30:**214-218.

42. Poupa, O., K. Krofta, J. Procházka, and Z. Turek. 1966. Acclimation to simulated high altitude and acute cardiac necrosis. Fed. Proc. **25:**1243-1246.

43. Poupa, O., K. Krofta, J. Procházka, and M. Chvapil. 1965. The resistance of the myocardium to anoxia in animals acclimated to simulated altitude. Physiol. Bohemoslov. **41:**233-237.

44. Meerson, F. Z., O. A. Gomazkov, and M. V. Shimkovich. 1973. Adaptation to high altitude hypoxia as a factor preventing development of myocardial ischemic necrosis. Am. J. Cardiol. **31:**30-34.

45. Bowers, W. D., Jr., R. F. Burlington, B. K. Whitten, R. C. Daum, and M. A. Posiviata. 1973. Ultrastructural and metabolic alterations in myocardium from altitude acclimated rats. Am. J. Physiol. **220:**1885-1889.

46. McGrath, J. J., B. Ostadal, J. Procházka, M. Wachlova, and V. Rychterova. 1975. Experimental cardiac necrosis in hypobaric and anemic hypoxia. J. Appl. Physiol. **39:**205-308.

47. McGill, H. C., Jr., ed. 1968. The geographic pathology of atherosclerosis. Williams & Wilkins Co., Baltimore.

48. Ruiz, L. 1973. Epidemiologia de la hipertension arterial y de la cardiopatia isquemica en las grandes alturas: prevalencia y factores relevantes a sus historia natural. Doctoral Thesis, Universidad Peruana Cayetano Heredia, Instituto de Investigaciones de la Altura, Lima, Peru.

49. W.H.O. chronicle. 1969. International work in cardiovascular diseases, 1959-1969. World Health Organization, Geneva.

50. Tucker, A., and S. M. Horvath. 1971. Metabolic responses to normoxia and hypoxia in the altitude-adapted rat during swimming. J. Appl. Physiol. **31:** 761-765.

51. Dawson, C. A., R. B. Roemer, and S. M. Horvath. 1970. Body temperature and oxygen uptake in warm- and cold-adapted rats during swimming. J. Appl. Physiol. **29:**150-154.

52. DeFeo, J. J., I. Baumel, and H. Lal. 1970. Drug environment interactions: acute hypoxia and chronic isolation. Fed. Proc. **29:**1985-1990.

53. LeBlanc, J. 1975. Man in the cold. Charles C Thomas, Publisher, Springfield, Ill.

54. Brauer, R. W., D. E. Parrish, R. Oway, P. C. Pratt, and R. L. Pessotti. 1970. Protection by altitude acclimatization against lung damage from exposure to oxygen at 825 mm Hg. J. Appl. Physiol. **28:**474-481.

12 | Functional responses to experimental starvation and chronic undernutrition of adults

A basic principle of living organisms is that they require a continuous supply of energy and nutrients to maintain their normal metabolic activities, to continue tissue replacement, and to grow. Therefore a drastic reduction of dietary intake, as in experimental starvation or weight loss programs, affects the individual's biological and behavioral functions. These effects are reflected in the use of body tissue such as fat and muscle as fuel and decreased energy expenditure and work capacity. Findings derived from such studies are important for understanding both body composition and physiological work performance of populations living with chronic low dietary intakes, such as in developing nations. In this chapter physiological and behavioral responses to both experimental and chronic starvation will be discussed.

FUNCTIONAL PERFORMANCE AND EXPERIMENTAL STARVATION

Depending on the caloric restriction, the various forms of starvation can be classified as (1) acute starvation, which involves an intake of less than 600 calories per day for less than 2 weeks, (2) semiacute starvation with an intake ranging from 900 to 1100 calories per day for less than 30 days, and (3) moderate semistarvation with an intake ranging from 1300 to 1600 calories per day for as long as 24 weeks.

Behavior

All three forms of starvation cause a number of psychological effects that alter normal individual and group behavior.[1-3] The most important behavioral characteristics of the starving person include (1) apathy and reluctance to engage in any new activity, (2) unresponsiveness to external stimuli, (3) spontaneous reduction in all physical movements, (4) sensations of muscle weakness, which are reflected in movements requiring muscular strength, and (5) adoption of energy-sparing movements. The result of these behavioral changes is a marked reduction in energy expenditure and thus a slowdown in the rate of deterioration of the starving organism.

Body weight and composition

The most conspicuous manifestation of calorie restrictions in acute or semiacute starvation is the drastic reduction in body weight.[3] As shown in Fig. 12-1, rate of weight loss follows the law of diminishing decrements; during the first 2 weeks of semiacute starvation weight loss is greater than during the last 4 weeks. On the other hand, rate of weight loss is directly proportional to the amount of caloric restriction.

In semiacute and acute starvation between 40% and 55% of the reduction in body weight is accounted for by loss of body fat, and loss in body water accounts for 20%. As shown in Fig. 12-2, acute starvation for 10 days produces a loss of 17% body fat, only a minimal muscle loss (1%), and a 10% reduction in "active tissue."[4,5] (Active tissue equals body weight minus body fat, body minerals, and extracellular water weights.) On the other hand, moderate semiacute starvation for 24 weeks produces marked body fat losses to as much as 69% and muscle losses up to 41%, whereas active tissue is reduced by only 27%. These changes reflect the organism's sequential use of body food stores. During the first 16 hours of starvation the organism derives its energy mostly from the 300 g of carbohydrate stored in the liver (100 g) and muscle (200 g) cells in the form of glycogen. Thereafter, during the first 2 weeks of starvation, the body preferentially uses fat rather than protein for metabolism, but when starvation continues for as long as 24 weeks both fat and protein are used for metabolism.

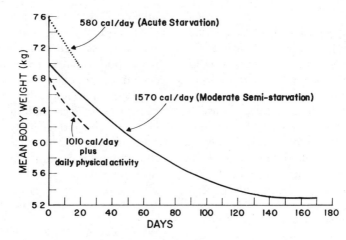

Fig. 12-1. Decrease in body weight during starvation. In all three forms of starvation rate of weight loss is greater during first 4 weeks, and thereafter weight is lost at minimal rates. (Modified from Grande, F. 1964. Man under caloric deficiency. In D. B. Dill, E. F. Adolph, and C. G. Wilber, eds. Handbook of physiology. vol 4. Adaptation to the environment. American Physiological Society, Washington, D.C.)

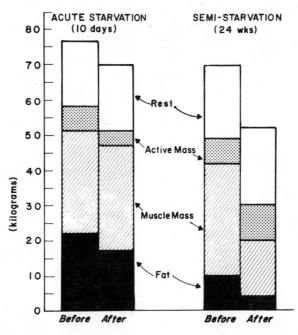

Fig. 12-2. Changes in body composition during starvation. Reduced body weight during acute starvation is accounted for mostly by loss of fat and active tissue (active tissue = body weight − body fat − body mineral − extracellular water), whereas during long-term semistarvation greatest losses occur in body fat and muscle. (Modified from Viteri, F. E., and O. Pineda. 1972. Effects on body composition and body function. Psychological effects. Symposia of the Swedish Nutrition Foundation **9**:25-40.)

Metabolic rate

Acute calorie restriction for 10 days does not affect the metabolic rate. However, as shown in Fig. 12-3, semiacute starvation for as long as 24 weeks does result in reduced basal oxygen consumption. This decrease appears related to a differential decrease in the mass and metabolic activity of body organs or tissues that have high metabolic rates, rather than a generalized decrease in all body cell rates.[1,2] The observed reduction in metabolic rate represents an adaptive response in that it conserves body energy in the face of reduced energy input.

Physical work performance

Acute starvation, although it may produce many adverse effects such as hypohydration and protein catabolism, does not appear to affect physical work performance significantly. The oxygen uptakes during standardized submaximal and maximal exercises performed on the treadmill during acute calorie restriction for 10 days were not significantly different from those during normal calorie

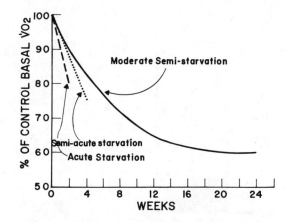

Fig. 12-3. Decrease in metabolic rate during starvation. As in reduction of body weight, decrease of metabolic rate during first 4 weeks of starvation is faster than thereafter. (Modified from Viteri, F. E., and O. Pineda. 1972. Effects on body composition and body function. Psychological effects. Symposia of the Swedish Nutrition Foundation **9:**25-40.)

intake.[1,2,6] However, during longer periods of calorie restriction, such as observed during semiacute starvation, a reduction in physical work performance does occur.[1] This was shown by the fact that after 24 weeks of semiacute starvation the maximal oxygen intake, expressed as milliliters per kilogram of body weight and grip strength, was drastically reduced. This decrease reflects the concomitant reduction in the efficiency of the cardiovascular, respiratory, and hematological systems, which results in limiting the capacity to supply oxygen to the muscles.

WORK CAPACITY, PRODUCTIVITY, AND CHRONIC UNDERNUTRITION

For practical purposes an individual or population is considered to be undernourished when the daily dietary intake provides less than 2000 calories per day. Using this criteria a large segment of the populations of developing nations live with chronic undernutrition. An important question to consider is whether populations living with chronic low dietary intakes have a decreased work capacity like that seen in populations subjected to experimental calorie restriction. In 1968 the Food and Agriculture Organization (FAO) pointed out the possibility that chronic undernutrition during growth may result in impaired physical work capacity. Because low work capacity may also be associated with low productivity, several investigations have been conducted, both under laboratory and field conditions.

Aerobic work capacity

As discussed in Chapter 9 the maximum oxygen intake per unit of body weight per minute (or aerobic capacity) is an adequate measure of the individual's work capacity because it reflects the capacity of the working muscles to use oxygen and the ability of the cardiovascular system to transport and deliver oxygen to the tissues.

The work capacity of four groups of Guatemalan subjects with different nutritional and socioeconomic backgrounds was studied in Guatemala.[7] The study included (1) army recruits with adequate dietary intakes, (2) nutritionally supplemented subjects who had been supplemented for 3 years prior to the study with a diet (Incaparina) supplying 5.5 g of high quality protein and 250 calories per day, (3) a group of poorly nourished, nonsupplemented rural subjects, and (4) military cadets of good current nutritional status as well as good nutritional background. The maximum oxygen intake was evaluated while the subjects performed maximal work on a treadmill. This study showed that maximum oxygen intake (L/min) corresponded to the nutritional status of each of the samples; thus the highest values are among the

well-nourished military cadets, and the lowest are among the poor, nonsupplemented subjects. However, when aerobic capacity was expressed as milliliters of oxygen intake per kilogram of body weight or kilogram of lean body weight (LBW) as shown in Fig. 12-4, the poor, nonsupplemented subjects attained values similar to the army recruits and the nutritionally supplemented subjects, although the military cadets still attained higher values.

Productivity

To complement laboratory studies, time-motion studies with nutritionally supplemented subjects and poorly nourished rural subjects were also conducted.[7] The measurements were made while the subjects performed almost identical assigned agricul-

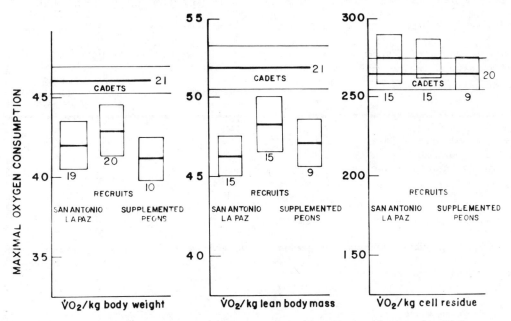

Fig. 12-4. Comparison of maximal oxygen consumption of four Guatemalan samples. Well-nourished cadets had higher maximum oxygen intake than all other groups. However, there are no major differences between the three contrasting nutritional status groups. (Modified from Viteri, F. E. 1971. Considerations on the effect of nutrition on the body composition and physical working capacity of young Guatemalan adults. In N. S. Scrimshaw and A. M. Altschul, eds. Amino acid fortification of protein foods. The M.I.T. Press, Cambridge, Mass.)

tural tasks, which were done without time restrictions. As summarized in Table 8, the nonsupplemented subjects, despite their similar total average caloric expenditures, went into a higher negative caloric balance, evidenced by their greater loss of body weight. Table 8 also indicates that the non-supplemented subjects were active a smaller percent of the time after their work tasks were completed and spent more time resting or sleeping. A review of the German World War II data on heavy working coal miners and steel workers revealed that as the caloric intake dropped from 2200 kcal per day to 1800 kcal per day in 1946, coal and steel production was greatly reduced.[8] As shown in Fig. 12-5 steel production between 1938 and 1945 decreased gradually year by year as the caloric intake decreased.

Investigations among Swedish lumber-jacks found that those with maximum oxygen intake (L/min) had a greater work output than those with maximum oxygen intake.[9] Among East African sugarcane cutters a significant correlation ($r = 0.46$) between daily productivity and maximum oxygen intake (L/min) was found.[10] Similarly, an extensive study of Colombian sugarcane cutters through multiple regression analysis found that productivity (metric tons/day) was positively related to maximum oxygen intake and height and negatively related to percent body fat.[11,12] The authors suggest that the observed associations may be related to the effects of chronic undernutrition during growth as well as physical fitness; undernu-trition in the adult would bring about its effect on productivity primarily through its effect on maximum oxygen intake.[12] In other words, productivity is affected indirectly by

Table 8. Summary of time-motion studies and energy cost of work in the field (24-hour values, average of 3 to 6 days)*

	Supplemented peons (N = 19)	San Antonio (La Paz) (N = 20)
Total caloric intake	3446	2693
Basal caloric expenditure	1594	1526
Calories available for work	1852	1167
Total caloric expenditure	3697D†	3396A
	3568A†	
Caloric balance	−251D	−703
	−122A	
Weight change (g)	−35D	−125
	−19A	
Caloric expenditure during different periods of 1 day (average of 3 to 6 days) (calories per minute)		
Type of work	Day	Assignment	Assignment
Activity period			
Work	4.1	5.2	4.6
After work	2.7	2.7	2.5
At rest or asleep			
After work	1.12-1.28	1.12-1.28	1.06-12.6
At night	1.12	1.12	1.06

*Based on data from Viteri, F. E. 1971. Considerations on the effect of nutrition on the body composition and physical work-ing capacity of young Guatemalan adults. In N. S. Schrimshaw and A. M. Altschul, eds. Amino acid fortification of protein foods. The M.I.T. Press, Cambridge, Mass.
†Type of work: D = Day; A = Assignment.

nutritional status through the influence of the latter on height, fat content, and maximum oxygen consumption. A recent study of industrial workers in India found that work output was significantly correlated to body weight and lean body weight; total daily work output was higher in those with greater body weight and high lean body weight.[13]

Although the available data are only suggestive, this problem is especially significant for developing nations. If reduction in adult body size is associated with lower productivity, then programs oriented to increasing productivity must be concerned with increasing the developmental, nutritional status of a population, which in turn would increase adult stature and productivity. However, it should not be assumed that bigger always means better. Just because better producers are bigger does not follow that bigger is better in other ecological condi-

tions. In Peru, when exposed to poor socioeconomic conditions, tall mothers, who probably grew up under more favorable conditions leading to their height, had fewer surviving offspring than their short counterparts.[14] Short body size may well be more adaptive under such conditions or when considering different parameters.

CONCLUSION

Experimental studies on starvation have provided valuable information about the organism's capacity to readjust its needs and redistribute its energy reserves. Both acute and semiacute starvation severely affect the individual. At the behavioral level irritation and apathy are prominent features of acute starvation. In terms of body composition the available data indicate that during acute starvation fat is used as an energy source, whereas during prolonged semistarvation energy

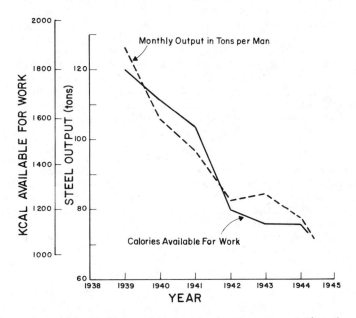

Fig. 12-5. Relationship of kilocalories, work output, and years among steel workers. Along with decline in calories available for work, monthly output in tons per man declined drastically. (Modified from Keller, W. D., and H. A. Kraut. 1963. World Rev. Nutr. Diet **3:**65-81.)

is derived from both fat and muscle. These data reveal the organism's hierarchical utilization of nutritional reserves stored in the forms of fat and muscle. The effects of short-term (less than 10 days) caloric restriction on physical performance are minimal, but prolonged starvation affects the individual's cardiovascular, respiratory, and circulatory systems resulting in a reduction of work capacity.

It appears that chronic undernutrition does not affect aerobic capacity when expressed as milliliters of oxygen per kilogram of body weight. However, as shown by measurements of energy expenditure, time-motion studies, and the relationship of aerobic capacity to body size, chronic undernutrition, through its influence on adult stature, lean body weight, and aerobic capacity, negatively affects work productivity. The extent to which these findings are applicable to other work conditions, ecological factors, and populations is not presently known. Therefore, further research in this area is warranted.

REFERENCES

1. Keys, A., J. Brozek, A. Henschel, O. Mickelsen, and H. L. Taylor. 1950. The biology of human starvation. University of Minnesota Press, Minneapolis.
2. Grande, F. J., T. Anderson, and A. Keys. 1958. Changes of basal metabolic rate in man in semistarvation and refeeding. J. Appl. Physiol. **12**:230-238.
3. Grande, F. 1964. Man under caloric deficiency. In D. B. Dill, E. F. Adolf, and C. G. Wilber, eds. Handbook of physiology. vol. 4. Adaptation to the environment. American Physiological Society, Washington, D.C.
4. Krzywicki, H. J., C. F. Consolazio, L. O. Matoush, and H. L. Johnson. 1968. Metabolic aspects of acute starvation. Body composition changes. Am. J. Clin. Nutr. **21**:87-97.
5. Viteri, F. E., and O. Pineda. 1972. Effects on body composition and body function. Psychological effects. Symposia of the Swedish Nutrition Foundation **9**:25-40.
6. Dawe, T. A., C. F. Consolazio, S. L. Hilty, H. L. Johnson, H. J. Krzywicki, R. A. Nelson, and N. F. Witt. 1972. Evaluation of cardiopulmonary function and work performance in man during caloric restriction. J. Appl. Physiol. **33**:211-217.
7. Viteri, F. E. 1971. Considerations on the effect of nutrition on the body composition and physical working capacity of young Guatemalan adults. In N. S. Scrimshaw and A. M. Altschul, eds. Amino acid fortification of protein foods. The M.I.T. Press, Cambridge, Mass.
8. Keller, W. D., and H. A. Kraut. 1963. Work and nutrition. World Rev. Nutr. Diet **3**:65-81.
9. Hansson, J. E. 1965. The relationship between individual characteristics of the worker and output of work in logging operations. Studia Forestalia suecia 29. Skogskolan, Stockholm.
10. Davies, C. T. 1973. Relationship of maximum aerobic power output to productivity and absenteeism of East African sugar cane workers. Br. J. Ind. Med. **30**:146-154.
11. Spurr, G. B., M. Barac-Nieto, and M. G. Maksud. 1975. Energy expenditure cutting sugar cane. J. Appl. Physiol. **39**:990-996.
12. Spurr, G. B., M. Barac-Nieto, and M. G. Maksud. 1977. Productivity and maximal oxygen consumption in sugar cane cutters. Am. J. Clin. Nutr. **30**:316-321.
13. Satyanarayana, K., A. Nadamuni Naidu, B. Chatterjee, and B. S. Narasinga Rao. 1977. Body size and work output. Am. J. Clin. Nutr. **30**:322-325.
14. Frisancho, A. R., J. Sanchez, D. Pallardel, and L. Yanez. 1973. Adaptive significance of small body size under poor socioeconomic conditions in southern Peru. Am. J. Phys. Anthropol. **39**:255-262.

13

Influence of protein-calorie malnutrition and chronic undernutrition on human growth

Malnutrition is one of the most pressing problems confronting the developing nations. A nutrition survey of over 190,000 children in forty-six communities in South America, Africa, and Asia between 1963 and 1972 indicates that the presence of severe forms of protein-calorie malnutrition (PCM) ranges between 0.5% and 20% of the population, whereas about 3% to 74% suffer from moderate malnutrition.[1] Furthermore, the interamerican investigation of mortality in childhood in Latin America points out that malnutrition was either directly or indirectly responsible for over 50% of the deaths of children under 5 years of age.[2] In view of the fact that an individual's adult biological and behavioral performance is profoundly influenced by environmental factors operating during growth and development, an understanding of the effects of malnutrition on human growth is of prime importance. In this chapter the characteristics of protein-calorie malnutrition and their relationship to brain growth, infection, and immunity are discussed. In addition the growth of populations living in chronic undernutrition is discussed.

SEVERE PROTEIN-CALORIE MALNUTRITION

The term *protein-calorie malnutrition*, abbreviated as PCM, has been widely used to designate the spectrum ranging from pure protein deficiency to deficiencies of both protein and calories. PCM is a disease with a multiple etiology, observed principally in developing nations or populations undergoing cultural transition and/or urbanization. In all forms of PCM there is a reduction of both protein and calorie intake, but the ratio of protein to total calorie intake may vary widely in different conditions. In general two main forms of PCM are recognized: marasmus and kwashiorkor.

Marasmus

Marasmus is a term applied to a child with exhausted protein and calorie stores. It results from a chronic, symmetrical reduction of all nutrients that approaches starvation levels. Its origin is traceable to the prenatal period and is usually manifested during the first year of postnatal life. It causes a drastic reduction in growth and development such that the marasmic child is short and lightweight for its age, as well as retarded in skeletal maturation. The child exhibits extreme muscular wasting and a near lack of subcutaneous fat (Fig. 13-1, *A*); these conditions reflect an attempt by the organism to use its own tissues as a source of nutriment in the face of a chronic and generalized decrease in nutrient resources. The marasmic child also has a reduced brain weight, cortical atrophy, hypotonia, reduced activity, and displays constant hunger behavior.

Kwashiorkor

Kwashiorkor is caused primarily by an acute protein deficiency occurring in the presence of relatively adequate caloric intake, often from foods rich in carbohydrates such as starch but poor in protein. The name kwashiorkor is used by the Ga people of Ghana to whom the disorder is well known. This disease is usually manifested after the first year, most often between the second and fourth years of postnatal life. The kwashiorkor child is normal in growth and development through the first postnatal year, but after the first year growth in height and weight is drastically reduced to between 60% and 80% of the expected standard. A typical kwashiorkor (Fig. 13-1, *B*) child is the so-called "sugar baby," with a round moon face, pitting edema, variable degrees of dermatosis with depigmentation, and hyperkeratosis. The child's hair is often depigmented, and when malnutrition alternates with periods of relatively adequate dietary intake, depigmented bands appear in the hair, often referred to as "flag signs." In addition, the implantation of the hair is affected such that it falls out spontaneously or can be painlessly removed. Also serum albumin and protein are reduced.

The kwashiorkor child is apathetic, lethargic, anorexic (not hungry), withdrawn, and highly irritable. Sometimes the child becomes immobile, lying quietly in a fetal po-

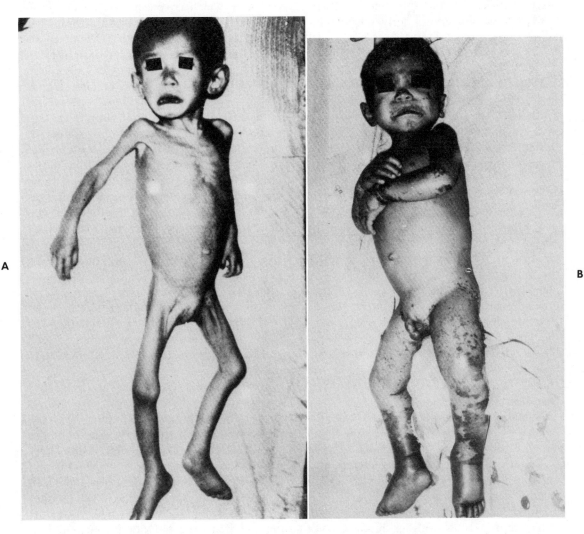

Fig. 13-1. Typical appearance of children with, **A,** marasmus and, **B,** kwashiorkor. Note the drastic reduction of subcutaneous fat and muscle wasting of the marasmic child. In contrast, the child with kwashiorkor exhibits edema and changes in skin and hair pigmentation. (From Suskind, R. M. 1975. Pediatr. Clin. North Am. **22:**873-883. Photographs courtesy medical staff, Anemia and Malnutrition Research Center, Chiang Mai, Thailand.)

sition with open, nonfixating eyes. Often the kwashiorkor child maintains a monotonous whimper. Like the marasmic infant, the kwashiorkor child exhibits hypotonia and poorly developed motor skills to such an extent that in some cases the child does not respond, in any measurable sense, to standard psychomotor stimuli derived from mental developmental scales.

Marasmus and kwashiorkor

The term *marasmus-kwashiorkor* is used to describe conditions in which signs of both syndromes are present. The child with marasmus-kwashiorkor has reduced growth in stature and weight and a drastic reduction in subcutaneous fat and muscle.

Critical periods of vulnerability of the brain

At present the dominant thesis is that the effects of malnutrition on brain growth depend on the developmental stage at which the individual is subjected to the stress; if malnutrition occurs during the period of high growth velocity or "growth spurt," the effects are permanent, but if it occurs after this critical period, the effects are reversible. Evidence in support of this thesis has been derived from experimental studies on animals and autopsies of children who died from severe malnutrition.

Animal studies. Experimental studies on rats have demonstrated that the growth and structure of the brain of an animal may be profoundly altered by events occurring during critical periods of development.[3-9] These studies have shown that if body growth is retarded at the time of the brain growth spurt, there is a resulting brain growth deficit associated with a disproportionate reduction of the cerebellum and neuron cells that resist subsequent nutritional rehabilitation. On the other hand, if body growth is retarded after the brain growth spurt, the

brain growth deficit and structural components fully recover with restoration of a good diet. On the basis of these investigations it has been suggested that growth and development of the organs follow a sequential pattern for cell multiplication and growth in cell size, which is specific to a given organ system. The development of the brain follows three phases of growth: (1) hyperplasia —in this stage there is an increase in brain weight, protein content, and DNA content; (2) hyperplasia plus concomitant hypertrophy—the increase in DNA content falls behind the increase in brain protein content and weight; and (3) hypertrophy—there is no additional increase in DNA content, but the existing cells enlarge resulting in increases in net protein synthesis and brain weight at the same rate. Because of the sequential pattern of growth the theory of vulnerable periods maintains that malnutrition inflicted during hyperplastic (proliferative stage) growth results in an organ with a permanent deficit in cell number. Biochemically, there may not be complete recovery. On the other hand, malnutrition imposed during the hypertrophic (cell enlargement stage) phase results in a reduction of cell size that can be restored by rehabilitation to normal.

Human studies. Postmortem studies of children who suffered from severe malnutrition support in part the findings from experimental animal studies.[6-10] These studies show that children who suffer from severe malnutrition are characterized by a reduction in brain weight and size and a reduction in number of cells. Such a deficit in cell number occurs only among children who died during the first year but not among children who died of kwashiorkor after the first year, presumably because they were well nourished during the first year of life. Furthermore, in brains of children who died during the first year of life, total cholesterol and total phospholipid content was reduced in proportion to the reduction in cell number, and if the malnutrition extended into the second year of life before the infant died, an actual decrease in lipid quantity occurred.

In summary, both experimental studies on animals and postmortem observations of children provide evidence for lasting structural changes in the brain being related to the timing of early malnutrition. It appears that the brain growth spurt is by far the most vulnerable period, and malnutrition at this stage may result in quantitative and qualitative physical distortion.

Critical periods and intellectual development. As shown in Fig. 13-2, the brain growth spurt in humans begins during the last trimester of fetal life and terminates by the second postnatal year. Thus, in humans the vulnerable period for the permanent effects of malnutrition would be from the last trimester of the prenatal period to the end of the first year. Conversely, the effects of malnutrition on brain growth and structural distortions after the second year would not be permanent. An obvious question is whether these quantitative and structural changes of the brain are also found among survivors of severe malnutrition.

Investigators have attempted to test this hypothesis with little success.[11-14] Studies during treatment and recovery in the hos-

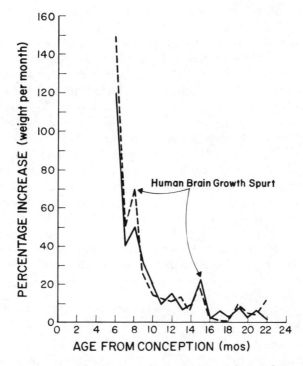

Fig. 13-2. Brain growth expressed by percent of increase in weight in relation to conceptual age. There are two "spurts" of brain growth, one during last trimester of gestation and another at 5 months of postnatal period. (Modified from Cheek, D. B., A. B. Holt, and E. D. Mellits. 1972. Malnutrition and the nervous system. Pub. 251. Pan American Health Organization, Washington, D.C.)

pital of returning competence in Mexican children hospitalized from severe malnutrition revealed that behavioral recovery was less complete in the children who were hospitalized before 6 months of age than in older children.[15] This finding supports the hypothesis that during the critical period of infancy the individual is more susceptible to permanent effects of malnutrition and hence more resistant to intellectual recovery. However, these results are questionable because the follow-up period after malnutrition was too short, and the period of hospitalization was not the same in both groups of children.[13] Furthermore, studies of Jamaican[16] and Ugandan[17] school age children who suffered an episode of acute or severe malnutrition prior, during, and after the age of 2 years found no relationship between the scores obtained in psychological or intellectual tests and the age when the subjects were hospitalized. Similarly, a study of school-age Nigerian children who suffered from severe malnutrition (kwashiorkor) when they were 1 to 3 years old found no relationships between scores on psychological tests and the ages at which they were hospitalized.[18]

It is evident that evaluations of cognitive or intellectual development have failed to determine whether malnutrition has long-lasting biological consequences on brain function. This is not surprising in view of the fact that all cognitive or behavioral measurements are influenced by the individual's social and environmental experience, and therefore such measurements where malnutrition coexists with poor socioeconomic conditions are useless for testing the hypotheses that malnutrition per se has long-lasting effects on neurological development. For this reason, to test hypotheses of vulnerable periods of brain growth, what is needed are biological quantifiable measurements of brain growth and function that are not influenced by social environmental factors.

MALNUTRITION AND INFECTIONS
Frequency and effects on morbidity and mortality

Because of poor socioeconomic and hygenic conditions, malnourished populations are constantly subject to infectious diseases. As learned from studies of immunoglobulin levels on cord blood, infectious diseases among malnourished populations start at the intrauterine stage. About 50% of malnourished Guatemalan children were born with high immunoglobulin (IgM) levels when compared to well-nourished children.[19,20]

Infectious disease, because of its debilitating effects, plays an important role in the development of malnutrition, morbidity, and mortality of young children in developing nations. The mortality rate from measles for children in a malnourished rural Guatemalan population was 189 times greater than that for children in the United States in 1959.[21] In the same manner the measles case-fatality rates reported among malnourished infants and children living in Nigeria, India, Senegal, and Guatemala over the last decade have ranged from 6% to 17% compared to the low United States and European rates.[22] Furthermore, 93% of 426 malnourished Senegalese children with measles had diarrhea, and 57% of 83 malnourished Nigerian children with measles had pneumonia as complications.[23] Of 35,095 deaths in children under 5 years of age reported in thirteen Latin American projects, 60.9% of the deaths from malnourishment were due to infectious diseases.[2]

Synergic interaction of infection and malnutrition

All infections have an adverse effect on the nutritional status and growth of the child, but they especially affect the malnourished child because they reduce food intake and increase urinary metabolic losses of nitrogen, ascorbic acid, iron, and other important nutrients that are already in short supply.[24,25] Therefore the requirements for protein and other nutrients are increased during both the infection and recovery phases. If these increased requirements are not met by the insufficient diet, the individual is left in a depleted state, becoming increasingly more vulnerable to the development of clinical and nutritional diseases as a result of additional infectious episodes. Furthermore, these infections may, in themselves, depress cell-mediated immunity and therefore new infections may emerge or existing ones may become more severe. In other words, there is a reciprocal and synergistic interaction between infection and malnutrition in which each exacerbates the other, and the combination of the two have more profound consequences for the individual than would be predicted from the presence of either alone.[25]

Infections and immunity: causation

The fact that malnourished populations are more vulnerable to the effects of infectious diseases suggests a defective immune response with malnutrition. In general, however, malnourished children have greater immunoglobin levels than well-nourished children, suggesting both an increased frequency of infections and an enhanced immunity system. In other words, the malnourished child is more susceptible to infections and at the same time has a greater defense mechanism. As schematized in Fig. 13-3 this apparent contradiction results from the fact that malnutrition has two different effects depending on the immunosystem. First, malnutrition per se decreases production of immunoglobulins (IgA) in nasopharyngeal salivary secretions, such as those found in the mucosa, tears, and saliva.[26,27] The low production of immunoglobulins facilitates colonization of the mucosal surface by microorganisms and therefore predisposes the malnourished child to increased incidence of infection. Second, malnutrition does not affect the capacity to produce antibodies.[26,27] In fact, once infected, the

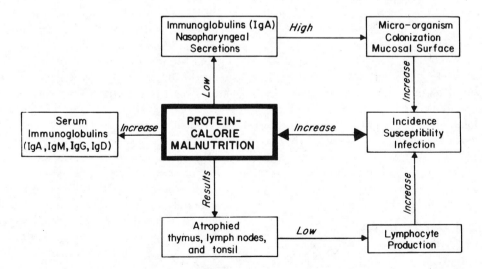

Fig. 13-3. Schematization of synergic interaction of protein-calorie malnutrition and infection. Malnutrition, although it does not impair capacity to produce serum antibodies, does decrease production of antibodies in nasopharyngeal secretions, which, in turn, become a focus of infection. This resulting infection exacerbates malnutrition effects.

malnourished child responds with an elevated production of serum immunoglobulins (IgA, IgM, IgG, IgD).

Third, another mechanism whereby malnutrition predisposes to infections is through an inhibition of cell-mediated responses.[27-30] The cell-mediated immune response is affected by the capacity of the thymus glands, lymph nodes, and tonsils to produce lymphocytes. The thymus of malnourished children is atrophied, and the lymph nodes, tonsils, and spleen are smaller than in well-nourished children[30-33]; hence their capacity for the production of lymphocytes is impaired. This is manifested by the loss of lymphocyte killer function. The resulting immunofunction deficiency is manifested by an increased susceptibility to infections, decreased reactivity to delayed skin test antigens.[28,29] In fact the degree of reduced cellular immune response in malnourished children is comparable to that observed in patients with primary cellular immunodeficiency states. This depressed cellular immunity contributes to the marked susceptibility of malnourished children to many infections such as measles, herpes simplex, tuberculosis, and gram-negative infections.[34]

In summary, as illustrated in Fig. 13-3, a vicious cycle between malnutrition, infections, and immunodeficiency is established, further intensifying malnutrition, facilitating new infections, or permitting an existing infection to become more severe. The existence of this synergic interaction calls attention to the fact that nutritional programs oriented to improving growth must also include programs of disease control.

GROWTH WITH CHRONIC UNDERNUTRITION
Prenatal growth

Birth weight and concomitants. Among populations living in poor socioeconomic conditions in which daily dietary intakes do not exceed 2000 calories and are derived mainly from carbohydrates, which are of poor protein quality, prenatal growth is retarded. In the rural villages of Mexico the average birth weight was 2999 g, and the percentage of prematurity (birth weight less than 2500 g) equaled 12.3.[35] Among four rural Guatemalan villages about 40% of all newborns weighed less than 2500 grams, 11% of these were born prior to 37 weeks gestational age (true prematures), and 20% were born at term (after 37 weeks of gestation).[24] These values are significantly different from those found in well-nourished populations in which the birth weight averages between 3300 and 3500 g, and the percentage of births below 2500 g is approximately 8%.[36,37]

The resulting reduction in average birth weight appears to be more reversible than previously suspected. Large calorie supplements given to undernourished mothers at any term of pregnancy improved birth weights to values close to those found in normal United States populations.[38,39] These investigations estimated that for every 10,000 calories of supplementation during pregnancy the birth weight could be increased between 19 and 20 g.

One of the functions of maternal weight gain during pregnancy is to provide energy stores for the growth of the fetus as well as for future lactation. This weight gain is reflected in increases in subcutaneous fat and body muscle. As previously discussed calorie and protein reserves are deposited in the form of body fat and body muscle. Consequently, differences in the amounts of subcutaneous fat and body muscle would reflect, to a certain extent, the differences in calorie and protein reserves,[40-48] which during pregnancy could influence prenatal growth.

Fig. 13-4 summarizes the results of an extensive study of the relationship between maternal nutritional status and prenatal growth in a Peruvian urban population.[47,48] The data show a direct relationship between the type of maternal nutritional reserves and prenatal growth. Increased maternal reserves of protein and calories (high muscle and high fat) are associated with increased weight and enhanced recumbent length of the newborn. On the other hand, mothers with high protein and low calorie (high muscle and low fat) have newborns with greater weight and greater recumbent length than

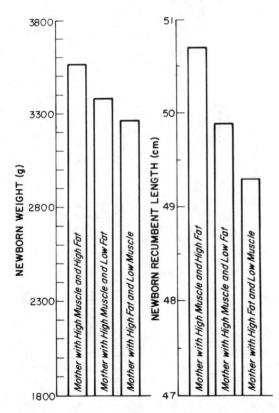

Fig. 13-4. Relationship of maternal muscularity and fatness to newborn weight and recumbent length. Mothers with high muscularity have longer and heavier newborns than fat mothers. (Based on data from Frisancho, A. R., J. E. Klayman, and J. Matos. 1977. Am. J. Phys. Anthropol. **46:**265-274; Am. J. Clin. Nutr. **30:**704-711.)

mothers who have high calorie and low protein (high fat and low muscle) reserves. In other words, increase in maternal protein reserves has a greater influence on prenatal growth than increase in calorie reserves. Furthermore, from these and other investigations it is now evident that differences in pregnancy weight gain and prepregnancy weight and/or differences in calorie and protein reserves override the influence of maternal stature—short mothers with high calorie reserves have newborns with comparable weights to those of tall mothers with similar calorie reserves.[47-50]

A recent study indicates that Mexican mothers who migrated to Mexico City from poor rural areas after attaining puberty had smaller newborns than their counterparts who migrated to Mexico City during childhood,[51] suggesting a possible intergenerational effect on prenatal growth. This problem is of interest to both basic and applied human biology because if indeed the environmental influences on prenatal growth are intergenerational, attempts to improve health and nutritional status of chronic undernourished populations may take a longer time than previously thought.

Consequences of low birth weight. Low birth weight neonates, especially those born at term (those considered small-for-date babies), have a profoundly different survival rate and developmental status during childhood than those born at average weights. As inferred from recent works,[52] the low birth weight infants are associated with (1) a greater incidence of inadequate respiratory function resulting in hypoxia, cyanosis, and respiratory distress; (2) poor thermoregulatory control in the face of changing environmental temperatures, resulting in a number of metabolic disturbances; (3) poor resistance to infection because of impaired development of immunity; (4) inadequate nutritional metabolism as shown by their intolerance of fat, incidence of hypoglycemia, and concomitant energy shortages; (5) a higher incidence of anemia; and (6) inadequate renal function because of a decreased glomerular filtration rate.

All the aforementioned functional handicaps are probably influential in producing increased mortality in the small-for-date newborn. The neonatal mortality among those born under 2500 g in the United States white and nonwhite populations is about three times greater than that in those populations with infants of average weight at birth. These same differences in United States neonatal mortality are observed among developing nations. Moreover, the observed physiological handicaps of the low birth weight newborns are also associated with lower indices of neurological status and higher incidence of neurological abnormalities. Finally, low birth weight infants score lower, through 7 years of age, than full weight subjects on various measurement scales of mental development, language development, school readiness, and academic achievement.[53] A recent study in Guatemala indicates that an increase in birth weight of Guatemalan rural populations characterized by chronic low birth weight results in increased psychomotor development at 6 months of age.[54] These findings suggest the functional significance of an improved birth weight.

Postnatal growth

Height. From a recent summary of worldwide variation in growth,[55] it can be inferred that the populations living with chronic low dietary intakes have a pattern of growth characterized by (1) slow growth during childhood and adolescence, (2) late adolescence growth spurt, and (3) prolonged period of growth (Fig. 13-5).

On the average the slow growth rate in height becomes evident after birth and con-

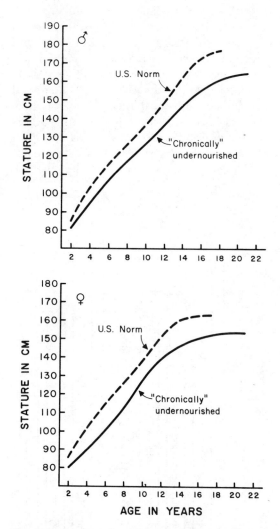

Fig. 13-5. Pattern of growth of chronically undernourished population compared to United States norm. With chronic undernutrition for all ages growth rate is slow and continues into early twenties. (Based on data from Hamill, P. V., T. A. Drizd, C. L. Johnson, R. B. Reed, and A. F. Roche. 1977. NCHS growth curves for children birth-18 years United States. Pub (PHS)78-1650. U.S. Department of Health, Education, and Welfare, Public Health Service, National Center for Health Statistics, Hyattsville, Md.; and Eveleth, P. B., and J. M. Tanner. 1976. Worldwide variation in human growth. Cambridge University Press, New York.)

tinues through the early 20s. Most populations attain adult height by about 22 to 24 years for males and 20 to 22 years for females. These values when compared to the United States standards amount to an increase of 10% in the duration of the period of growth. Despite this increase in the period of growth the adult height of undernourished populations is reduced by 10%. This difference is mostly accounted for by the uniform slow growth rate that characterizes undernourished populations.[55-57,69]

Skeletal maturation. Along with retarded growth in height undernourished populations, when compared to the Gruelich-Pyle, Tanner-Whitehouse, or Garn-Rohman-Silverman standards, exhibit a drastic retardation in skeletal maturity.[55,56] It must be noted, however, that irrespective of the method of evaluation the effects of undernutrition on skeletal maturation are greater during childhood than during adolescence. For example, among Central American rural populations (Fig. 13-6) when compared to the Garn-Rohman-Silverman standards, the delay in the appearance of ossification centers between the ages of 0 to 10 years averages about 20%, whereas the delay in the appearance of adolescence markers such as the adductor sesamoid and epiphyseal fusion of the digits does not exceed 10%.[56] The 10% delay in epiphyseal closure coincides with the increase in the age of attainment of adult stature, which as previously indicated is prolonged by about 10% in most undernourished populations. Since the age at epiphyseal closure and termination of growth is proportionally less retarded than the delay experienced during childhood, environmentally related differences in adult stature are mostly caused by environmental influences that retard growth and maturation during childhood.

Cortical bone thickness. Radiogrammetric measurements of the total bone width of the second metacarpal and width of the medullary cavity have demonstrated that malnutrition reduces the absolute and relative amount of cortical bone. Severely malnourished (kwashiorkor) Guatemalan children, when compared to rural nonmalnourished Guatemalan children, were found to be deficient in cortical bone.[58,59] Further studies have shown that the loss of cortical bone occurs mainly at the endosteal (inner) surface of the bone, whereas the periosteal (outer) surface of the bone continues to increase.[60] For this reason during malnutrition the medullary cavity is enlarged, and the total width of the bone is either maintained or continues to grow.

Sexual development. Menarche is the most widely used indicator of sexual maturity in females. In general age at menarche is derived either through the status quo or through retrospective or prospective methods. Age at menarche, by whatever method of assessment, is delayed among populations in poor socioeconomic conditions.[55] However, within a population the effects of socioeconomic indicators on age at menarche are less than on childhood maturity markers. For example, based on the status quo method, age at menarche for well-off Bantus varies between 13 and 15 years, and for poor or lower class Bantus it ranges from 14.8 to 15.4 years.[55,61] In the same manner the median age at menarche in United States high income whites averaged 13 years and 13.5 years for the low income groups, and United States undernourished white girls averaged 14.4 years compared to 12.4 in the well-nourished controls.[62] For the well-off, middle-class, and lower-income Chinese (Hong Kong) the age of menarche averaged 12.5, 12.8, and 13.3 years respectively.[63] In India and Mexico similar differences have been indicated.[64,65] In other words delay among the poor or undernourished does not appear to exceed 15% of the well-off average

age. However, this does not mean that age of menarche is not delayed in other populations. Among New Guinea natives and Himalayan Sherpas the age of menarche, based on the less reliable retrospective method, has been reported to be as late as 18 and 19 years, respectively.[57,66]

CONCLUSION

In conclusion, at present there is considerable evidence indicating that the effects of protein-calorie malnutrition on brain growth and function might have long-lasting consequences depending on the critical period at which the nutritional insult occurs.

Both experimental studies on animals and autopsies of children who died of malnutrition indicate that if malnutrition occurs during the period of brain growth spurt, the effects on neuronal cells and biochemical composition might be permanent; but if it occurs after the growth spurt or critical period, the effects can be reversible and not permanent. However, the extent to which these findings are applicable to living populations or survivors of malnutrition is not known.

Using behavior or psychological measurements, investigators have unsuccessfully attempted to test the critical period

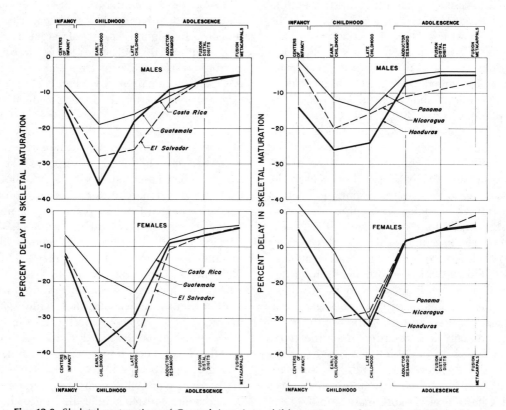

Fig. 13-6. Skeletal maturation of Central American children expressed as percent delay with respect to United States standards. Note that in both males and females retardation in skeletal maturation during childhood is systematically greater than that observed during adolescence. (From Frisancho, A. R., S. M. Garn, and W. Ascoli. 1970. Am. J. Phys. Anthropol. **33:**325-336; Am. J. Clin. Nutr. **23:**1220-1227.)

hypothesis. Results of studies involving children who were hospitalized for severe acute malnutrition at different ages during infancy and childhood are inconclusive to support or reject the hypothesis that systematic differences in intellectual level at school age are related to severe malnutrition that occurred at different vulnerable age periods in human development. This inconclusiveness is not surprising in view of the fact that severely malnourished children are exposed to decreased learning opportunities because of both the inherent inactivity and lethargy associated with malnutrition the poor socioeconomic conditions with which malnutrition coexists, and the tests employed to measure cognitive processes are based on traits that are particularly sensitive to social-environmental influences. Therefore possible effects of undernutrition on biological-neurological development are confounded by the influence of external environmental factors.

Laboratory and epidemiological studies suggest that there is a synergistic interaction between malnutrition and infection, whereby malnutrition predisposes the organism either through low production of immunoglobulins on the mesopharyngeal secretions or inhibition of the cell-mediated immunoresponse. The infection in turn exacerbates the effects of malnutrition, and therefore new infections may emerge or existing ones become more severe. Thus a vicious cycle between malnutrition, infections, and immunodeficiency is established. This synergic interaction calls attention to the fact that nutritional programs oriented to improving and understanding the etiology of malnutrition must also include programs for control of infection.

There is conclusive evidence indicating that maternal chronic undernutrition retards prenatal growth; thus variations in maternal calorie and protein reserves are the most important factors affecting newborn body size and composition. These findings and those derived from the Dutch famine[67,68] suggest that in conditions of drastic dietary restriction maternal calorie and protein reserves are not sufficient to maintain adequate prenatal growth. The relationship between maternal nutritional status and prenatal growth is so well defined that any changes in maternal calorie intake or change in calorie

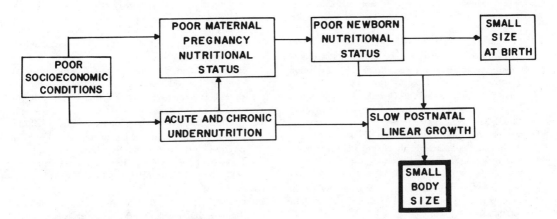

Fig. 13-7. Schematization of effects and interaction of prenatal and postnatal undernutrition on human growth and adult body size. Reduction in adult body size among populations living under poor socioeconomic conditions results from compound effects of prenatal and postnatal undernutrition manifested in acute and chronic forms.

and protein reserves are reflected in dramatic changes in birth weight. Indeed, it can be safely concluded that about one half of the incidence of prematurity (10%) observed among developing nations (12% to 20%) is either directly or indirectly related to malnutrition. In view of the negative concomitants of prematurity, improvements of maternal nutritional status must be a prime priority of public health programs.

During the postnatal period populations living in chronic undernutrition or poor socioeconomic conditions exhibit slow growth in stature and weight, decreased bone cortex, and late age at menarche. Although the period of growth is extended, undernourished populations do not attain the adult stature of well-nourished populations. Experimental studies indicate that an animal's postnatal growth is to a large extent determined by the size and nutritional status attained at birth. Those born small who did not have a tall parent and continue to experience undernutrition are likely to grow slowly and remain small for their age in spite of the fact that they may continue to grow for a longer time.[69] In Fig. 13-7 these findings have been summarized in schematic form. It shows that among populations living in poor socioeconomic conditions undernutrition in its acute or chronic manifestations (through its effect on maternal pregnancy status) leads to poor newborn nutritional status and reduced size at birth. Because of the cumulative effects of prenatal undernutrition, prenatal growth retardation, and chronic undernutrition after birth linear growth during the postnatal period is slow and eventually leads to reduced adult body size.

REFERENCES

1. Bengoa, J. M. 1974. The problem of malnutrition. W.H.O. Chron. **28:**3-7.
2. Puffer, R. R., and C. V. Serrano. 1973. The role of nutritional deficiency in mortality. Boletin de la Oficina Sanitaria Panamericana 7:1-25.
3. Dobbing, J. 1968. Effects of experimental undernutrition in development of the nervous system. In N. S. Scrimshaw and J. F. Gordon, eds. Malnutrition, learning, and behavior. The M.I.T. Press, Cambridge, Mass.
4. Cobbing, J., and J. Sands. 1972. Vulnerability of developing brain. Part 9. The effect of nutritional growth retardation on the timing of the brain growth-sprint. Biol. Neonate **19:**363-378.
5. Chase. H. P., J. Dorsey, and G. M. Mckhann. 1967. Malnutrition and the synthesis of myelin. Pediatrics **40:**551-558.
6. Winick, M., and P. Rosso. 1969. Head circumference and cellular growth of the brain in normal and marasmic children. J. Pediatr. **74:**774-778.
7. Winick, M., P. Rosso, and J. Waterlow. 1970. Cellular growth of cerebrum, cerebellum, and brain stem in normal and marasmic children. Exp. Neurol. **26:**393-398.
8. Winick, M., and A. Noble. 1966. Cellular response in rats during malnutrition at various ages. J. Nutr. **89:**300-306.
9. Benton, J. W., H. W. Moser, P. R. Dodge, et al. 1966. Modification of the schedule of myelination in the rat by early nutritional deprivation. Pediatrics **38:**801-807.
10. Winick, M. 1969. Malnutrition and brain development. Pediatrics **74:**667-679.
11. Winick, M. 1973. Relation of nutrition to physical and mental development. Bibl. Nutr. Dieta. **18:** 114-122.
12. Manocha, S. L. 1972. Malnutrition and retarded human development. Charles C Thomas, Publisher, Springfield, Ill.
13. Pollit, E., and C. Thomson. 1977. Protein-calorie malnutrition and behavior. A view from psychology. In R. J. Wurtman and J. J. Wurtman, eds. Nutrition and the brain. Raven Press, New York.
14. Lloyd-Still, J. D. 1976. Clinical studies on the effects of malnutrition during infancy on subsequent physical and intellectual development. In J. D. Lloyd-Still, ed. Malnutrition and intellectual development. Publishing Sciences Group, Inc., Littleton, Mass.
15. Cravioto, J., and B. Robles. 1965. Evolution of adaptive and motor behavior during rehabilitation from kwashiorkor. Am. J. Orthopsychiatry 35:449-464.
16. Hertzig, M. E., H. G. Birch, S. A. Richardson, and

J. Tizard. 1972. Intellectual levels of school children severely malnourished during the first two years of life. Pediatrics **49**:814-824.

17. Hoorweg, J., and P. Stanfield. 1972. The influence of malnutrition on psychological and neurological development: preliminary communication. In Nutrition, the nervous system and behavior. P.A.H.O. Scientific Publication 251. Pan American Health Organization, Washington, D.C.

18. Nwuga, V. C. B. 1977. Effect of severe kwashiorkor on intellectual development among Nigerian children. Am. J. Clin. Nutr. **30**:1423-1430.

19. Lechtig, A., and L. J. Mata. 1971. Cord IgM levels in Latin American neonates. J. Pediatr. **78**: 909-910.

20. Mata, L. J., J. J. Urrutia, C. Albertazzi, O. Pellecer, and E. Arellano. 1972. Influence of recurrent infections on nutrition and growth of children in Guatemala. Am. J. Clin. Nutr. **25**:1267-1275.

21. Gordon, J. E., A. A. Jansen, and W. Ascoli. 1965. Measles in rural Guatemala. J. Pediatr. **66**:779-786.

22. Morley, D. 1969. Severe measles in the tropics. Br. Med. J. **1**:297-300.

23. Stare, F. J. 1968. Measles and malnutrition. Nutr. Rev. **26**:232-234.

24. Mata, L. J., J. J. Urrutia, and A. Lechtig. 1971. Infection and nutrition of children of a low socioeconomic rural community. Am. J. Clin. Nutr. **24**:249-259.

25. Scrimshaw, N. S. 1975. Interactions of malnutrition and infection: advances in understanding. In R. E. Olson, ed. Protein-calorie malnutrition. Academic Press, Inc., New York.

26. Sirisinha, S., R. Suskind, R. Edelman, C. Asvapaka, and R. E. Olson. 1975. Secretory and serum IgA in children with protein calorie malnutrition. Pediatrics **55**:166-170.

27. McMurray, D. N., H. Rey, L. J. Casazza, and R. R. Watson. 1977. Effects of moderate malnutrition on concentrations of immunoglobulins and enzymes in tears and saliva of young Colombian children. Am. J. Clin. Nutr. **30**:1944-1948.

28. Edelman, R., R. Suskind, S. Sirisinha, and R. E. Olson. 1973. Mechanisms of defective cutaneous hypersensitivity in children with protein-calorie malnutrition. Lancet **1**:506-508.

29. Suskind, R. M. 1977. Characteristics and causation of protein-calorie malnutrition in the infant and preschool child. In L. S. Green, ed. Malnutrition, behavior and social organization. Academic Press, Inc., New York.

30. Neumann, C. G., G. J. Lawlor, Jr., E. R. Stichm, M. E. Swendseid, O. Newton, J. Herbert, A. J. Ammann, and M. Jacob. 1975. Immunologic responses in malnourished children. Am. J. Clin. Nutr. **28**:89-104.

31. Mugerwa, J. W. 1971. Lymphoreticular system in kwashiorkor. J. Pathol. **105**:105-109.

32. Work, T. N., A. Ikekwunigwe, D. B. Jellife, P. Jelliffee, and C. G. Neumann. 1973. Tropical problems in nutrition. Ann. Intern. Med. **79**:701-711.

33. Smythe, P. M., M. Schonland, K. K. Breton-Stiles, H. M. Coovadia, H. J. Grace, W. E, K. Leoning, A. Mafoyane, M. A. Parent, and G. H. Vos. 1971. Thymolymphatic deficiency and depression of cell-mediated immunity in protein calorie malnutrition. Lancet **2**:939-943.

34. Becker, W., W. E. Naude, A. Kipp, and D. McKenzie. 1963. Virus studies in disseminated herpes simplex infections: association with malnutrition in children. S. Afr. Med. J. **37**:74-76.

35. Cravioto, J., and E. Delicardie. 1972. Environmental correlates of severe clinical malnutrition and language development in survivors from kwashiorkor or marasmus. In Nutrition, the nervous system and behavior. P.A.H.O. Scientific Publication 251. Pan American Health Organization, Washington, D.C.

36. Niswander, K. R., and M. Gordon. 1972. The women and their pregnancies. W. B. Saunders Co., Philadelphia.

37. Chase, H. C. 1969. Infant mortality and weight at birth: 1960 United States birth cohort. Am. J. Public Health **59**:1618-1628.

38. Habicht, J.-P., A. Lechtig, C. Yarbrough, and R. F. Klein. 1974. Maternal nutrition, birth weight and infant mortality. In Size at birth. Ciba Foundation Symposium 27. A.S.P., Amsterdam.

39. Lechtig, A., C. Yarbrough, H. Delgado, J.-P. Habicht, R. Martorell, and R. E. Klein. 1975. Influence of maternal nutrition on birth weight. Am. J. Clin. Nutr. **28**:1223-1233.

40. Jelliffe, D. B. 1966. The assessment of the nutritional status of the community. W.H.O. Monograph Series 53. World Health Organization, Geneva.

41. Stini, W. 1972. Reduced sexual dimorphism in upper arm muscle circumference associated with protein-deficient diet in a South American population. Am. J. Phys. Anthropol. **36**:341-352.

42. Johnston, F. E., and A. Beller. 1976. Anthropometric evaluation of the body composition of black, white and Puerto Rican newborns. Am. J. Clin. Nutr. **29**:61-65.

43. Martorell, R., C. Yarbrough, A. Lechtig, H. Delgado, and R. E. Klein. 1976. Upper arm anthropometric indicators of nutritional status. Am. J. Clin. Nutr. **29**:46-53.

44. Frisancho, A. R. 1975. Triceps skin fold and upper arm muscle size norms for assessment of nutritional status. Am. J. Clin. Nutr. **27**:1052-1058.

45. Frisancho, A. R., and S. M. Garn. 1971. Skinfold thickness and muscle size: implications for developmental status and nutritional evaluation of children from Honduras. Am. J. Clin. Nutr. **24**:541-546.

46. Frisancho, A. R., and S. M. Garn. 1971. Relationship of skinfolds and muscle size to growth of children. Part 1. Costa Rica. Am. J. Phys. Anthropol. **35**:85-90.

47. Frisancho, A. R., J. E. Klayman, and J. Matos. 1977. Influence of maternal nutritional status on prenatal growth in a Peruvian urban population. Am. J. Phys. Anthropol. **46**:265-274.

48. Frisancho, A. R., J. E. Klayman, and J. Matos. 1977. Newborn body composition and its relationship to linear growth. Am. J. Clin. Nutr. **30**:704-711.

49. Weis, W. E., E. C. Jackson, and K. R. Niswander. 1969. The influence on birth weight of change in maternal weight gain in successive pregnancies in the same woman. Int. J. Gynecol. Obstet. **7**:210-223.

50. Rush, D., H. Davis, and M. W. Susser. 1972. Antecedents of low birthweight in Harlem, New York City. Int. J. Epidemiol. **1**:375-387.

51. Weinstein, R. S. 1978. Early stress, maternal phenotypic variability and fetal growth in Mexico. Am. J. Phys. Anthropol. (Abstract) **48**:447.

52. Reed, D. M., and F. J. Stanley, eds. 1977. The epidemiology of prematurity. Urban and Schwarzenberg, Baltimore, Munich.

53. Rubin, R. A., C. Rosenblatt, and B. Balow. 1973. Psychological and educational sequelae of prematurity. Pediatrics. **52**:352-363.

54. Lasky, R. E., A. Lechtig, H. Delgado, R. E. Klein, P. Engle, C. Yarbrough, and R. Martorell. 1975. Birth weight and psychomotor performance in rural Guatemala. Am. J. Dis. Child. **129**:566-569.

55. Eveleth, P. B., and J. M. Tanner. 1976. Worldwide variation in human growth. Cambridge University Press, New York.

56. Frisancho, A. R., S. M. Garn, and W. Ascoli. 1970. Childhood retardation resulting in reduction of adult body size due to lesser adolescent skeletal delay. Am. J. Phys. Anthropol. **33**:325-336.

57. Malcolm, L. A. 1970. Growth and development of the bundi child of the New Guinea highlands. Hum. Biol. **42**:293-328.

58. Blanco, R. A., R. M. Acheson, C. Canosa, and J. B. Salomon. 1975. Height, weight, and lines of arrested growth in young Guatemalan children. Am. J. Phys. Anthropol. **40**:39-48.

59. Garn, S. M., C. G. Rohmann, M. Behar, F. Viteri, and M. A. Guzman. 1964. Compact bone deficiency in protein-calorie malnutrition. Science **145**:144-45.

60. Frisancho, A. R., S. M. Garn, and W. Ascoli. 1970. Subperiosteal and endosteal bone apposition during adolescence. Hum. Biol. **42**:639-664.

61. Burrell, R. J. W., J. M. Tanner, and M. J. R. Healy. 1961. Age at menarche in South African Bantu girls living in the Transkei reserve. Hum. Biol. **33**:250-261.

62. Dreizen, S., C. N. Spirakis, and R. E. Stone. 1967. A comparison of skeletal growth and maturation in undernourished and well nourished girls before and after menarche. J. Pediatr. **70**:256-264.

63. Chang, K. S. F. 1969. Growth and development of Chinese children and youth in Hong Kong. University of Hong Kong, Hong Kong.

64. Malina, R. M., C. Chumlea, C. D. Stepick, and F. G. Lopez. 1977. Age of menarche in Oaxaca, Mexico schoolgirls with comparative data for other areas of Mexico. Ann. Hum. Biol. **4**:551-558.

65. Roberts, D. F., S. Chinn, B. Girija, and H. D. Singh. 1977. A study of menarcheal age in India. Ann. Hum. Biol. **4**:171-178.

66. Pawson, I. G. 1977. Growth characteristics of populations of Tibetan origin in Nepal. Am. J. Phys. Anthropol. **47**:473-482.

67. Stein, Z., and M. Susser. 1975. The Dutch famine 1944-1945, and the reproductive process. Part 1. Effects on six indices at birth. Pediatr. Res. **9**:70-75.

68. Stein, Z., and M. Susser. 1975. The Dutch famine, 1944-1945, and the reproductive process. Part 2. Interrelations of caloric relations and six indices at birth. Pediatr. Res. **9**:76-82.

69. McCance, R. A., and E. M. Widdowson. 1974. The determinants of growth and form. Proc. R. Soc. Lond. (Biol.) **185**:1-17.

14

Westernization of dietary habits and disease expression

Beriberi

Sickle cell anemia

Cancer and diverticulosis
Breast and colon cancer
Environmental factors
Genetic factors
Diverticulosis

Conclusion

The advance of human civilization has created conditions, which in many ways are unlike those which existed during the last 3 million years of human evolution. These new conditions have certainly had a beneficial impact on human survival, and, indeed, without these advances humans would not have attained their present biological status. However, the advances of civilization have also created negative conditions, which if continued unchecked may constitute a grave threat to the survival, let alone the well-being, of humanity. In terms of human adaptation and nutrition the most significant changes are quantitative and qualitative differences in food consumption and variations in food use. Knowing how the human organism is reacting biologically to these changes is important for understanding the expression of various diseases. The influence of nutrition on disease expression is great and cannot be adequately treated in one single chapter. Thus this chapter is limited to a discussion of the interaction of westernization of dietary habits and disease expression. Within this context the diseases of beriberi, sickle cell anemia, cancer, and diverticulosis will be discussed.

BERIBERI

Beriberi is a disease caused by deficiencies of thiamine or Vitamin B_1. There are two types of beriberi: dry beriberi and wet beriberi. Dry beriberi is characterized by muscular weakness, muscle pain, paralysis of the limbs, and sometimes mental confusion. Wet beriberi is typified by edema and cardiac failure. Infants born of thiamine-deficient mothers are liable to contract the disease because the mother's milk fails to supply sufficient thiamine to meet the infant's needs.

Beriberi in both its dry and wet forms is still common in Thailand and other countries. Its origin is traced to consumption of polished or millet rice. Thiamine is located in the outer layer of cereal grain, which is removed during the polishing process. Thus the polished rice product is deficient in thiamine. With acculturation and westernization polished rice became preferred, and with it beriberi became a serious health problem.[1] In other regions where western patterns of food consumption have been acquired, the desire for white, highly refined cereal flour containing minimal amounts of thiamine is spreading, and concomitant with this practice symptoms of beriberi are manifested.[2] Evidence that beriberi is caused by the loss of thiamine resulting from rice and not by actual vitamin deficiency in the cereal itself is derived from the fact that in other populations in which rice is consumed in parboiled form, beriberi is less frequent than in rice eating areas where this is not a practice.[3] In India through the process of parboiling, in which unhusked rice is steamed and then dried before milling, the vitamin is not lost. This is because thiamine is water soluble, and through parboiling the vitamin from the outer layer of the grain is distributed more evenly in the inner parts of the rice. For this reason and to reduce the risk of vitamin deficiencies in the United States, all white flour used in the manufacture of bread is fortified with vitamins by law. However, other flours used in the manufacture of pastries and pasta are not fortified with vitamins. Since at present there is a trend to increased consumption of pastries, cake, and pizza, it would not be surprising if even in the United States there may be a risk of vitamin B_1 deficiency.

It must be noted, however, that beriberi might also occur when thiamine intake is adequate. Raw, fermented fish consumed daily (mean = 56 gr) by the northeastern Thais contains about 225 U of antithiamine factor in the form of the thermolabile enzyme thiaminase I, which alters the structure and reduces the biological activity of the vitamin.[4,6] In addition, fermented tea leaves chewed as stimulants by the Thais also contain an antithiamine factor that has deleterious effects on the biological activity of thiamine.[5,6] It is evident, then, that food consumption and cultural factors are symbiotically related to human health and well-being now more so than ever.

SICKLE CELL ANEMIA

The sickle cell trait of red blood cells is one of the best examples of genetic adaptation to malaria.[7,8] In Africa and other malaria regions the homozygous normals develop malaria, many die early, and vitality of the survivors is impaired. On the other hand, the homozygotes for the sickle cell trait develop sickle cell anemia, whereas the heterozygous sicklers do not develop malaria. For this reason in Africa and other regions where malaria is endemic, the heterozygous condition occurs in up to 25% of the population.[9-11] However, despite the high frequency of heterozygous sickle cell trait in Africa, the West Indies, and the Mediterranean, the percentage of individuals who suffer from the clinical manifestations of sickle cell anemia is much lower than in the United States.[10,12,13] The usual explanation for the low frequency of sickle cell anemia in Africa or other regions where malaria is endemic is that the majority of victims die in early infancy.[7,10,14] Nevertheless, other studies suggest that the clinical manifestations of sickle cell anemia may be diminished by foods containing cyanate, thiocyanate, folic acid, and ascorbic acid and iron-deficient foods.[15,16]

Various studies have shown that the clinical symptoms of sickle cell anemia are decreased when treated with cyanate.[17-20] Hematological improvement and a decrease in hemolytic anemia occur on oral administration of cyanate.[18] However, since the cells

inhibited from sickling are eventually replaced by new sicklers, cyanate oral therapy would have to be continued for life.[18] It has been postulated that the low frequency of clinical manifestation of sickle cell anemia in Africa and other regions is related to the high consumption of cyanate- and thiocyanate-containing foods such as cassava (manioc), yams, sorghum, millet grains, sugarcane, and dark varieties of lima beans.[13,15,16] This is supported by the finding that Jamaican subjects with mild clinical manifestations of sickle cell anemia, on migration to the United States or England, experience severe crises of sickle cell anemia, which are eliminated on return to the original environment.[13] Therefore there must be an environmental factor that is responsible for the mild symptoms of sickle cell anemia in Jamaica.[13] Specifically, the decrease in clinical manifestation of sickle cell anemia in Jamaica is attributed to the high consumption of cassava, dark varieties of lima beans, and sugarcane,[16] all of which contain large amounts of cyanate and thiocyanate. According to food analysis cassava flour contains about 70 to 80 mg/100 g of thiocyanate and yam flour between 50 to 60 mg/100 g of thiocyanate.[21] Thus it would appear that the full expression of sickle cell anemia in blacks in the United States represents an unrelieved nutritional dependency on cyanate precursors.[15,16] In other words, those with sickle cell anemia constitute another such group in which the disease is rooted in a special nutritional need as the interface between heredity and pathology. Since present-day diets in the tropics provide foods considerably richer in cyanate and thiocyanate, or nitrilosides, than diets of the United States and other western countries,[22] the clinical manifestation of sickle cell anemia may be viewed as the result of changed patterns of food consumption associated with westernization. It may also be noted that according to laboratory studies cyanate, to be effective in decreasing sickling, requires that about 50% of the hemoglobin tetrads be attached to cyanate. To achieve this goal the dosage reaches toxic levels. Oral administration of cyanate, to be effective, might have to be continued for the life span of the patient.[18] Therefore natural sources, such as those found in the diet, might prove to be more practical. It would not be surprising to find that other natural sickling inhibitors exist in the diet of populations in which the genetic trait is prevalent.

In some regions of West Africa cassava and yams are seldom given to infants, yet the frequency of sickle cell anemia is low.[23] In this region, as in much of Africa and in the southern United States, geophagia, a form of pica (the eating of nonfood items) in which earth or clay is consumed, is common among children and adults.[24] Although the actual positive or negative nutritional value of geophagia is questionable, in view of the possible role of natural diets in the etiology of sickle cell anemia, further research in the area is needed.

CANCER AND DIVERTICULOSIS
Breast and colon cancer

Environmental factors. From a nutritional standpoint the most important changes associated with westernization of dietary habits include increased consumption of animal protein and fat and a marked decrease in the intake of fiber, particularly cereal fiber. As shown in Fig. 14-1, in the United States between 1900 and 1970, the per capita consumption of meat, poultry, and fish increased by 50%, whereas the consumption of crude fiber derived from fruits and vegetables has declined by a similar proportion.[25,26] Concomitant with these changes has been a drastic increase in the use of refined flour and the replacement of whole cereal grains with ready-made breakfast cereals.[25,26] Di-

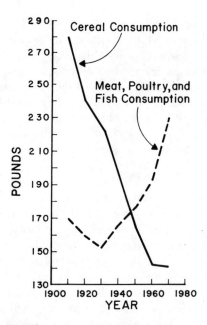

Fig. 14-1. Changes in per capita consumption of cereal, meat, poultry, and fish. As consumption of meat, poultry, and fish has increased, intake of cereals has decreased. (Data from U.S. Department of Agriculture, Economic Research Service. 1975.)

etary patterns in the western world a century ago compared with today show major differences that are similar to those between foods consumed in the developing nations and in economically developed countries today.[27,28]

Recent epidemiological studies have called attention to these changes in diet being associated with the increased incidence of colon and breast cancer. The National Cancer Institute estimates that 60% of all cancers in women and 41% of cancers in men may be related to diet and nutrition.[29-31] As shown in Fig. 14-2, the breast and large intestine cancer mortality of Polish immigrants to the United States far exceeds the rates of Polish natives and approaches the rates of United States natives.[32] Similarly, from Fig. 14-3 it is evident that colon and stomach cancer mortality for Japanese immi-

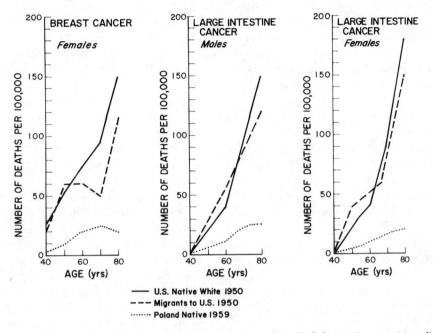

Fig. 14-2. Breast and large intestine cancer mortality trends in Polish immigrants. Mortality of Polish who immigrated in 1950 differs markedly from mortality of their native Polish counterparts, but is similar to mortality of United States natives. (Modified from Staszewski, J., and W. Haenszel. 1965. J. Natl. Cancer Inst. **35**:291-297.)

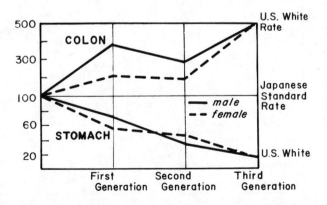

Fig. 14-3. Colon and stomach cancer mortality trends: Japanese immigrants to United States. With residency in United States colon cancer mortality increases in both male and female Japanese, whereas stomach cancer mortality declines; in both cases rates are similar to those of United States whites. (Modified from Haenszel, W., and M. Kurihara. 1968. J. Natl. Cancer Inst. **40**:43-68.)

grants residing in the United States changes; by the third generation their rates approach those prevalent in the United States.[33] These changes are associated with increases in the Japanese immigrants' calorie, protein, and fat intake.[34] The same trend toward increased cancer incidence has been found for rural-urban migrants in Israel, Hong Kong, and Cali, Colombia.[35,36]

In the United States the lowest rates of cancer incidence and mortality from all tumors are found among vegetarian populations such as the Seventh Day Adventists,[37,38] whose intake of protein is low and intake of dietary fiber and unrefined carbohydrates is high.[40] Similarly, Mormons living in Utah have a lower incidence of cancer of all tumor types than non-Mormons also living in Utah,[39-41] suggesting the possible role of dietary habits.[42]

Epidemiological data derived from world populations also indicate that the age-adjusted mortality rate from colonic and breast cancer is positively correlated with the per capita daily consumption of fats and oils and negatively correlated with dietary fiber intake.[43-45] That is, the higher the consumption of fats and oils and the lower the intake of dietary fiber, the greater the breast cancer mortality (Fig. 14-4).

Studies of humans and experimental animals suggest that the relationship between types of dietary intakes and breast cancer may be mediated through developmental factors. That is, increased dietary intakes are associated with accelerated growth and maturation, which, in turn, is associated with increased incidence of breast cancer. For example, Polish women with early menarche have been found to have a higher risk of developing breast cancer than those with late menarche.[46] Similar results have been found in Greece,[47] Japan,[48] and the United States.[49] Experimental studies on animals indicate that calorie restriction generally inhibits tumor formation and increases life expectancy.[50-52] A lower protein intake inhibits the development of spontaneous or chemically induced tumors.[50-52] Conversely, an increase of fat has been found

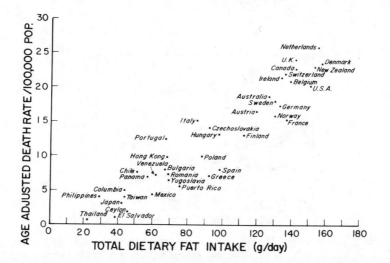

Fig. 14-4. Relationship between breast cancer death rate and dietary fat intake. Internationally, the higher the dietary fat intake, the greater the age-adjusted death rate. (Modified from Carroll, K. K. 1975. Cancer Res. **35:**3374-3383.)

to enhance the incidence of breast tumors, and the tumors also occurred earlier in the life of the animal.[53] Furthermore, the incidence of tumors tends to be consistently greater in heavier rats than in lean rats.[51]

Genetic factors. Although a large proportion of breast cancer may be attributed to environmental agents, not all persons similarly exposed develop cancer, indicating that genetic factors may account for this variability. There is abundant evidence that for women whose mothers or sisters had breast cancer the risk of developing breast cancer is about two or three times greater than for controls.[54,55] Studies on twins indicate a higher rate of concordance of breast cancer in monozygotic than dizygotic twins.[56] The influence of familial or hereditary factors may be expressed through differences in hormonal secretion. Studies of teenage daughters of breast cancer patients found higher prolacting levels during certain days of the menstrual cycle than in daughters of control women.[57]

Among the several genetic markers studied in relation to breast cancer, investigations of cerumen type have produced fruitful results. Human cerumen (earwax) has two phenotypic forms, wet and dry, which are inherited in a simple mendelian fashion. It is well known that oriental countries have a lower incidence of breast cancer than western countries.[58] It has been postulated that the low risk of breast cancer in orientals is partially caused by their overall decreased breast secretion activity which is associated with dry cerumen.[59] This hypothesis is based on the following associations. First, there is a direct relationship between the frequency of wet cerumen and world breast cancer mortality.[60] Second, breast secretory activity of nonlactating nonpregnant women is associated with differences in cerumen type; in women with dry cerumen there is a lower proportion of breast secretions.[59] Third, the

lowest proportion of breast secretory activity is found among orientals and American Indians.

Given the fact that earwax glands and breast glands are apocrine in structure and function, the association of breast cancer incidence with cerumen type is not implausible. Since breast gland secretions have been found to contain a variety of environmentally derived chemicals and nutrients,[61] it is quite possible that a low or absent breast secretory activity may minimize contact of the breast with exogenous carcinogens.[62] Viewed in this manner, the observed lower frequency of breast cancer in oriental women may be related to their lower breast secretory activity.[62] However, this does not explain the increased frequency of breast cancer found among Japanese migrants to Hawaii and California and their American born offspring.[63] On the other hand, a relationship to changes in breast-feeding practices is possible; the decrease in breast-feeding may result in an increased retention of carcinogenic agents in the breast.

Diverticulosis

Diverticular disease is characterized by small "blow out" protrusions (diverticular) in the large intestine, which become inflamed. The resulting condition is diverticulitis. Diverticulitis is generally associated with an increase in the segmenting pressures produced by the contracting colon. It has been postulated that the increased pressure results from a fiber-deficient diet, which causes colonic contents to be more viscous and harder to propel, as occurs in constipation.[64] Among those with a fiber-depleted diet, the colonic lumen is narrower because of the smaller bulk of the diet, which in turn causes a greater segmentation of the colon and the buildup of intraluminal pressure. This increased pressure eventually produces diverticula.[65] There appears to be a strong negative correlation between the epidemiology of diverticular disease and crude fiber intake.[65,66] The fiber deficiency theory of the etiology of diverticular disease is supported by clinical studies, which showed that symptoms of the disease are effectively alleviated following the addition of 20 to 30 g/day of wheat bran to the diet.[67] Deficiency of dietary fiber has also been related to circulatory and metabolic diseases such as varicose veins, ischemic heart diseases, obesity, diabetes mellitus, and other diseases of the gastrointestinal tract (appendicitis, hemorrhoids, etc.).

CONCLUSION

Evidence suggests that among populations in which westernization of dietary habits is associated with refined flour replacing parboiled rice as the food of choice, the disease of beriberi, which is caused by a deficiency of Vitamin B_1, is manifest. In the same manner, there is evidence supporting the hypothesis that the full expression of homozygous sickle cell anemia is mediated by the lack of cyanate-containing foods that characterize western diets.

Available data suggest that some factors, such as differences in the consumption of proteins and fiber characteristic of modern western civilization, play a significant role in the etiology of breast cancer, colon cancer, and diverticulosis. The expression of these diseases is dependent on differences in exposure to these factors. The fact that breast and colon cancers are not more prevalent in occupational groups in which exposure to environmental carcinogens is high reinforces the view that environmental pollutants per se are not influential factors in the observed relationship between nutrition and cancer incidence and mortality.[68]

However, the available data are only circumstantial, and the specific role of diet and nutrition in cancer etiology is still un-clear. It appears that diet, depending on its content of carcinogenic components, may modulate organ susceptibility and response to causative factors.[68] A recent theory, illustrated in Fig. 14-5, postulates that an excessive fat intake modifies the metabolism of cholesterol, bile acids, and neutral steroids in the intestine, as well as the metabolism and secretion of steroid hormones in circulation.[69] On one side the bile acids secreted in the intestines are degraded by bacteria growing in the intestine to form carcinogenic substances that may initiate colon cancer.[70] This process of degradation and transformation of bile acids is modulated by the presence of fiber in the diet, which is known to decrease the food transit time, and as a result the contact between concentrated stool content and the mucosa is decreased. This in turn decreases the production of bacterial flora capable of forming carcinogens from the degradation of bile salts.[71] Furthermore, the altered metabolism of steroid hormones could impose unnatural burdens on cellular receptors of specific target tissues, such as uterus or breast, again initiating cancer in those tissues.[68]

At the present time there is no doubt that in terms of quantity and quality a western diet differs markedly from the diet of indigenous or nonwesternized populations. What is not clear is how these changes affect the expression of disease in westernized populations. In Fig. 14-6 the interaction of westernization of diet, change in growth patterns, change in breast-feeding practices, environmental carcinogens, and incidence of breast cancer is summarized in schematic form. From these data the following points are important. First, westernization as a result of the increased availability of fats and proteins leads to an increased storage of body fat and accelerated rate of growth and maturation, which in turn are associated with an increased incidence of breast cancer.

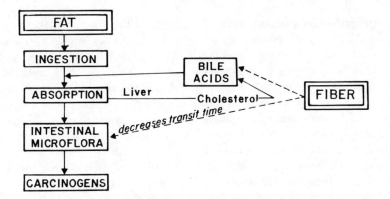

Fig. 14-5. Schematization of interaction of fat and fiber dietary intake and its influence on incidence of intestinal cancer. Dietary fiber, through its action on formation of bile acids and effect on food transit time, is said to influence rate of accumulation of carcinogens. (Modified from Diet, Nutrition and Cancer Program Status Report. Sept. 30, 1977. Diet, Nutrition and Cancer Program, National Cancer Institute, National Institute of Health, Bethesda, Md.)

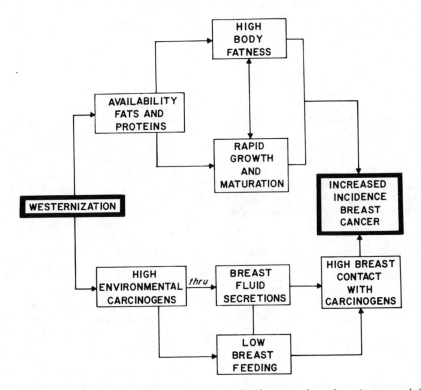

Fig. 14-6. Schematization of interaction of dietary, developmental, and environmental factors influencing increased incidence of breast cancer. Westernization as a result of industrialization has simultaneously increased availability of dietary fats and proteins and environmental carcinogens and decreased the practice of breast-feeding. As a result of complex interaction of these factors, incidence of breast cancer increases.

Second, westernization concomitant with increased industrialization has resulted in an increased concentration of environmental carcinogens. These carcinogens through circulation and breast fluid secretions reach the breast alveolar and ductal epithelium, and as a result the risk of breast cancer increases. Third, westernization because of low breast-feeding practices can also lead to increased contact of breast epithelium to carcinogenic agents and in turn affect the incidence of breast cancer. Viewed in this context increased breast cancer in oriental women, despite their low breast fluid secretions, may be associated with both changes in dietary intakes and breast-feeding practices.

With respect to diverticulosis, the protective role of dietary fiber has been attributed to the fact that crude fiber provides bulk to the food and thereby affects intestinal functions such as transit time, fecal weight, and bowel habits. It has been observed that ingestion of large quantities of dietary fiber decreases the food transit time.[27,64,65] Among Rhodesian subjects consuming a western diet of highly refined carbohydrates, the food transit time was much longer than for those eating a traditional Bantu diet of mainly unrefined carbohydrates.[72] However, the mechanisms by which the fiber exerts these effects are not presently known. The fact that the incidence of these diseases continues to increase among western populations calls for intensive research to determine the specific mechanisms whereby a dietary factor can become a carcinogen.

REFERENCES

1. Robson, J. R. K. 1972. Malnutrition, its causation and control. vols. 1 and 2. Gordon & Breach, Science Publishers, Inc., New York.
2. Latham, M. C. 1967. Present knowledge of thiamin. In Present knowledge in nutrition. Nutrition Foundation Inc., New York.
3. Katsura, E., and T. Oiso. 1976. Beriberi. In G. H. Beaton and J. M. Bengoa, eds. Nutrition in preventive medicine. World Health Organization, Geneva.
4. Vimokesant, S., N. Nimitmongkol, P. Phuwastein, S. Nakornchai, S. Sripojanart, S. Dhanamitta, and D. M. Hilker. 1973. In Proceedings of the IX International Congress of Nutrition. S. Karger, Basel.
5. Vimokesant, L., S. Nakornchai, S. Dhanamitta, and D. M. Hilker. 1974. Effect of tea consumption on thiamin status in man. Nutr. Rep. Int. 9:371-376.
6. Tanphaichitr, V. 1976. Thiamin. In M. Hegsted, C. O. Chichester, W. J. Barby, K. W. McNutt, R. M. Stalvey, and W. H. Stotz, eds. Present knowledge in nutrition. Nutrition Foundation, Inc., Washington, D.C.
7. Neel, J. V. 1956. Genetics of human hemoglobin differences. Ann. Hum. Genet. 21:1-30.
8. Livingstone, F. B. 1967. Abnormal hemoglobins in human populations. Aldine Publishing Co., Chicago.
9. Raper, A. B. 1950. Sickle-cell disease in Africa and America: a comparison. J. Trop. Med. 53:49-53.
10. Motulsky, A. G. 1973. Frequency of sickling disorders in U.S. blacks. N. Engl. J. Med. 288:31-33.
11. Bernstein, R. E. 1973. Mass screens for sickle cell disease. J.A.M.A. 288:31-33.
12. Song, J. 1971. Pathology of sickle cell disease. Charles C Thomas, Publisher, Springfield, Ill.
13. Serjeant, G. R. 1973. Sickle cell anemia: Clinical features in adulthood and old age. In H. Abramson, J. F. Bertles, and D. L. Wethers, eds. Sickle cell disease. The C. V. Mosby Co., St. Louis.
14. Lambotte, C. 1970. Disorders of the blood and reticuloendothelial system—sickle cell anaemia. In D. B. Jelliffe, ed. Diseases of children in the subtropics and tropics. Arnold, London.
15. Houston, R. G. 1973. Sickle cell anemia and dietary precursors of cyanate. Am. J. Clin. Nutr. 26:1261-1264.
16. Houston, R. G. 1975. Sickle cell anemia and Vitamin B_{17} a preventive model. Am. Laboratory 7:51-63.
17. Cerami, A. 1972. Cyanate as an inhibitor of red cell sickling. N. Engl. J. Med. 287:807-812.
18. Gillette, P. N., C. M. Peterson, J. M. Manning, and A. Cerami. 1972. Decrease in the hemolytic anemia of sickle cell disease after administration of sodium cyanate. J. Clin. Invest. 51:36.

19. May, A., A. J. Bellingham, and E. R. Huehns. 1972. Effect of cyanate on sickling. Lancet **1**:658-660.

20. Manning, J. M., A. Cerami, P. N. Gillette, F. G. De Furia, and D. R. Miller. 1972. Chemical and biological aspects of the inhibition of red blood cell sickling by cyanate. Adv. Exp. Med. Biol. **28**:253-260.

21. Oke, O. L. 1969. The role of hydrocyanic acid in nutrition. World Rev. Nutr. Diet. **11**:170-198.

22. Krebs, E. T., Jr. 1970. The laetriles-nitrilosides— in the prevention and control of cancer. McNaughton Foundation, Sausalito, Ca.

23. Thomas, H. M. 1972. Some aspects of food and nutrition in Sierra Leone. World Rev. Nutr. Diet. **14**:48-58.

24. Hunter, J. M. 1973. Geophagy in Africa and in the United States: a culture-nutrition hypothesis. Geogr. Rev. **63**:171-195.

25. Scala, J. 1974. Fiber, the forgotten nutrient. Food Technology **28**:34-36.

26. U.S. Department of Agriculture, Economic Research Service (USDA/ERS). 1975.

27. Trowell, H. 1976. Definition of dietary fiber and hypotheses that it is a protective factor in certain diseases. Am. J. Clin. Nutr. **29**:417-427.

28. Burkitt, D. P. 1977. Relationships between diseases and their etiological significance. Am. J. Clin. Nutr. **30**:262-267.

29. Wynder, E. L. 1969. Introductory remarks in nutrition in the causation of cancer. Cancer Res. **35**:3238-3239.

30. Wynder, E. L., and G. B. Gori. 1977. Contribution of the environment to cancer incidence: an epidemiological exercise. J. Natl. Cancer Inst. **58**:825-832.

31. U.S. Department of Health, Education and Welfare. 1975. Third national cancer survey: incidence data. DHEW Pub. (NIH)775-787.

32. Staszewski, J., and W. Haenszel. 1965. Cancer mortality among the Polish born in the United States. J. Natl. Cancer Inst. **35**:291-297.

33. Haenszel, W., and M. Kurihara. 1968. Studies of Japanese migrants. Part 1. Mortality from cancer and other diseases among Japanese in the United States. J. Natl. Cancer Inst. **40**:43-68.

34. Hirayama, T. 1975. Epidemiology of cancer of the stomach with special reference to its recent decrease in Japan. Cancer Res. **35**:3460-3463.

35. Correa, P., and G. Llanos. 1966. Morbidity and mortality from cancer in Cali, Colombia. J. Natl. Cancer Inst. **36**:717-745.

36. Correa, P., C. Cuello, and E. Dugue. 1970. Carcinoma and intestinal metaplasia of the stomach in Colombian migrants. J. Natl. Cancer Inst. **44**:297-306.

37. Lemon, F. R., R. T. Walden, and R. W. Woods. 1964. Cancer of the lung and mouth in Seventh Day Adventists. Cancer **17**:486-497.

38. Wynder, E. L., F. R. Lemon, and I. J. Bross. 1959. Cancer and coronary artery disease among Seventh Day Adventists. Cancer **12**:1016-1028.

39. Lyon, J. L., M. R. Klauber, J. W. Gardner, and C. R. Smart. 1976. Cancer incidence in Mormons and non-Mormons in Utah, 1966-70. N. Engl. J. Med. **294**:129-133.

40. Enstrom, J. E. 1974. Cancer mortality among Mormons. Cancer **36**:825-841.

41. Weathersbee, P. S., L. K. Olsen, and J. R. Lodge. 1977. Selected beverage consumption patterns among Mormon and non-Mormon populations from the same geographic location. Am. J. Clin. Nutr. **30**:3513-3522.

42. Phillips, R. L. 1975. Role of lifestyle and dietary habits in risk of cancer among Seventh Day Adventists. Cancer Res. **35**:1162-1165.

43. Wynder, E. L. 1975. The epidemiology of large bowel cancer. Cancer Res. **35**:3388-3394.

44. Howell, M. A. 1974. Factor analysis of international cancer mortality data and per capita food consumption. Br. J. Cancer **29**:328-336.

45. Haenszel, W., J. W. Berg, M. Segi, M. Kurihara, and F. B. Locke. 1973. Large bowel cancer in Hawaiian Japanese. J. Natl. Cancer Inst. **51**:1765-1779.

46. Staszewski, J. 1971. Age at menarche and breast cancer. J. Natl. Cancer Inst. **47**:935-940.

47. Valaoras, V. G., B. MacMahon, and D. Trichopoulos. 1969. Lactation and reproductive histories of breast cancer patients in greater Athens, 1965-1967. Int. J. Cancer **4**:350-363.

48. Yuasa, S., and B. MacMahon. 1970. Lactation and reproductive histories of breast cancer patients in Tokyo, Japan. Bull. W.H.O. **42**:195-204.

49. Salber, E. J., D. Trichopoulos, and B. MacMahon. 1969. Lactation and reproductive histories of breast cancer patients in Boston, 1965-1966. J. Natl. Cancer Inst. **43**:1013-1024.

50. Ross, M. H., G. Bras, and M. S. Ragbeer. 1970. Influence of protein and caloric intake upon spontaneous tumor incidence of the anterior pituitary gland of the rat. J. Nutr. **100**:177-189.

51. Ross, M. H., and G. Bras. 1971. Lasting influence of early caloric restriction of prevalence of neoplasms in the rat. J. Natl. Cancer Inst. **47**:1095-1113.

52. Carroll, K. K. 1975. Experimental evidence of dietary factors and hormone-dependent cancers. Cancer Res. **35**:3374-3383.

53. Tannenbaum, A. 1942. The genesis and growth of tumors. Part 3. Effects of a high-fat diet. Cancer Res. **2**:468-475.

54. Post, R. H. 1966. Breast cancer, lactation and genetics. Eugen. Quart. 13:1-28.

55. Tokuhata, G. K. 1969. Morbidity and mortality among offspring of breast cancer mothers. Am. J. Epidemiol. 89:139-153.

56. Kundson, A. G., I. C. Strong, Jr., and D. E. Anderson. 1973. Heredity and cancer in man. Prog. Med. Genet. 9:113-158.

57. Henderson, B. E., V. Gerkins, and I. Rosario. 1975. Elevated serum levels of estrogen and prolactin in daughters of patients with breast cancer. N. Engl. J. Med. 293:790-792.

58. Doll, R., C. Muri, and J. Waterhouse, eds. 1970. Cancer incidence in three continents. vol. 2. International union against cancer. Springer Verlag New York, Inc., New York.

59. Petrakis, N. L., L. Mason, R. Lee, B. Sugimoto, S. Pawson, and F. Catchpool. 1975. Association of race, age, menopausal status, and cerumen type with breast fluid secretion in nonlactating women, as determined by nipple aspiration. J. Natl. Cancer Inst. 54:829-833.

60. Petrakis, N. L. 1971. Cerumen genetics and human breast cancer. Science 173:347-349.

61. Petrakis, N. L., L. D. Gruenke, T. C. Beeler, N. Castagnoli, Jr., and L. C. Craig. 1978. Nicotine in breast fluid of nonlactating women. Science 199: 303-304.

62. Petrakis, N. L. 1977. Genetic factors in the etiology of breast cancer. Cancer 39:2709-2715.

63. Buell, P. 1973. Changing incidence of breast cancer in Japanese-American women. J. Natl. Cancer Inst. 51:1457-1479.

64. Burkitt, D. P. 1976. Some mechanical effects of fibre-depleted diets. In W. W. Hawkins, ed. Dietary fibre. The Nutrition Society of Canada and Mile Laboratories, Ltd. Ontario, Canada.

65. Painter, N. S. 1975. Diverticular disease of the colon: a deficiency disease of western countries. Heinemann Educational Books Ltd., London.

66. Painter, N. S., and D. P. Burkitt. 1975. Diverticular disease of the colon, a 20th century problem. Clin. Gastroenterol. 4:3-21.

67. Findlay, J. M., A. N. Smith, W. D. Mitchell, A. J. B. Anderson, and M. A. Eastwood. 1974. Effects of unprocessed bran on colon function in normal subjects and in diverticular disease. Lancet 1:146-149.

68. Gori, G. B. 1977. Diet, nutrition and cancer program. Status report of diet, nutrition and cancer program. National Institutes of Health, Bethesda, Md.

69. Hill, M. J. 1975. Metabolic epidemiology of dietary factors in large bowel cancer. Cancer Res. 35:3398-3402.

70. Reddy, B. S., A. Mastromarino, and E. L. Wynder. 1975. Further leads on metabolic epidemiology of large bowel cancer. Cancer Res. 35:3403-3406.

71. Moore, W. E. C., and L. V. Holdeman. 1975. Discussion of current bacteriological investigations of the relationship between intestinal flora, diet, and colon cancer. Cancer Res. 35:3326-3331.

72. Lubbe, A. M. 1971. Dietary evaluation. A comparative study of rural and urban Venda males. S. Afr. Med. J. 45:1289-1297.

Index